Playing in the bush

Recreation and national parks
in New South Wales

Edited by Richard White and Caroline Ford

SYDNEY UNIVERSITY PRESS

Published 2012 by Sydney University Press
SYDNEY UNIVERSITY PRESS
University of Sydney Library
sydney.edu.au/sup

National Library of Australia Cataloguing-in-Publication entry
Title: Playing in the bush : recreation and national parks in New
           South Wales / edited by Richard White and Caroline Ford.
ISBN: 9781743320020 (pbk.)
Notes: Includes bibliographical references and index.
Subjects: Wilderness area users--New South Wales--Attitudes
           Wilderness areas--Recreational use--New South Wales
           Natural areas--Public use--New South Wales--History
           National parks and reserves--New South Wales--Management
           Outdoor recreation--New South Wales--Management.
Other Authors/Contributors:
           White, Richard
           Ford, Caroline M
Dewey Number:
           333.7809944

Cover design by Miguel Yamin, the University Publishing Service

Contents

Foreword

National parks are eminently cultural, a fact that is obvious to those working in fields like history and heritage. The value of this present collection of essays is that it demonstrates to a broader readership, in park-based case studies, just why and how this is so. There was a time, of course, when the uncleared, un-farmed parts of New South Wales were – or at least seemed to be – wide open to those who wanted to stroll in the bush, camp below the banksias on a quiet beach, or watch kangaroos browsing in the late afternoon sunlight. These days, such experiences will almost inevitably take place in a national park. The young historians who make up the majority of the contributors to this volume show us how this shift has occurred. They also show how, along the way, the national park experience became inextricably tangled up in the way we imagine Australian nature, the way we define the national character, the ways in which we think about and experience fire, camping, and a range of other things.

These essays will prove to be an important resource for present and future scholars of environmental and recreational history. But there is so much between these covers which is surprising, intriguing, amusing and thought provoking that I hope the volume will also find its way into the hands and backpacks of ordinary campers and indeed anyone who remembers a good time in a national park.

Denis Byrne
Office of Environment and Heritage NSW

Acknowledgements

The then NSW Department of Environment and Climate Change (now Office of Environment and Heritage) provided the inspiration, financial and in-kind support for the research phase of this project. We would also like to thank all those past and present staff who assisted us in a variety of ways: especially Sharon Veale who conceived and initiated the project and Denis Byrne who has provided ongoing support; Denis, Bronwyn Batten, Steve Brown and Damian Lucas for providing comment on draft chapters; Melissa Harper for her time and knowledge of bushwalking history; and Dave Redman, Mark Williams, Megan Khempster, Victor Harnadi, Rosie Garthwin and the many others who shared their thoughts and knowledge about park management with us.

Thanks also to the many visitors at Murramarang, Meroo, Yuraygir and Georges River national parks who took time out of their holidays or weekends to chat with us about their experiences in national parks.

We would also like to thank Susan Murray-Smith and Agata Mrva-Montoya from Sydney University Press for their enthusiasm and faith in the project.

Notes on contributors

Ella Barnett has a long association with national parks around NSW, which includes many fond childhood memories of holidaying with family and friends around Jervis Bay, the Blue Mountains, the Royal National Park, the Barrington Tops and the Snowy Mountains. Having grown up in Sydney's inner west, Ella developed a keen interest in local history, studied history and heritage studies in her undergraduate years and completed honours in Australian history. She now works for a Federal Member of Parliament and is studying psychology part-time.

Isobelle Barrett Meyering grew up in Sydney. She spent most of her childhood holidays at her uncle's home in Wooli, where she was never far from the walks, mountain bike trails and beaches of Yuraygir National Park. In 2011, Isobelle began a PhD in history at the University of New South Wales. She is also a research assistant at the Australian Domestic and Family Violence Clearinghouse, where she has worked since 2009.

Julia Bowes grew up in Boronia Park, Sydney. Her house was metres from the beginning of the Great North Walk in Lane Cove National Park and so her appreciation of national parks, perhaps forced at first, began at an early age. She completed an honours degree at the University of Sydney in 2008 and is currently undertaking a PhD in history at Rutgers, the State University of New Jersey.

Claire Farrugia grew up near Georges River National Park and spent a great deal of time exploring the many areas of the park that intrigued her. She graduated with honours in history from the University of Sydney in 2008 and spent the following six months travelling in the Middle East and attempting to learn Arabic. After living in London for a further ten months she returned to Sydney with a renewed passion for the outdoor opportunities that the national parks provide. She began a PhD in refugee and migrant related areas at Macquarie University in 2012.

Caroline Ford grew up in Sydney's southern suburbs, close to the Royal National Park. She has fond memories of walking, swimming and driving in the park, although her high school's annual walk to Audley is not one of them. Caroline completed her PhD on the history of Sydney's beach culture at the University of Sydney in 2008 and is now a Cultural Heritage Researcher with the Office of Environment and Heritage NSW. She is the author of *Sydney's beaches: a history* (UNSW Press, forthcoming).

Justine Greenwood spent her annual childhood holidays at Huskisson, on the NSW South Coast, visiting the beaches scattered through the nearby Jervis Bay National Park. As a PhD candidate in history at the University of Sydney she has continued to work on aspects of recreation in people's lives, focusing on the role tourism and holiday-making have played in migrant settlement experiences in postwar Australia. She is also the Assistant Editor of *History Australia*, the journal of the Australian Historical Association.

Fiona Howie is a native Tasmanian. Her childhood memories include annual summer camping at Coles Bay, Freycinet National Park, visiting the family shack at Eaglehawk Neck on the Tasman Peninsula and picnicking and bushwalking in Mt Field National Park. Her education in national parks in Sydney has included the Bundeena to Otford overnight walk in the Royal National Park, and getting knocked on the head by a falling tree in the Blue Mountains. Luckily, it was only a very small tree. Fiona graduated with honours in history from the University of Sydney and then worked in publishing. She is currently living in Hanoi, Vietnam.

Tess Mierendorff was born in Tamworth NSW and has been visiting Arakoon and rambling around the gaol, beach and bushland since she could walk. She has always seen national parks as places carved out for adventure, fun and family. In 2008 Tess graduated from the University of Sydney with honours in history and she is currently completing a Bachelor of Laws.

Richard White grew up in Sydney where the Royal, Ku-ring-gai Chase and Lane Cove National Parks were essential venues for family picnics. He teaches Australian history and the history of travel and tourism at the University of Sydney and his books include *Inventing Australia*, *The Oxford book of Australian travel writing*, *On holidays: a history of getting away in Australia* and *Symbols of Australia*. He is currently researching the emergence of the past as a tourist destination in Australia.

Introduction

Richard White and Caroline Ford

National parks have always had to strike a balance between two underlying principles: recreation and conservation. Historically, the balance has not been easy to achieve. Recreation and conservation are frequently presented as competing forces, and often there are direct conflicts involved. Yet it is also worth recognising how often these two fundamental components of any national park mission have worked together. The whole purpose of recreation in national parks revolves around their conservation values: the recognition that recreation in a national park is qualitatively different from other forms of recreation, and that what makes national parks different needs to be protected. A national park can no longer fill this role if turned into a crowded playground or even a golf course. On the other hand, conservation of national parks generally recognises that the greatest support for limiting human impacts in national parks has come from a desire to hold on to those special places for recreation, both now and into the distant future. While rationales for national parks have moved from anthropocentric to biocentric ones over the twentieth century, most conservationists themselves are keen participants in recreational activities in national parks.

The relative importance of recreation and conservation in the thinking behind national parks has fluctuated over their 130-year existence in Australia. The professionalisation of national park management in the 1960s coincided with the ascendancy of a conservationist rationale, and as a result the recreational rationale behind national parks was often sidelined. Recreation was seen as less important than, and competing with, scientific management and at worst, certain recreational users were stereotyped as blunderingly inept and environmentally destructive.

The project which informs this book grew out of a recognition that while a lot of research has been done on the 'science' of national parks – the animals, the plants, the geology and the issues of management – and much still needs to be done there, recreation has had less attention and we know very little about the recreational uses to which parks have historically been put. How have people used national parks in the past? What feelings of attachment have been inspired by their use for recreation? What impacts have users had and how has that popular enjoyment of the park been negotiated with the parks' authorities? And where does the balance between recreation and conservation stand in relation to the increasing recognition being given to the presence of Indigenous Australians in national parks on the one hand, and the use of national parks by recent migrants on the other? For generations Aboriginal people have been conserving and living on the land given over to national parks, but they have also had longstanding economic connections to the land that do not sit easily with non-Indigenous assumptions about the purpose of national parks. At the same time, the ways non-Anglo migrants use national parks can often fall outside the particular culturally bound assumptions behind the establishment of national parks: what then are the implications for management?

In 2008 a group of fourth-year history honours students at the University of Sydney took part, with the generous support of the (then) Department of Environment and Climate Change, in a project that sought to answer some of those questions. Each developed a line of enquiry that investigated a particular aspect of the history of recreation in New South Wales (NSW) national parks, undertaking individual research but also drawing on group work and an oral history project developed in association with their honours program. The topics spread across the range of experiences that people, from locals to international travellers, have had in NSW national parks, from the family picnic to the pioneering rock climb, a remarkable range of activities stretching from the nineteenth to the twenty-first centuries. Some activities have persisted throughout this time: picnicking, bathing, sightseeing (and photography), bushwalking, horse riding, fishing, as well as a range of traditional activities of Indigenous Australians. Gradually new ones –

skiing, motoring, and later, rock climbing, mountain biking, paragliding and four-wheel driving – were added. Despite the variety of recreational uses, what they had in common was the fact that they were all undertaken for enjoyment. They shared a belief that a national park, in providing a natural setting where the impacts of human activity were curtailed, and where, somehow, they could see themselves as getting 'back to nature' (though they would disagree about what that might mean), gave the recreational experience a special quality. Both the growing popularity of older recreational activities and the emergence of new ones posed a variety of challenges for those responsible for managing the parks.

The eight chapters that follow are based on the research of these honours students. Richard White's overview of the origins of Sydney's first national park provides the historical and international context for the discussions which follow. Ella Barnett investigates how the national park became a setting for 'romance' and how nineteenth-century understandings of romanticism applied to nature gave the national park, even into the twenty-first century, an association with romantic relationships. Justine Greenwood addresses the complex issue of regulation in national parks, the ways in which the 'freedom' the park promises is constrained by a framework of regulation, and the conflict and contestation that this can bring about. Julia Bowes considers the role of fire in national parks, with a particular focus on users' attachment to the camp fire. Fiona Howie takes as her subject the provision of amenities which, in a similar way to regulation, treads a fine line between enhancing and diminishing the appeal of 'nature'. Isobelle Barrett Meyering goes to another extreme – extreme sport – and examines the development of more adventurous forms of recreation in national parks, giving particular attention to rock climbing. Claire Farrugia analyses the various ways in which recreational activity in national parks has been seen as beneficial, teaching people how to be 'good citizens', in the belief that an appreciation of nature, gained through innocent enjoyment of the bush, could turn children into responsible adults, working people into useful citizens and immigrants into proud Australians. Finally, Tess Mierendorff discusses the special problems posed by the presence of cultural rather than natural heritage, places that have historical significance because of the human activity that produced them. Her emphasis is on the built heritage of the park system, commonly known as the 'historic heritage'.

Together, these chapters highlight the diversity of ways in which people engage with protected landscapes. In particular, they shed light on the emotional attachment that so many recreational park users have developed to the park landscape of NSW, and to the activities they enjoy within those parks. We are beginning to understand the nature and extent of the attachment to national parks felt by people who were associated with those landscapes prior to their becoming public land.[1] The attachments which recreational park users form to the same landscapes are no less valid or complex and can also create particular challenges for park management. This book shows that the spectrum of attachments people hold to places, behaviours and objects within parks creates an equally diverse but often passionate spectrum of opinions about how these places and behaviours should be managed.

The chapters in this book focus on the parks close to Sydney, in particular the Royal, Ku-ring-gai Chase and Blue Mountains National Parks. These are among the oldest national parks in the country, and, together with the coastal national parks and Kosciuszko National Park, which also feature heavily, attract high numbers of visitors. We recognise that there is far greater diversity across the NSW park system than is represented in this book: diversity in landscapes, ecosystems, history and recreational uses. However, with a focus on those parks that have had the longest and most extensive histories of recreation, we hope to provide insight into some of the major themes and issues in the history of recreation in NSW national parks.

References

Kijas, Johanna (2009). There were always people here: a history of Yuraygir National Park. Sydney: Department of Environment and Climate Change.

Veale, Sharon (2001). *Remembering country: history and memories of Towarri National Park*. Sydney: National Parks and Wildlife Service.

---

1 Sharon Veale (2001).

Chapter 1

The recreational rationale in NSW national parks

Richard White

This chapter seeks to provide a broad introduction to the development of national parks in NSW and the role of recreation within them. National parks in NSW have a proud history of international significance. NSW can lay claim to establishing in 1879 what is generally accepted as the world's second national park, 'The National Park' (becoming, after the Queen's visit in 1954, the Royal National Park) on Sydney's southern outskirts. Some, on the basis of the first use of the term 'national park' in the legal language creating a park, would claim it to be the first.[1] In 1894 NSW gained a second, Ku-ring-gai Chase, to Sydney's north, and other colonies and then states also set aside land as national parks. Others were sporadically added in NSW until 1967 when an overarching National Parks and Wildlife Service (NPWS) was established based on the American model. With the balance shifting from an emphasis on recreation to a relatively greater emphasis on conservation, particularly following a new *National Parks and Wildlife Act* in 1974, new parks were rapidly established. Today there are over 820 protected areas in NSW, covering 6.8 million hectares, or nearly nine percent of the state, and attracting over twenty million visitors a year. The nearly 200 national parks now cover over five million hectares.

The original concept of the national park – a large tract of land left in what was regarded as its natural state, protected and managed

---

1 This claim is somewhat weakened by the fact that the park was gazetted as a single park, called 'The National Park', not as a new category of park.

for 'ecosystem conservation and recreation'[2] – was invented in the late nineteenth century, a gift from the 'new world' to the old. The first wave of national parks appeared in British settler societies: in the United States (Yellowstone, 1872), Australia (Sydney's National Park, 1879), Canada (Banff, 1885) and New Zealand (Tongariro, 1887). In each of these countries, additional national parks were proclaimed before the concept was adopted elsewhere – next in Sweden in 1909, but not in Britain until 1951.

The reasons national parks should first appear in these places at this time are not hard to find.[3] These were self-consciously modern, advanced and wealthy societies, aware that nature was endangered by the advance of civilisation. They were becoming more conscious of their national histories, which told of initially precarious settlement spreading into and conquering a forbidding wilderness. The parks were created at the point where the balance swung, when wilderness was more threatened by settlement than settlement was by wilderness. They defined themselves against Europe as the old world. Their nation-making looked to a romanticised nature rather than culture or history, to the vastness of geographical space rather than an immensity of historical time. Conscious of a relative lack of history compared to Europe, they were confident in their control of abundant natural resources, all awkwardly and often violently appropriated from indigenous populations. They assumed a shared obligation to settle 'white men's countries' in the interests of modern global race politics.[4] Their governments were used

---

2   The full International Union for Conservation of Nature (IUCN) definition of a Category II (National Park) Protected Area: 'Protected areas are large natural or near natural areas set aside to protect large-scale ecological processes, along with the complement of species and ecosystems characteristic of the area, which also provide a foundation for environmentally and culturally compatible spiritual, scientific, educational, recreational and visitor opportunities'. This chapter draws on a paper, Harper & White (2008), a version of which is to be found in Harper & White (2012). We would like to thank Jane Taylor for the research assistance she provided for this chapter.

3   Hall & Shultis (1991), for example, emphasise similarities. Jane Carruthers (1997) argues for an imperial tradition in British colonies (including South Africa) distinct from the Yellowstone model. Note also Frost & Hall (2009).

4   Lake & Reynolds (2008); Griffiths & Robin (1997). Tracey Banivanua-Mar

Fig. 1.1. View of Stanwell Park, at the southern end of the National Park, c1947. State Records NSW.

to setting aside tracts of land for future use and, being among the world's most advanced democracies, they claimed to act in the interests of their people. They recognised the economic value of a new tourism industry (stimulated by spreading railway networks), but also that uncontrolled entrepreneurial tourism could destroy the very aesthetic values on which it was based. Conveniently, the land set aside was seen as having little other economic value. Moreover, the British settler societies often self-consciously modelled themselves on the US. The Australian colonies, for example, were seen as another America throughout the nineteenth century.[5] Many commentators have taken it for granted that those parks established in the wake of Yellowstone were necessarily imitations of a Yellowstone model: 'following the American precedent.'[6]

(2010) has gone further to suggest that the designation of national parks was a logical end-point to the dispossession of Indigenous owners and the triumph of private property: a final insistence that even wasteland, which they could see no prospect of improving, had some meaning for the invaders, and hence justified their ownership.

5   White (1981), 47–50.
6   Hall & Shultis (1991), 57, 65.

Yet there were significant differences in the national parks themselves and the national meanings that underpinned them. While they all straddled the uneasy tension between recreation and conservation, all setting out to provide for the enjoyment of visitors in natural surroundings, there were important differences. In particular, in the NSW case, recreation played a more significant role. Whereas Yellowstone and Banff were on the very frontiers of white settlement, and Tongariro was also a significant distance from New Zealand's two main cities, NSW's first and second national parks, and South Australia's first, made a virtue of – and derived their very rationale – from their proximity to the city. As the National Park Trust's *Official guide* put it in 1902:

> several public men argued for the government to provide public parks, pleasure grounds and places of recreation adjacent to all thickly populated centres in NSW ... to ensure sound health and vigour of the community it was necessary that all cities, towns and villages should be possessed of parks and pleasure grounds as places of recreation.

The wealthy radical, Sir John Robertson, had made his name in 1860 with his land acts opening up the land to small farmers (selectors) rather than large pastoralists (squatters). As acting premier, he conceived and developed the idea of bequeathing 'to the people of this colony a national domain for rest and recreation'. The 'immense people's reserve' (18 000 acres doubled the following year to 36 300 acres) was dedicated to 'the use of the public forever' in the belief that the 'air of these uplands is pure and invigorating to the jaded citizen of Sydney or her suburbs'.[7] It was push rather than pull: the emphasis was not on what the park contained, but what the people needed; there was a sense that any large undeveloped tract of land would do. In that regard, Yellowstone was *not* a model for Australian parks, which were instead closer in spirit to on those on the outskirts of London – Hampstead Heath, Epping Forest – and even New York's Central Park. While the

---

7   *Official guide to the National Park* (1902), 7–10.

National Park's 36 300 acres (or 147 square kilometres) was no match for Yellowstone's 8987 square kilometres, it was significantly larger than Hampstead Heath's 220 acres (less than one square kilometre) protected in 1871, and the twenty-two square kilometres protected under the *Epping Forest Act* of 1878. South Australia's 'National Park', established in 1891, was more like the English examples with a mere 2000 acres (eight square kilometres). The National Park and Ku-ring-gai Chase, Sydney's second, 35 000 acres gazetted in 1894 and always seen as the equivalent of 'the' National Park for Sydney's north, cannot be seen as simply copies of either the American or English models.

One reason is that although all of them were dedicated to the people, the imagined users of these parks were significantly different: Yellowstone and Banff provided for an urban elite who could afford to travel long distances for extended holidays, whereas the Australian parks enabled far more democratic use. This vital difference was recognised by an American journalist who visited Sydney with the Great White Fleet in 1908:

> We, by whom I mean the Americans now in Sydney, are delighted to learn that you have vast national parks within Australia close to your principal cities … Our national parks are too far away from our great centres of population. The Yellowstone is almost inaccessible to the man of moderate means unless he lives near; Yosemite has been inaccessible until recently to all who have not the means to enable them to travel on mere sight-seeing errands.[8]

The landscapes differed too: Yellowstone, Banff and Tongariro were noted for their dramatic scenery and natural wonders and curiosities such as the Yellowstone geysers and mud volcanoes, the dramatic mountains, valleys and lakes of the Rockies and the three volcanoes

---

8   Franklin Matthews. 'An American view, Australia as seen by Brother Jonathan, distinguished journalists' impressions, where we succeed and where we fail'. Unknown newspaper/date. Vernon Family Papers MLMSS 6571, Vernon family – papers, 1880–1994, Mitchell Library. Thanks to Justine Greenwood for this reference.

Fig. 1.2. Boating at Lane Cove National Park. State Records NSW.

of Tongariro. All contained hot springs. They fitted what was, by the late nineteenth century, conventional and indeed hackneyed notions of the sublime, which despite its clichéd quality, still carried something of Edmund Burke's original sense of natural phenomena that inspired awe and reflections on God's infinite power and the insignificance of humanity. While Sydneysiders were not immune to the appeal of the sublime – they celebrated it in the nearby Blue Mountains (now a world heritage site) – the landscapes of the first Australian national parks were admired for a less celebrated, more intimate beauty. These were landscapes not to admire from a distance but to immerse oneself in through picnics, boating and bushwalking.

Arguably, it was this recreational purpose that gave the NSW parks their national meaning. Whereas in the other cases, popular understandings of nation were bound up with the grandeur of nature and the natural wonders were seen as somehow characteristic of the national ethos, the nature protected by the NSW parks was more valued for its recreational possibilities. Before federation and the creation of the new nation of Australia, many people in NSW – especially in authority – were beginning to think of themselves in national terms. Once they gained self-government in 1856, people began to think of themselves as an emerging nation and so could establish national schools, a national art gallery and national parks.

It is possible to identify three ways in which it could be conceived as appropriate to see NSW parks as national parks. Recreation was seen as a democratic right which the state should provide (in the same way it provided national galleries and national schools); a love of recreation was increasingly being seen as a part of the emerging Australian character (for many it was a negative feature but others saw it as something to be encouraged); and finally, in the context of broadly social Darwinist beliefs about racial competition and the survival of the fittest, the idea of healthy recreation contributed to notions of national fitness. When the first Australian national parks were established, the idea of the recreational nation was well understood. The potential for a national park to serve the nation through its recreational benefits was the fundamental stimulus. This is not to say other national parks did not embrace recreation, or that other societies did not establish parks primarily for the purpose of recreation, only that it was in Australia that recreation was a sufficient justification for making a park national.

* * *

While the balance was weighted towards recreation in Australia's first national parks, it should not be assumed that conservation was not a consideration. The natural bushland was a fundamental premise of their existence. There was a growing appreciation of the natural landscape and a desire to preserve its primitive character. Sydney had formal parks (Hyde Park and the Domain) and would acquire another,

Centennial Park, in 1888, in which decorous tree-plantings, ornamental flower-gardens and elegant statuary were the attractions. But in the national parks it was the natural bush setting that was the drawcard for recreation, and protection of that landscape was one of the primary roles of those managing the parks.

A common tendency, popular and academic, is to downplay aesthetic appreciation and protection issues, concentrating, from a later environmentalist standpoint, on the readiness of the early trustees to clear land, improve the surrounds and introduce exotic species. Certainly all the early national parks were improved, usually around a central base for visitors. Much is made of the terms of the original grant which allowed the trustees of the National Park:

> in their discretion to set apart and use such portions of the said Park as they may from time to time think necessary for the purposes following, that is to say, first, ornamental plantations, lawns and gardens; second, zoological gardens; third, race-course; fourth, cricket, or any other lawful game; fifth, rifle butt or artillery range; sixth, exercise or encampment of Military or Naval Forces; seventh, bathing-places; eighth, for any public amusement or purpose which the Governor for the time being may from time to time, by notification in the *Government Gazette*, declare to be an amusement or purpose for which the said National Park, or any portion or portions thereof, may be used.[9]

The trustees acted on a number of these, most notoriously introducing deer, which soon escaped from their enclosure. Had it not been for the Depression of the 1890s they may have done more. In 1900 Eccleston du Faur himself – the foremost advocate of the need for a national park in Sydney's north and of the need to protect native flora and fauna – was proposing rifle ranges and 'a golf link or two' for Ku-ring-gai Chase.[10] Improvements were common elsewhere, and indeed

---

9   Land Grant Register Book, vol. 827, fol. 755, 19 January 1887, 2.

10 Cited in Stanley (unpublished), 6.

in Banff huge luxury hotels and golf courses aimed to turn the area into a resort that would rival the spas of Switzerland.

But access to the unimproved bushland remained the central rationale for the NSW parks. Above all, the trustees said, they were determined to effectually preserve the flora and fauna committed to their care. It was a penal offence to discharge firearms, interfere with birds and animals, remove, cut or deface any trees, shrubs, plants, rocks, fences or gates. This was even more pronounced in Ku-ring-gai Chase, where raiding parties were sent out to ambush flower-gatherers. There the trustees inserted what must be one of the earliest regulations concerning Indigenous cultural heritage:

> The defacing or removing of any Aboriginal drawings or chippings on rocks is especially prohibited under this Regulation, as also the digging up or removal of any banks of shells and refuse, presumedly Aboriginal Kitchen-middens, in search of skulls, bones or other Aboriginal remains.[11]

Workmen involved in road-building in the National Park were required to sign a list of rules, which included:

> Great care must be taken that remarkable or handsome trees, tree ferns, cabbage tree palms, stag horn ferns, Christmas bushes, waratahs, creepers or other trees, plants, shrubs &c, of an interesting or remarkable character are injured, (even when they may seem to interfere with necessary road making &c), to as slight a degree, or as seldom as possible.[12]

In Ku-ring-gai, du Faur, the managing trustee, explained the thinking of the trustees. While recognising the need to provide public access, they considered as a duty of even greater importance the

---

11 Webb (2004)., 41.

12 William Freeman. Secretary, National Park Trust. 'Rules to be observed by, and conditions of employment of workmen engaged upon Road making, and in other capacities at the National Park Port Hacking'. Miscellaneous Papers re proposed National Park, NRS 10723, NSW Archives.

'preservation of the Native Flora within its limits for the gratification of future generations, when ruthless spoliation shall have exterminated it as utterly on the Lower Hawkesbury, as Gosford, and elsewhere'. It would create

> a domain where the typical flora of the east coast of NSW may flourish undisturbed, and where the native birds and animals, such as the Eagle Hawk, the Lyre Bird, Pigeons and many lesser varieties, as well as the smaller marsupials, may enjoy safety from the guns and dogs of so-called sportsmen.[13]

Guns, it was thought, had no place in a national park. The trustees were not simply concerned with vandalism, hunting or the unintentional depredations of picnickers. The possibilities of commercialisation drew their particular ire. They were determined to

> prevent the modern abomination of advertising ... so prevalent almost everywhere else; so that here at least Nature's beauties can be enjoyed without notifications concerning So-and-so's soap, or Somebody's Embrocation, or Otherman's Pills vulgarising everything.[14]

By-laws explicitly prohibited advertising and 'No person, unless authorised by the trustees, shall expose any article for sale in the Park'.[15] They knew the natural beauty of other tourist sights had been destroyed once commercial interests saw their money-making potential. The landscapes of the national parks were to be 'safe beyond the reach of plunder, safe from the machinations of ambitious schemers, and secured to the people of this country'.[16]

The attractions of Sydney's national parks were in a sense less celebrated than those in other national parks. They were less focused on

13 Eccleston du Faur. 'Kuring-gai Chase: The Northern National Park of Sydney'. *Dalgety's Monthly Review*, 15–19. Press clippings, Ku-ring-gai library. 994.41 KUR Appendices SR.

14 *Official guide to the National Park* (1902), 20.

15 *Official guide to the National Park* (1902), 97.

16 *Official guide to the National Park* (1902), 95.

a particular spectacle and, instead, were more modest, more intimate, in a sense more democratic. The language used to describe the Australian national parks was not of the sublime but the picturesque: 'the scenery, though not on a scale of grandeur, charms with its quiet but varied beauty'.[17] There were on the coastal edge some spectacular cliffs from which waterfalls dropped, but the attraction at Audley, Wattamola and Bobbin Head was more of a generic bushland and gentler scenery of water and trees. Rather than a landscape of tall poppies, this was one of Sydney angophoras, Christmas bush, Gymea lilies, tree ferns, bush orchids, 'a wealth of picturesque and quiet beauty' not to be admired as a set piece from a distance, but one to enter and surround oneself with.[18] Far from being neglected by an alienated English aesthetic that could not appreciate the beauty of the Australian bush, this sort of landscape was in desperate need of protection from its admirers. The threat came from walkers, flower pickers and fern stealers who were loving the landscape to death. The early meetings of the National Park Trust were taken up with the question of how to deal with a respectable solicitor who had brazenly removed 'a large and valuable Tree Fern, sundry Staghorn Ferns & Rock Lily plants' from the park to decorate his garden.[19] The threat also came from the spread of the villa, which made the most of a native bush setting. Increasingly picturesque landscapes, particularly those with water views and natural bush settings, were being favoured as housing sites.[20] Moreover, the population pressures were expected to increase with the development of the valuable coal seams to the south of the park as well.[21]

Certainly that appreciation of the aesthetic value of the park does not add up to a fully fledged conservationist rationale. A flurry of recent

---

17 'In Kuring-gai Chase'. *Sydney Morning Herald*, 22 September 1902, 5.

18 *Official guide to the National Park* (1902), 10.

19 Miscellaneous Papers re proposed National Park Draft Minute and notes on cross-examination, 1885. NRS 10723, NSW Archives.

20 For the attraction of the villa see Ford (2008); Taylor (2008); Webb (2004), 35.

21 W Freeman, Surveyor-General's office, to Sir John Robertson, 24 February 1879. 79–7836; Miscellaneous Papers re proposed National Park, NRS 10723, NSW Archives.

scholarship has agreed the Australian tradition failed to show much concern about protecting environmental values.[22] Despite the inchoate variety of organisations springing up – scientific and amateur naturalists, bird-watchers and acclimatisers – they did not articulate a coherent conservationist philosophy. Recent scholars rightly point out there was nothing in Australia yet that compared to the articulate American conservation movement represented by John Muir and George Perkins Marsh for example. However, the desire of these scholars to trace the pioneers of contemporary environmentalist perspectives in the past misses the point that while the Australian advocates for national parks fitted more into a recreational tradition than an environmental one, the recreation they had in mind was entirely dependent on the protection of the surrounding bushland.

This lack of an articulated philosophy on the recreational value of bushland had parallels with what has been called colonial socialism. Late in the nineteenth and especially early in the twentieth century, the Australian colonies were seen as social laboratories where the state played a major role in the economy – running railways, regulating industrial conditions, even establishing butcher shops – and was intent in part, to protect working people from the more brutal aspects of capitalism. It attracted notice around the world and the French social theorist Albert Métin labelled it 'socialisme sans doctrines'.[23] It was a set of policies derived from accumulated pragmatic interventions, rather than the product of a coherent philosophical position. Similarly, when it came to the establishment of national parks, there was no underlying philosophy. When the need arose to articulate a philosophy, the vacuum was filled by the more coherent, proto-environmentalist philosophy being articulated in the US. Yellowstone came to be seen as a precedent for the national parks in NSW in retrospect as it were, when arguably they had developed independently from a set of more pragmatic recreational concerns.

* * *

22 Beginning with Powell (1976), but more recently with Mulligan & Hill (2001); Hutton & Connors (1999). See also Whitelock (1985); Goldstein (1979).

23 Métin (1910).

The first national parks had considerable popular support, attracting large numbers of visitors. A railway station opened at the National Park in 1886 and made it a convenient day's outing. In 1892 the trustees recorded 38 000 visitors; in 1903, 170 000.[24] Park users became increasingly attached to their parks, with definite ideas of what kinds of recreation were appropriate and what could be considered to be overdevelopment. As Fiona Howie shows in her chapter, there was public opposition when trustees proposed allowing sawmilling and a golf course in the National Park in 1922, and again when in 1938 they announced plans for 'the greatest playground in Australia'. A National Parks Association was eventually established in 1957 to represent those with a particular attachment to the national park ideal.

There was an exponential increase in the number of national parks in NSW over the twentieth century. At first the few new national parks that were established continued the emphasis on recreation. A number were established but were not initially named national parks. Mooted in 1925, Lane Cove National Park was a third urban park for Sydney. It was left over from the old Field of Mars common and developed largely as an unemployment relief project, opening in 1938. Kosciuszko State Park, established in 1944, was developed in association with the Snowy Mountains Hydro-Electric Scheme largely to provide a controlled space for the increasingly popular recreation of skiing. It attempted to promote the sustainability of winter sports at the expense of pastoral uses.

But as the growing popularity of skiing shows, recreation patterns were changing. The car had a major impact, at first as a middle-class luxury but after World War II increasingly as a popular means for people to get away more adventurously. The early rhetoric of individualistic car travel meshed in surprising ways with the national park ideal, offering adventure, spontaneity and the opportunity to escape from the crowds into nature. While originally the car gave a particular stimulus to camping, as it became available to a mass market, it came to be seen as a threat to national parks. Apart from encouraging access to more remote locations there was a sense that the car represented a contradiction to

---

24 Stanley (unpublished), 29.

Fig. 1.3. Port Hacking River, Royal National Park. Mass car ownership would put new pressures on national parks. State Records NSW.

what a national park stood for. Other than creating new pressures to provide parking spaces, cars ultimately had relatively little impact on the recreational activities within the parks.[25]

_____

25 White et al. (2005), 96–100, 133–39.

In terms of the impact on recreational experiences within national parks, perhaps the most significant development was the emergence of an organised bushwalking movement. This movement was made up of serious bushwalkers and from the 1920s drew increasingly sharp distinctions between different types of recreation, distinguishing themselves from frivolous hikers who did not share their knowledge of the bush or their enthusiasm for wilderness. Bushwalkers would actively campaign for primitive areas where the sort of recreational infrastructure that had been a feature of the early national parks – the roads, kiosks and picnic facilities – would not be allowed.

Solicitor and enthusiastic bushwalker Marie Byles was largely responsible for mobilising bushwalking clubs to campaign for the establishment of Bouddi Natural Park in 1935, based around Maitland Bay, which she knew well from some of her early camping trips.[26] Myles Dunphy was another active campaigner, for sixty years, for new national parks and the protection of wilderness areas. He argued for national parks on the Yellowstone model, in particular campaigning from 1932 for a Greater Blue Mountains National Park of 1800 square miles for 'the purposes of preservation of scenery and areas of natural bushland, for conservation of wildlife, and for the furtherance of all kinds of recreation not destructive to the essentials of the proposal.'[27] In 1937 the government gazetted 150 square miles as a flora and fauna reserve which became, in 1959, the Blue Mountains National Park. This area was slowly augmented to eventually form the world heritage site it is today.[28] After a walking trip in 1925 Dunphy had also advocated a national park at Gloucester Tops which was eventually established in 1959 and which became part of Barrington Tops National Park ten years later. In 1936 bushwalkers and rock climbers also proposed a park for the spectacular Warrumbungles, where a National Park was established in 1953. Dunphy established the National Parks and Primitive Areas Council to campaign for parks throughout the state, to educate the

---

26 Harper (2007), 262.
27 Dunphy (1934).
28 Prineas & Gold (1997), 68–69.

public and governments of the necessity of permanent protection, and to agitate for the construction of paths and tracks.[29]

The impetus for many of these national parks too was recreation, but of a different sort from what was originally imagined. Their supporters developed a more coherent conservationist philosophy, often looking explicitly and enviously at US models. Along with a stronger conservationist ethic and a determination to seek out more primitive areas came a somewhat disdainful dismissal of mere recreation. Between the wars the term bushwalking was invented to distinguish between two types of recreational activity. Bushwalkers mocked hikers, whom Dunphy depicted as 'A crowd of flappers of both sexes straggling through the bush in street attire with ukuleles and hampers to impede their progress, tripping over rocks and vines and leaving scraps of paper lying around to mark their halting places'.[30] Serious bushwalker Marie Byles, on a trip in 1934, lamented with some irony the invasion of Mount Solitary by noisy hikers with their frivolous cooeeing and their orange-peel droppings.[31] Bushwalkers brought a more professional attitude to their recreation and began to satirise the improvements of trustees and their clumsy attempts at protection. Dunphy argued that 'a hotch-potch all-purposes national park' would, in time, cease to be 'a national repository of the natural history of the region'.[32] The attitude was neatly summed up in 1958, when the *Australian encyclopaedia* was snootily scathing of NSW's two chief national parks, 'largely patronized by picnickers who have merely "come out to play", and who sometimes extend their activities into the stealing of flowers and other examples of vandalism'.[33] But while Dunphy and others maintained the view that wilderness ought to be available as recreation to serious bushwalkers,

29 'National Parks and Primitive Areas Council: objects and scope' in Thompson (1986), 171.

30 Harper (2007), 201–02, 231–34. Dunphy cited, 233.

31 'Ten year's progress on Mount Solitary', *Sydney Bushwalker*, 19 June 1934, 11–12. Thanks to Bronwyn Powell for this reference.

32 Letter NPPAC to Roy Vincent (Minister for Mines and Forests), 25 June 1935. Dunphy papers, MLK3336.

33 *Australian encyclopaedia* (1958), vol. 6, 247.

some were beginning to advocate the protection of wilderness with strict limits on all human activity. This signalled the beginning of a challenge to the recreational emphasis in Australia's national parks.[34]

These renewed tensions between recreation and conservation emerged as national parks in NSW underwent dramatic reorganisation. Since the 1930s Dunphy and others had been arguing for a central administration for national parks in NSW on the model of the US National Parks Service, which had been established in 1916. In 1967 the New South Wales *National Parks and Wildlife Act* replaced the trustees of individual parks with a National Parks and Wildlife Service. This act was, in turn, replaced by a more comprehensive act in 1974 and supplemented by a dedicated *Wilderness Act* of 1987, which designated specific areas within national parks as wilderness, defined as land that had not seen significant human interference and that should be left to evolve in that state.[35]

After 1967 there was a rapid increase in the number of national parks, the rationale for which was more often conservation than providing new areas of recreation. A balance, however, a was still being struck between the two. Wilderness was still seen as providing certain kinds of recreation, providing opportunities for solitude and self-reliant bushwalking which had no detrimental impact. Within more intensely used parks, moves were made to remove many of the exotic plantings and facilities provided by earlier generations of managers. But then from the 1990s it was recognised that these earlier modified landscapes, especially around the base camps of the earliest national parks, had *cultural* heritage value of their own. Cultural as well as natural heritage was recognised as being in need of protection as well as part of the attraction for visitors to national parks.

The nature of recreation itself also continued to change. Tourism became a more important element in the economy and evolved, with increasing government support, into a self-conscious, articulate and increasingly influential industry. The tourist experience – or at least the experience promoted by the industry – became increasingly

34 Mosley (1999), 56–63.
35 Prineas & Gold (1997), 250–51.

commercialised: leisure became not simply an absence of work but a new consumer product. The idea of a relaxed holiday where nothing much happened gave way to the packaged experience, though it should be recognised many holidays took place outside this framework.[36] Moreover, governments, which had long been active in the provision of tourism ever since the dominance of the railways, were making way for private operators. Recreation was increasingly being catered for by a growing commercial tourism industry. The idea of state provision of space for healthy, spiritually uplifting recreation was perceived as interference in the market and the value of recreation shifted from being measured in terms of benefit to the people to being measured by what it contributed directly to the economy. Nature tourism, often imagined as a romantic escape from such pressures, was not immune, as can be seen in the emergence of ecotourism (or sustainable nature tourism) as a profitable high yield niche market.[37]

After decades of pressure from the tourism industry, the government established a NSW Taskforce on Tourism and National Parks in 2008 to explore 'opportunities for an enhanced level of sustainable nature tourism' in national parks. With a membership drawn largely from tourism lobby groups, the Taskforce tended to see national parks as a resource that had been locked away from the tourism industry. Their very definition of tourism skewed their findings towards the commercialisation of recreation: 'the travel of people outside of their usual environment and those activities undertaken that typically attract some form of commercial fee by a supplier'.[38] The report was particularly interested in targeting what was defined as 'comfort in nature' tourists, the eighty-five percent of the nature tourism market who require guides, 'appropriate accommodation and facilities' and access to 'a broader range of tourism experiences, including food and wine and cultural heritage'. Crucially, '[c]omfort in nature participants are a higher yielding market' than those national park users who prefer

---

36 White (2005), 167–73, 180–84.

37 Davidson & Spearritt (2000), 244–45; Allcock et al. (1994), 3.

38 New South Wales Taskforce on Tourism and National Parks (2008), iii, xviii.

Fig. 1.4. The causeway at Audley was built to provide swimming and boating opportunities. State Records NSW.

'remote locations with limited or no facilities'.[39] This is quite a different notion of recreation from the inspiration behind the first national parks that motivated the great majority of park users in NSW through the twentieth century. There should, the report said, 'be adequate consideration given to current "unstructured" minimal impact activities and quiet enjoyment of undeveloped settings', but the implication was that this was a minority interest relatively marginal to the new vision for commercialised recreation in national parks.[40]

---

39 New South Wales Taskforce on Tourism and National Parks (2008), vi; citing Tourism Victoria *Victoria's nature-based tourism strategy 2008–2012*.

40 New South Wales Taskforce on Tourism and National Parks: Final Report (2008), xiii.

For over a century, the notion of recreation provided by national parks in NSW had always implied an opportunity for the people to escape into nature to a world outside commercial transactions. Established on the principle that 'the health of the people should be the primary consideration of all good Government', national parks were conceived of as democratic spaces to which all would have access, 'safe from the machinations of ambitious schemers'.[41] These ideas distinguished the first NSW national parks from those established elsewhere. The conception of tourism promoted by the Taskforce challenged these ideas, implying they were no longer relevant to modern needs. On the issue of access and equity, its main concern was the access given to commercial tourism interests to compete in the national park market, recommending that:

> To improve access, fairness, cost recovery, visitor management and proper pricing, the Taskforce recommends DECC [Department of Environment and Climate Change] … Review fees for DECC accommodation against cost recovery, competitive neutrality and comparable industry rate benchmarks to ensure DECC is neither under nor over pricing product.[42]

Understandably, more traditional users of the parks, represented by the National Parks Association, opposed the Taskforce report, seeking to uphold 'the primary nature conservation purpose' of the Act and ensure that 'parks remain accessible to everyone as the most democratic spaces we have, free of elite commercial precincts'.[43] In 2010 the NSW government decided not to act on the Taskforce's report, though no doubt the tourism industry will continue to seek to commercialise the recreational experience provided by national parks.

Understandings of both recreation and conservation changed markedly over the twentieth century and the Taskforce report was part

---

41 *Official guide to the National Park* (1902), 7, 95.

42 New South Wales Taskforce on Tourism and National Parks: Final Report (2008), x.

43 Resolution passed at public meeting organised by the National Parks Association of NSW, University of Sydney, 26 February 2009.

of those shifts, reasserting the priority of recreation over conservation as the core of the national park experience. However the experience the Taskforce envisaged would be unrecognisable to those who, in the nineteenth century, had established an Australian tradition of the recreational national park as 'a national domain for rest and recreation'.[44]

References

Allcock, Alison et al. (1994). *National ecotourism strategy*. Canberra: Commonwealth Department of Tourism.

Australan encyclopaedia (1958). Sydney: Andus & Robertson.

Banivanua-Mar, Tracey (2010). 'Carving wilderness: Queensland's parks movement and the unsettling of emptied lands, 1890–1910', in Penny Edmonds & Tracey Banivanua-Mar (eds). *Making space: settler-colonial perspectives on land, place and identity*. London: Palgrave.

Carruthers, Jane (1997). 'Nationhood and national parks: comparative examples from post-imperial experience', in Tom Griffiths & Libby Robin (eds). *Ecology and empire: environmental history of settler societies*. Melbourne: Melbourne University Press.

Davidson, Jim & Peter Spearritt (2000). *Holiday business: tourism in Australia since 1870*. Melbourne: Miegunyah Press.

Dunphy, Myles (1934). 'Blue Mountains National Park Scheme'. *Katoomba Daily*, 24 August.

Ford, Caroline (2008). The first wave: the making of a beach culture in Sydney, 1810–1920. PhD thesis, Department of History, University of Sydney.

Frost, Warwick & C Michael Hall (eds) (2009). *Tourism and national parks: international perspectives on development, histories and change*. London: Routledge.

Goldstein, Wendy (1979). *Australia's 100 years of national parks*. Sydney: NPWS.

Griffiths, Tom & Libby Robin (eds) (1997). *Ecology and empire: environmental history of settler societies*. Melbourne: Melbourne University Press.

---

44 *Official guide to the National Park* (1902), 7.

Hall, C Michael & John Shultis (1991). 'Railways, tourism and worthless lands: the establishment of national parks in Australia, Canada, New Zealand and the United States'. *Australian-Canadian Studies* 8(2).

Harper, Melissa (2007). *The ways of the bushwalker: on foot in Australia*. Sydney: UNSW Press.

Harper, Melissa & Richard White (2012). 'How transnational were the first national parks? Comparative perspectives from the British settler societies', in Bernhard Gissibl, Sabine Höhler & Patrick Kupper (eds). Civilising nature: national parks in global historical perspective. Munich: Berghahn Books.

Harper, Melissa & Richard White (2008). 'The "nationalisms" of the first national parks: was the Australian model different?' Conference paper. Civilising nature: national parks in transnational historical perspective. Washington DC: German Historical Institute. 12–14 June.

Hutton, Drew & Libby Connors (1999). *A history of the Australian environment movement*. Melbourne: Cambridge University Press.

Lake, Marilyn & Henry Reynolds (2008). *Drawing the global colour line: white men's countries and the question of racial equality*. Melbourne: Melbourne University Press.

Métin, Albert (1910). *Socialisme sans doctrines: Australie et Nouvelle Zelande*. Paris: Felix Alcan, translated by Russel Ward (1977). *Socialism without doctrine*. Sydney: Alternative Publishing Co-operative.

Mosley, Geoff (1999). *Battle for the bush: the Blue Mountains, the Australian Alps and the origins of the wilderness movement*. Sydney: Envirobook in conjunction with the Colong Foundation for Wilderness.

Mulligan, Martin & Stuart Hill (2001). *Ecological pioneers: a social history of Australian ecological thought and action*. New York: Cambridge University Press.

Official guide to the National Park (1902). Sydney: Government Printer.

New South Wales Taskforce on Tourism and National Parks: Final Report (2008). Sydney: Department of Environment and Climate Change.

Powell, JM (1976). *Environmental management in Australia, 1788–1914, guardians, improvers and profit: an introductory survey*. Melbourne: Oxford University Press.

Prineas, Peter & Henry G Gold (1997). *Wild places: wilderness in eastern New South Wales*. Sydney: Colong Foundation for Wilderness.

Stanley, Howard. History of Ku-ring-gai Chase National Park. Unpublished, DECC Library.

Taylor, Jane (2008). 'An incubus upon the district': civilisation, private property and the Field of Mars Common. Honours thesis, Department of History, University of Sydney.

Thompson, Patrick (1986). *Selected writings: Myles Dunphy*. Sydney: Ballagirin.

Webb, Joan (2004). *Eccleston du Faur: man of vision*. Sydney: Deerubbin Press.

White, Richard et al. (2005). *On holidays: a history of getting away in Australia*. Melbourne: Pluto.

White, Richard (1981). *Inventing Australia: images and identity, 1688–1980* Sydney: Allen & Unwin.

Whitelock, Derek (1985). *Conquest to conservation: history of human impact on the South Australian environment*. Adelaide: Wakefield Press.

Chapter 2

Flirting with the picturesque: the effects of Romanticism and romance

Ella Barnett

A marriage proposal in a national park is a grand romantic gesture in an ideal location. A 'Wedding of the week' in Sydney's *Sunday Telegraph* in 2000 described a proposal in the Royal National Park, where after a 'riverside picnic breakfast' of strawberries, champagne and pastries, 'David got down on bended knee, took the engagement ring from his pocket and asked Tanya to be his bride.'[1] In this instance the natural beauty of the riverside landscape enhanced the beauty associated with the experience, while the secluded setting complemented its intimacy. David, down on one knee, completed this fairytale-like story of romance. Stories of romance emanating from national parks are not uncommon. 'She had her wedding on the beach, with a little arch, and she rode a horse … the waves were splashing around the arch and he had to pick her up … it couldn't have worked better.' This is how park visitor Roland Mangos described a wedding he attended which took place on a beach in one of New South Wales' national parks.[2]

These sentiments indicate a present day understanding of national parks as romantic places. This chapter explores the historic relationship between national parks, Romanticism and romance. What makes a landscape romantic – in both senses? The question requires us to consider not only national park settings as playgrounds for romance but how some natural landscapes, before they were even gazetted as

1 'Wedding of the week', *Sunday Telegraph*, 8 October 2000, 142.
2 Roland & Julie Mangos. Interview, Termeil Beach, Meroo National Park, 22 January 2008.

national parks, came to be considered as romantic. What qualities in natural settings elicit romantic reflection and what makes them suitable for romance?

On his tour of the Blue Mountains area in 1815, Governor Macquarie described what he named Prince Regent's Glen as 'a very extensive deep romantic glen, full of very picturesque and wild scenery'.[3] Here, Macquarie was adapting notions of late eighteenth-century European Romanticism to the local landscape of the Blue Mountains. Throughout the nineteenth and early twentieth centuries, NSW landscapes continued to be interpreted according to the Romantic vision. The first part of this chapter considers how aesthetic notions of Romanticism were applied to NSW landscapes before I go on to look at national parks as locations where romance played out. I aim to show that the Romanticism of these landscapes in art and literature influenced popular understandings and impressions of national parks as appropriate settings for romance throughout the twentieth century; that the sublime and picturesque representations of national parks contributed to the construction of these locations as places conducive to romance.

The second part of this chapter turns from the park as a Romantic setting to the romantic behaviour of visitors. Charting a history of nature as sites of romantic recreation, I will show that, by the middle of the twentieth century, national parks had acquired a thoroughly romantic quality – one which they still retain today. I will demonstrate how national park landscapes evolved as spaces where men and women could socialise with one another, where opportunity provided inspiration for romance and where young lovers could escape supervision.

Throughout their history, national parks and other landscapes have provided shelter for discreet activities and thus have been the setting for a variety of romantic encounters ranging from innocent courting to more explicit forms of sexual and erotic behaviour. This essay predominantly focuses on socially approved forms of romance throughout the earlier part of twentieth century, specifically heterosexual activities such as

---

3   Macquarie (1956), 92.

courtship and honeymooning. Bushwalking, as an activity that inspires romance, is given particular attention. I will also examine national parks as popular locations for honeymoons, following the model of the renowned North American honeymoon destination, Niagara Falls, probing further the correlation between perceived sublime natural wonders and their popularity with lovers. Ultimately, I wish to draw attention to the history of NSW national parks as venues long appreciated by people for their beauty, wonder and, indeed, their romantic appeal.[4]

The Romantic view: the sublime to the picturesque

Romanticism, emerging from art and literature in eighteenth-century Europe, emphasised subjective emotion and the individual in nature. Romantics expressed an appreciation for natural beauty and the picturesque – a term given to visually pleasing landscapes which were deemed suitable for a picture. Of particular concern were notions of the sublime – extremely awe-inspiring scenery, capable of evoking strong emotion in the viewer for its grandeur, power or perfection – and the associated experiences of the emotional power of nature's grandeur, its contemplative qualities as well as its ability to inspire sensations of terror and awe.[5] Needless to say, the landscape of NSW was distinctly different from Europe. To nineteenth-century colonists who sought to claim and conquer the unusual terrain, these differences were often keenly felt.

---

4   Note that this study does not concentrate on one particular national park, although the Blue Mountains and the Royal National Park are given significant focus. Also, attention paid to national park sceneries often pre-dates the official declaration of these sites as national parks. The Blue Mountains National Park, for example, was not officially gazetted until 1959. Thus, this research surveys locations contained within the boundaries of contemporary national parks, with emphasis largely resting on the landscape, rather than the official designation of national parks.

5   For a concise history of Romanticism see Oxford Art Online, 'Romanticism', [Online] Available: www.oxfordartonline.com/subscriber/article/grove/art/ T073207 [Accessed 10 November 2008]. On Romanticism in Australia, see Horne (2005); Johns et al. (1998); Speirs (1981).

Thus began a process of adapting European Romantic ideologies of the sublime and picturesque to the local Australian landscape.

The application of a Romantic aesthetic to the Australian landscape can especially be observed in nineteenth-century Australian landscape painting. Eugene von Guérard and William Charles Piguenit are two noteworthy painters who created Romantic visions of the landscape. Von Guérard's *North-east view from the northern top of Mount Kosciusko* (1863) (see plate 1)[6] depicts members of his party on expedition to the Kosciuszko region. These minute figures stand in the foreground on mountain boulders, their human significance reduced when set against the snow-covered rocky outcrops and mountain ranges that lie in the distance. The rock formations in the picture have been exaggerated with the effect of intensifying the scale of the landscape. Piguenit's 1903 representation, *Kosciusko*, also portrays a majestic landscape. His misty, barren mountaintops generate a dramatic image of grandeur.[7]

The Blue Mountains was another focal point for Romantic interpretation. Particularly popular were depictions of waterfalls, which offered a picturesque aesthetic experience combining terror and transcendence. Augustus Earle's *Wentworth Falls* (c.1830) emphasises the dramatic aspect of the landscape by drawing attention to the imposing scale of the cliff face and its steep descent as the water cascades into the valley below. Von Guérard painted the same perspective in 1862 in *Weatherboard Creek Falls, Jamison's Valley, New South Wales*. This image, while still giving focus to the sheer gradient of the cliffs, also pays tribute to the wide mountain ranges that spread beyond the valley evoking an admiration for the immensity of the land.[8] JH Carse, choosing the same viewpoint in his work, *Weatherboard Falls* (c.1873), accentuates the scene by placing three figures in the foreground, dwarfed by the scale of the landscape. The mountain scene is made all the more

---

6   The spelling of Kosciusko has since been changed to Kosciuszko.

7   Both Johns et al. (2005), 157 and Horne (2005), 74, 224 provide insightful commentary on von Guérard's work. See also Horne for Piguenit's *Kosciusko*.

8   See Earle in Johns et al. (2005), 97. Guérard appears in Horne (2005), 102.

spectacular by mist floating through the gullies and the panorama that evokes a sense of majesty.[9]

The poetry of renowned nineteenth-century Australian poet Henry Kendall also typifies the adaptation of the Romantic sentiment of the sublime to Australia's mountain landscape:

> Peace hath an altar there. The sounding feet
> Of thunder and the 'wildering wings of rain
> Against fire-rifted summits flash and beat,
> And through grey upper gorges swoop and strain,
> But round the hallowed mountain-spring remain,
> Year after year, the days of tender heat.[10]

The scenery here is at once cast as forceful and majestic and steeped within a transcendent quality. In Kendall's verse we observe Romanticism translated to Australian conditions. What is also significant is that 'a local version of the sublime' was being characterised. Julia Horne has argued that unlike in Europe, where snow-capped mountain peaks provided a significant source of sublime inspiration, progressively it was the rocky gorges, waterfalls and deep valleys extending into the distance that stimulated Romantic sensibilities in NSW during the nineteenth century.[11]

A more prosaic example of Romanticism can be found in the writings of Nat Gould. A noted journalist and novelist who migrated to Australia from England in 1884, Gould produced an account of the Blue Mountains in 1896. In *Town and bush: stray notes on Australia* he dedicates ten pages to describing the Blue Mountains. He concludes his impression by exclaiming,

> The deep valleys and precipitous gorges are extraordinary … On every side the scenery is full of wild grandeur.

---

9   Carse printed in Johns et al. (2005).

10 Kendall (1970), 65.

11 Horne (2005), 222.

> The traveller looks upon it with a feeling akin to awe as he
> realises its vastness, and also the fact that the hand of man has
> nothing to do with it.[12]

Here, Gould employs the now somewhat conventional language of
the sublime. Indeed, he was inspired by the expansive and overwhelming
sense of the mountains, and implies he was struck by the insignificance
of man against nature and God. Yet Gould was particularly impressed
by the intimate spaces of mountain landscapes. He dedicated the first
nine pages of his account to casting the mountains in a picturesque
light. 'So delicate in tint', is the blue of the mountains; they offered so
many 'exquisite pictures', 'a shady gully of the most beautiful nature'
and 'a waterfall of small dimensions' that 'trickles down the rock and
wends it way through a bed of bright green moss'. He continued to
describe the gentle appeal of moist fern streams and beautiful flowers.
Gould's impressions of the landscape drew upon Romantic notions of
the sublime and the picturesque, but his Romantic sensibilities created
a distinction between them; between an appreciation of the small-
scale picturesque setting, and the transcendent notions of the sublime.
This is a significant separation of Romantic ideals and marks a shifting
response to the Australian landscape. Increasingly in the twentieth
century, bush landscapes across NSW were characterised according to
the Romantic notion of the picturesque, while representations of the
sublime gradually lessened, although they did not cease altogether.

The promotion of the picturesque in scenic landscapes was
fostered by an increase in travel and tourist literature from the end of
the nineteenth century. Areas such as the Blue Mountains, the (Royal)
National Park and Bundanoon in the Southern Highlands (on the edge
of what became Morton National Park) were spaces all made accessible
to the general public via the railways. C Michael Hall and John Shultis
have suggested that the railways usurped the Romantic image of
national parks for utilitarian purposes.[13] More importantly in this case,
rail and tourist promotions transmitted to the popular imagination the

---

12 Gould (1896), 205–14.
13 Hall & Shultis (1991), 57–74.

Romantic image of national parks that existed in art and literature. Ideas of the Romantic were translated into the vernacular through official tourist guides and advertising posters.

Government Printer publications were geared to promote rail travel and tourism with booklets such as *Pleasant places convenient to the railways*, *Holiday resorts: a tourist guide to the railways of NSW* and *Picturesque New South Wales*.[14] The National Park was a 'charming' pleasure ground, offering 'natural beauty' and 'scenery of the loveliest description'.[15] In the 1914 *Official guide to the National Park*, the Hacking River was touted as 'one of the most picturesque streams in Australia' upon which a name 'much more romantic and beautiful' could have been bestowed.[16] The bush scenery near Bundanoon was cast as 'picturesque' and 'the grandest' on the rail line.[17] The Blue Mountains traveller caught 'lovely glimpses of the silver-flowing stream meandering through the fertile plain', while the valleys offered a most picturesque view,

> In the depths of which the tall trees massed together look like a soft carpet of sombre verdure, fading away towards the horizon in blue and tender mauve. The shadows of the clouds creep in masses of indigo across the great gulfs and the sun lights up the bright cliffs, which are streaked red and yellow with stains of iron.[18]

This conceptual transition – from the sublime to the picturesque – holds significance for bush and national park landscapes, especially as they became recognised in the popular imagination as evocative of romance and romantic love.

---

14 *Pleasant places convenient to the railways: a tourists' guide* (1906); *Holiday resorts: a tourist guide to the railways of NSW* (1916); and Coghlan (1906).

15 *NSW Railway tourist guide, Illawarra Line*. Sydney: Government Printer (1889), 49.

16 *Official guide to the National Park* (1914), 39.

17 *Hotels, boarding houses etc. in the tourist districts: at or near railway stations* (1898), 13; *NSW Railway tourist guide*, 27; *Pleasant places*, 24.

18 Coghlan (1906), 149.

From Romanticism to romance

> Romance • noun 1. a pleasurable feeling of excitement and
> wonder associated with love.[19]

In her study of nineteenth-century beach culture in Sydney, Caroline
Ford points out that the relationship between Romanticism and
romance 'is certainly more than a mere coincidence of language' and
draws a parallel between the Romantic appeal of Sydney's beaches as a
natural space and their attraction as places of romance for young lovers.
Elaborating upon the link, she refers specifically to a sketch (c.1886) of
a young couple staring out to sea:

> Lovers who gazed at the sea invariably contemplated matters
> of the heart, but the scenery provided a focal point for that
> contemplation. This was, perhaps, quite similar to the Romantic
> idea of reflecting the inner soul while observing the purity of
> nature; a similar process but with an entirely different point of
> reflection.[20]

Although Ford focuses on beach scenery in particular, her argument
is significant because the suggested correlation between Romanticism
and romance can be applied to national park landscapes more generally.
Arguably, ideas of the Romantic and notions of romance are not only
compatible but interdependent experiences.

Many of the landscapes around Sydney which have since been
incorporated into national parks were recognised as settings for
romance from at least the turn of the nineteenth century. This is perhaps
most plainly reflected within the names of specific sites, as is especially
the case in the Blue Mountains. Lover's Nook is the name of a small cave
near Leura Falls and is recorded in the *Katoomba Times* as early as 1893.
In 1905 it was described in the *Sydney Mail*: 'Lover's Nook at the end of
a short and narrow path branching off to the left – surely an ideal spot in

---

19 AskOxford.com, Oxford Dictionaries, 'Romance'. [Online] Available:
oxforddictionaries.com/definition/romance [Accessed 10 November 2008].

20 Ford (2005), 08.8–08.9.

Fig. 2.1. Open displays of romantic affection: young couples picnicking at the National Park in 1947. Mitchell Library, State Library NSW.

which to tell the old, old story'.[21] The 'Bride and Bridegroom's Cave' close to Lover's Nook, is mentioned in the *Mountaineer* in 1908.[22] The name 'Bridal Veil Falls' was bestowed on the waterfall at Govett's Leap: 'this descending mass of water, white and misty as the driven snow, sways, as the wind blows to and fro, like the veil of a bride'.[23] The romantic themes of these place names linked these landscapes to romance by the early twentieth century. Most importantly, they began to suggest a connection between popular romance and notions of the Romantic as portrayed in art and literature.

What is the relationship between the Romanticism of national park landscapes and their role as settings for romance? What is it that makes

---

21 *The Katoomba Times*, 1 December 1893; *The Sydney Mail*, 6 September 1905, both cited in Fox (2006), 189.

22 *Mountaineer* (1908), 47.

23 *Pleasant places*, 30.

sunsets over mountain ranges, natural vistas, running rivers or secluded waterfalls attractive to lovers? For a romantically attached couple, the sensation of romance and the pursuit of romantic activities invariably intensifies the emotional experience of falling or being in love. Arguably, national park environments enhance this experience because the potential sensations aroused when immersed in culturally constructed nature complement feelings of romantic love. Whether captivated by the beauty of the scenery offered in natural environments, struck by their wonder or filled with a sense of exhilaration by their immensity, it becomes possible to recognise that these uplifting encounters with nature – experiences akin to the sublime sentiments of Romanticism – would intensify an impassioned mood between loving couples already sensitive to heightened emotions.

However, come the twentieth century, it was not just the sublime in nature that characterised national park landscapes as appropriate for romance. Small and serene spaces – small gullies or trickling waterfalls – would become equally compelling, in line with the picturesque imagery promoted in travel literature, where tenderness and an intimacy of feeling would complement the soft and affectionate – as well as the heightened emotional and sexual – sentiments of couples. As Melissa Harper has shown, it is arguable that for late Victorians, the idea of entering moist fern-clad gullies and dark caves had a direct erotic appeal.[24]

Indeed, the popularity of natural attractions as romantic places, appreciated for both their expansive and intimate spaces, was acknowledged in more tangible ways. A recent heritage study of the Blue Mountains walking tracks identifies, among other places, a bench carved into stone near Victoria Lookout, adorned with a heart and aptly named Lover's Seat. Resting spots such as these were provided at regular intervals along bush trails in the early part of the twentieth century. Blackheath is recorded as having 136 such rest-seats in the mid 1930s.[25] Besides simply offering a place of respite in the bush, the profusion of these seats would have conveyed the impression that it was

24 Harper (2000), 287–303.
25 Smith et al. (1999), 86.

Fig. 2.2. Audley, in the National Park, 1914: large picnic parties provided new opportunities for heterosexual intimacy in romantic surroundings. Mitchell Library, State Library NSW.

worthwhile to linger and appreciate these scenic spots. 'Seats were an encouragement for meditative pause, during which the sights, sounds and smells of the bush could be experienced.'[26]

Particularly for a couple in love, resting spots like Lover's Seat fostered an opportunity for contemplating matters of the heart – matters which were to be only further enhanced by the inspiring and reflective quality of the natural scenery, again feelings analogous with Romanticism. Importantly, areas like resting spots would have offered more than just an opportunity to ponder love – they would have given couples a degree of privacy and seclusion, and a chance to perhaps do more than just contemplate their relationship. In fact, the provision of such contemplative spaces leads to the conclusion that romantic pursuits along bush trails were indeed practices already prominent –

26 Smith et al. (1999), 86.

that is, that the construction of places like resting spots simply catered to activities by now already established.

Where romance existed as an attempt to maintain moral order, and national parks as an attempt to control nature, there is an interesting correlation between the construction of romance and park environments. It is perhaps ironic that, with the attempt to curtail inappropriate behaviour or sexual expression under the banner of romance within the tailored wilderness of national parks, national parks have in fact become renowned as romantic and erotic spaces.

National parks: a romantic rendezvous

My friends, the aim and purpose of Life is Love.[27]

In 1879 the NSW government, 'bequeathing to the people of this Colony a national domain for rest and recreation', created Australia's first national park. By 1918 the National Park boasted that it was 'one of the most magnificent recreation grounds in the world'.[28] Since their inception, national parks have been valued for their recreational benefits, in addition to their role as conservation landscapes. Bushwalking, picnicking, camping and sports were among the many activities visitors could, and still do, enjoy. The recreational impetus behind national parks goes a long way in helping to understand how they have functioned as playgrounds for romance throughout the twentieth century.

In a study of working-class women's leisure patterns in New York at the turn of the nineteenth century, Kathy Peiss examines the idea of homosocial and heterosocial culture. Peiss maintains that working-class men and women's leisure time was dominated by homosocial experiences. That is, men tended to socialise with men at work, in pubs and clubs; and women tended to socialise with women in the domestic sphere and with neighbouring wives and children. Examining urban leisure activities and social spaces wherein gender relations were played out, Peiss contends that new environments such as dance halls

---

27 Myles Dunphy, c.1920 cited in Thompson (1986), 102.

28 *Official guide to the National Park* (1894); *Guide to the National Park and Port Hacking* (1918), 1.

and nightclubs, picnic grounds and amusement parks, legitimised certain modes of interaction between the sexes, such as dating and close dancing.[29] This idea of heterosocial space and interaction, and its role in validating forms of behaviour between men and women, holds significance for national parks and pre-park landscapes, as they functioned as romantic venues.

Like the dance parties and amusement parks of New York, nature as a destination for popular recreation offered spaces where men and women of the early twentieth century had the opportunity to mingle and socialise with one another. In fact, certain national parks even hosted dances, such as those at Allambie House in the National Park. It is conceivable that as social venues, natural attractions and national parks were seen as respectable and uplifting because they were set in inspiring nature rather than the squalid city. Thus these spaces had none of the tawdry working-class associations of early dance halls, cinemas and other more urbanised forms of entertainment. In an era when social etiquette was certainly more rigid than it is today, particularly for the middle classes, these social gatherings were at the least an opportunity for innocent intermingling, if not an occasion for overt eroticism.

Images of visitors to the National Park depict large groups of men and women mingling with one another, relaxing on the grass and enjoying picnic lunches. Often, trips to the park involved groups of families and friends. The Allen family album depicts numerous trips to the National Park. An outing in 1898 shows a group of seven men and women boating. Photographs capture the party taking 'lunch at the head of the river' on the rocky bank and boiling the billy for 'tea at the backwater'.[30] A 1905 postcard of a guesthouse at Port Hacking shows a group of men and women sitting on the grass, while a man and woman are seated on a bench not far off, facing one another, their legs resting against each other.[31] Another image from 1914 shows a large picnic group of over 20 men and women sitting in the shade of

29 Peiss (1986).

30 Allen Family Album, Mitchell Library (ML), vol. 21, 12–16.

31 Guesthouse, Port Hacking NSW, postcard 1905 in Davidson & Spearritt (2000), 227.

Fig. 2.3. By the early twentieth century, honeymooners such as Rod and Ruby Whyte (pictured here in 1913 at Jenolan Caves) found romance in national parks and other romantic sites. Blue Mountains City Library.

a tree by a river.[32] All these images testify to the heterosocial nature of national park recreation. The Blue Mountains and Kosciuszko, amongst other places, were popular recreation areas. In 1914 the Kosciusko

---

32 NSW Government Printer series (1914). National Park, 'A typical picnic party in the National Park'. [GPO 1–16032 (ML)].

Hotel had had its most successful year to date, while the Jenolan Caves received close to 28 000 inspections.[33] As national parks and other popular sites flourished as natural settings for fashionable recreation, the opportunities for gender interaction of the sexes (and thus romantic encounters) also increased.

From the late 1920s, bushwalking became a popular mixed-gender recreation activity, exemplifying not only the role national parks played as spaces of heterosocial interaction but also the changes that were taking place in acceptable modes of behaviour between the sexes. Bushwalking as a serious recreation at the turn of the nineteenth century had invariably been a male activity. Melissa Harper suggests that going bushwalking freed men from 'formal dress and the need for idle social chatter'. Referring to Melbourne bushwalker Alexander Sutherland, Harper illustrates the freedom and opportunity which bushwalking provided for men to relax in the company of one another.[34] The formation of walking clubs gave structure to this male experience. The Mountain Trails Club of NSW, established in 1914, was a club for men that specialised in walking and camping excursions. 'Ladies' were 'not eligible for membership' although they had been known to participate in the 'easier' trips.[35]

By the 1920s women were active bushwalkers, yet it remained a somewhat segregated activity. The desire for change was evident. In 1927 Jack Derbert wrote to the *Sun*, advocating the formation of a hikers club, where all those who liked to hit the trail could meet and share their interest and knowledge with one another. 'Naturally' he urged, the club should 'be open to lady members, for one sees as many of the fair sex on the trail as men'.[36] In response to Derbert's suggestion, Myles Dunphy, an avid bushwalker and campaigner for national parks and secretary of the men's Mountain Trails Club, directed interested parties to attend his club's meetings. So great was the desire for a club open to both sexes that

---

33 Tourism New South Wales, 100 Years of NSW Tourism. [Online] Available: www.visitnsw.com/100years/history1910.asp [Accessed May 9 2008].

34 Harper (2007),119.

35 Myles Dunphy, *Sun*, 5 August 1927. Cited in Butler (1987), 3.

36 Jack Derbert, *Sun*, 2 August 1927. Cited in Butler (1987), 3.

a new club was created. It was to become the Sydney Bush Walkers. The importance of the social aspect of the club along with its keen love for experiencing nature is outlined in the club song:

> Beauty so enthralling,
>
> Bushland calling, calling,
>
> Come and make the best of friends.[37]

Imagining a group of bushwalkers singing these words in the remote depths of park landscapes, one can appreciate the social and potentially romantic bond that bushwalking inspired.

The monthly publication *The Sydney Bushwalker* records many group trips that Sydney Bush Walkers made together – to the Blue Mountains, the Barrington Tops, Kosciuszko, Bundanoon and the National Park. This formalised club gave legitimacy to the desire of men and women to accompany one another on day trips and overnight bushwalks in national parks. As has been seen, already by the 1920s national parks created opportunities for men and women to socialise on day trips. Activities such as picnics, boating and walks along bush tracks all provided a range of occasions for talking and touching, flirting and kissing. While in the early decades of the twentieth century social mores regarding acceptable forms of behaviour between men and women were becoming less stringent, the idea of young unmarried men and women spending nights in each other's company – especially when isolated and unchaperoned – was still regarded as inappropriate. Harper notes the recollection of bushwalker Jim Somerville who faced probing questions at work about sexual activity on his weekend trips. Reacting to this new form of social interaction, and in an attempt to curtail inappropriate behaviour, in 1931 the club registered its 'disapproval' and 'deprecation' of 'co-tenting'. Three couples were reprimanded for sleeping in the same tent on official walks.[38]

Despite this cautionary attitude, co-sex bushwalks provided ample opportunity for romantic liaisons. Dot Butler, an enthusiastic bushwalker,

---

37 *The Bushwalker*, August 1931, 1.

38 Harper (2007), 238; Butler (1987), 11.

joined the Sydney Bush Walkers in 1931. In her autobiography, Butler recounted romantic experiences as a member of the club. Meeting Edgar Yardly, another member of the club, at Era beach in the National Park, she details her first sensual, if not sexual, encounter,

> Moonlight trembled on the palm leaves … the boy and I lying on the beach under the stars … and for the first time I opened my eyes and saw the beauty of a boy's golden body kneeling above me.[39]

In the nineteenth century the untouched wilderness of Sydney's beaches provided ample space for young lovers to liaise.[40] As the urban environment of the twentieth century increasingly encroached upon Sydney's beaches, national parks presented an alternative avenue for escape. Young romantic couples could enjoy the seclusion and isolation that national parks offered. When getting away to nature, they were also escaping the watchful eyes of social, and more literally, parental bodies.

Members of the Sydney Bush Walkers often formed romantic attachments leading to engagements and marriages which were regularly announced in *The Sydney Bushwalker*. After 'two more weddings from our members the S.B.W. will soon be a married people's Club!' exclaimed Rene Brown in 1933.[41] The high incidence of marriage between its members demonstrates the potential within bush recreation for romances to develop. It also explains the club's jocular preoccupation with weddings. 'Rev. Dr. Hitchemup' married 'Mr Stan Well' and 'Miss Lily Vale', and 'Mr Hartley Vale' was the groomsman, *The Sydney Bushwalker* joked in 1931.[42] Two months later, the ceremony was recorded: 'Mr Stan Well' vowed,

---

39 Butler (1991), 45.

40 Ford (2005), 08.6.

41 *The Sydney Bushwalker*, February 1933, 17.

42 Note that both Stanwell Park and Hartley Vale are suburbs in NSW associated with national parks owing to their close proximity to the Blue Mountains and the National Park. *The Sydney Bushwalker*, August 1931, 17.

Fig. 2.4. The National Park was a favourite day trip for the Allen Family from their holiday home at Cronulla. Mitchell Library, State Library NSW.

> I, Stan Well, take thee Lily, to a splendid life, to walk and to eat,
> to climb and rockhop … in sunshine or rain, in daylight or dark,
> till Mondays come round and work do us part.[43]

Humorous renditions of romantic adventure in national parks in other formats, such as comic sequences and cartoons, also served to illustrate the parks' reputation as romantic spaces. Mystery hikes (as opposed to serious bushwalking) were a fad of the decade – another chance for men and women to socialise in national park environments. So popular were these organised hikes, where excursionists would travel by train to an unknown destination for a day of exciting adventure, that Sydney's third such hike, walking along the Hawkesbury River,

---

43 *The Sydney Bushwalker,* October 1931, 10.

attracted approximately 8000 people.⁴⁴ National parks were an ideal destination for the organised hike since space and transport were easily found. A cartoon in the *Sydney Mail* in 1932 tackled the battle that ensued between motorists and hikers over road space. 'Motorists are complaining loudly about the hikers – but love is also deaf'. The caption accompanied a picture of young hiking sweethearts so thoroughly besotted with one another they did not notice the honking car pursuing them.⁴⁵ The implication is that the hikers are far more concerned with each other than they are with anything else, including hiking. Most immediately, this representation emphasises the view that hiking, usually in national parks, was valued by many for its social benefits, particularly the romantic opportunities it presented. Furthermore, such sketches, which make light of amorous couples, reveal a cultural shift in attitudes towards romantic affection and a relaxation of moral codes that permitted more open displays of intimacy.

In fact, humorous jibes at the expense of young lovers may also have been a way of mitigating the seriousness and prevalence of what were considered to be immoral liaisons in places like the Blue Mountains. A cheeky sequence of cartoons was produced by Katoomba photographer Harry Phillips. In a pullout series intended for tourists, *Comic sights: Katoomba and Leura*, young lovers are shown at different viewpoints in the mountains. One mischievous drawing – 'The Three Sisters at Katoomba' – shows the rock formation of that name in the background while 'three sisters' canoodle with gentlemen at the lookout. Another image, and certainly the most sexually suggestive of them all, has a woman seated on her sweetheart's lap with Orphan Rock vertical behind them. Other couples can be seen embracing in the distance. 'The Orphan Rock(ed) at Katoomba' reads the heading. The implication is clear.⁴⁶

These humorous takes on romantic activity in national parks demonstrate that 1930s popular culture was keenly attuned to the

44 Harper (2007), 179.

45 *Sydney Mail*, 3 August 1932. Cited in Harper (2007), 191.

46 Harry Phillips (193?). *Comic sights: Katoomba and Leura*. (Ephemera/Postcards/Box1 [ML]).

romantic appeal of natural landscapes. As George Orwell explained of the 'dirty-joke' postcard format, these types of sketches also acted as popular forms of 'mental rebellion' against the 'fairly high standard of sexual morality' that still characterised Western culture in the early twentieth century.[47] The landscapes which were or would become national parks were spaces, and holidays were times, when challenges to conventional morality might be licensed.

Honeymooning

The modern honeymoon, renowned as a private romantic retreat, evolved from the nineteenth-century custom of the wedding tour where the bride and groom visited relatives who could not attend their wedding. It was an occasion used to reinforce family and social networks rather than an opportunity for a secluded romantic excursion.[48] In the twentieth century the honeymoon became an explicit and perhaps the most acceptable display of romance. National parks and pre-park landscapes became highly desirable locations in which to spend these excursions. The National Park itself, the Southern Highlands and especially the Blue Mountains gained reputations as popular honeymoon destinations in the early twentieth century.

The 1914 *Official guide to the National Park* makes it clear that newlyweds used park accommodation for honeymoons. Warumbul Cottage was offered as a 'charming' public accommodation to interested visitors, and an adjacent detached cottage gave 'seclusion to bachelor parties or honeymoon couples should this be desired'.[49] Allambie House was also remembered as popular for honeymoons in the 1930s. The Honeymoon track, a one-kilometre track descending from the hill to the Hacking River at Audley, was so named because it was the route taken by newlyweds from the National Park train station to Allambie House.[50] The Blue Mountains also became a favourite honeymoon

---

47 Orwell (1941).

48 Dubinsky (1999).

49 *Official guide to the National Park* (1914), 49.

50 McDougall (1992).

destination. In 1940, suggestions for the naming of a lookout on the eastern side of Cliff Drive were called for.[51] Honeymoon Lookout was chosen, illustrative of the mountains' reputation as a honeymoon haven. The Caves Express, a train and coach service running in the 1930s with connections to Jenolan Caves, was colloquially renamed the Honeymoon Express, further exemplifying the remarkable popularity of the mountains with newlyweds.[52] The Honeymoon Express was an open advertisement for the Blue Mountains as a contemporary honeymoon destination. Tourism promoters highlighted the appeal of the region to young couples.

As early as 1910, the Blue Mountains 'literally swarmed with young married couples'. The names of 13 couples who chose to honeymoon at the mountain's Carrington Hotel within a ten-day period were listed in *The Blue Mountains Echo*. The attraction of the mountains to these newlyweds was explained thus:

> The romantic side of honeymooning cannot be more admirably catered for in any part of Australia than in our midst. For here, in the sweet solitude of the Mountain glen, the gay and gloriously exhilarating trips of coach and motor car, or the ramble in the sequestered woods and caves love finds its fill to overflowing.[53]

This description reframes Romantic sentiment into an accessible experience for honeymooners seeking romance. Imbued with a picturesque Romanticism, the mountains were accordingly considered to offer the ideal backdrop for a honeymooning couple. This choice of locale for honeymoons demonstrates a romance–Romanticism continuum in the landscapes of national parks.

Niagara Falls as the honeymoon capital of the world serves as an interesting point of contrast to the popularity of the NSW national parks as honeymoon destinations. In the nineteenth century, Niagara was cast

---

51 Fox (2006), 148.

52 Belbin & Burke (1981).

53 'Katoomba for honeymoons', *The Blue Mountains Echo*, 13 April 1910. Cited in White et al. (2005), 62.

as an experience of the sublime – so profound it was often described as indescribable. In the twentieth century, as a symbol of wild and powerful nature, Niagara was often explicitly cast as a symbol of sexual passion, and yet now in the twenty-first century, it seems to have lost the sense of awe it once inspired, instead signifying 'the cheesy, outlandish, over-the-top'.[54] While Niagara Falls offers a distinctly different landscape to NSW national parks, it is interesting that these natural settings, both promoted for their sublime qualities in the nineteenth century, became havens for honeymooners in the twentieth century. Does this then affirm that experiences of the sublime were compatible with romance?

In her analysis of Niagara Falls, Elizabeth McKinsey has argued that 'containment and control of great power seems to be the key to the imaginative appeal of Niagara Falls as a honeymoon destination'.[55] Perhaps then, the idea of controlling or taming landscapes such as the Blue Mountains helps to explain why it became a popular honeymoon destination. McKinsey talks of containment in a psychological sense, arguing that the construction of Niagara in literature and later film, served to contain and thus control the wild and dangerous elements of the falls and suggests it is for this reason that Niagara remained a mecca for honeymooners. Niagara was more commercialised than most natural attractions – indeed it was an object lesson as to why national parks were needed to protect nature from commercialisation – but within the Romantic framework, sublime landscapes such as the Blue Mountains had become recognised as safe for the public to visit by the twentieth century. McKinsey's argument echoes that put forward by Kate Rossmansmith, who notes that, 'jagged cliffs became worth seeing, and seeing out from, at the same time that people began feeling relatively secure in nature'.[56] In many ways, controlled natural environments offered a sense of security against the perceived dangers of the wilderness. When honeymooning at the Blue Mountains, visitors could at once feel safe in their surroundings as well as comfortably secluded.

---

54 Dubinsky (1999), 41, 239.

55 McKinsey (1985), 188.

56 Rossmanith (2008), 17.

Much of the allure of a Blue Mountains honeymoon was the excitement of staying at one of the guesthouses or hotels such as the Hydro Majestic or Carrington Hotel, which combined the comfort of luxury with the natural attraction of the landscape. Lodging in hotels with large groups also made the honeymoon a social experience.[57] One honeymooner recalls sitting opposite two girls in the train carriage up to the mountains. These girls were also staying at the Carrington and accompanied the honeymooners on walks, had drinks in the lounge before dinner and sat together for every meal. They remained friends for many years.[58] Trips together with other people in charabancs (a type of open-air shuttle bus) or motorcars to locations such as Jenolan Caves were a typical activity and one that encouraged honeymoons to be social occasions.

The honeymoon experience could be a social one, but the mountain landscape provided an appropriately romantic setting for honeymooners specifically because it could also offer privacy. Honeymooners would go on walks together, climb the Giant Staircase and enjoy the many lookouts.[59] As with Dot Butler, to whom the National Park offered seclusion for young love, honeymooners could find privacy in the bush. 'Honeymoon Valley', recorded in The Blue Mountain Echo in 1913, was aptly named, as it was a 'pretty spot where a honeymoon couple escaped the stares and smiles'.[60]

Escaping for a honeymoon was a socially approved occasion for romance. While newlyweds could escape for moments of privacy in the depths of the park environment, the knowledge that they were honeymooning was open to the public, something a couple could either enjoy or find embarrassing. A consciousness of this public awareness

---

57 Burke (1985), 104.

58 Connie Cook. Interview conducted by Blue Mountains local historian Paul Innes, 20 September 2002. Cited with permission.

59 Barbara & Bruce Shand. Interview conducted by Paul Innes, 19 December 2002; Gwen Shappard. Interview conducted by Paul Innes, 13 November 2002; Aurdy Stewart. Interview conducted by Paul Innes, 20 May 2003. Cited with permission.

60 The Blue Mountains Echo, 31 October 1913. Cited in Fox (2006), 149.

may explain why one honeymooner in 1942 told her husband not to sit too close: 'we don't want them to know we're on our honeymoon'.[61] Thus, while the honeymoon was endorsed by society as a legitimate romantic occasion – most likely because it occurred within the framework of marriage – and the bush offered elements of privacy, the public negotiation of this private occasion could stifle romantic freedom. At the same time, public guessing (even perhaps sniggering) about who was on honeymoon gave the romance of parks a broader social acknowledgment.

A continuing romance with national parks

By the middle of the twentieth century a tone had been set: national parks and places such as the Blue Mountains and Kosciuszko evoked a sense of romance. Promotional material for national park locations in the first half of the century alluded to the romance of parks through landscape descriptions imbued with Romanticism. Increasingly, national parks were overtly promoted for their romantic qualities. A pamphlet from the late 1940s advertised the recently proclaimed Kosciusko State Park as a 'summer playground', picturing among its activities seeing the sights, horse riding, fishing and picking wildflowers. It also implied there were opportunities for romance, in photos of couples dancing and dining by candlelight.[62] There is no indication whether the couples advertised were married or not (perhaps the idea of a dirty weekend away was becoming more tolerated). This advertisement, with its promise of romance in national parks, certainly demonstrated a relaxation of the moral codes that had guided social etiquette in previous decades. The romantic encounter was by now promoted as a significant element of the national park experience. As the progression of romance and relationships shifted in the latter half of the twentieth century, traditional romance – courting, marriage and honeymooning – would no longer be the only permissible avenues of romance purused in national parks.

---

61 Connie Cook. Interview conducted by Paul Innes, 20 September 2002. Cited with permission.

62 'Kosciusko summer'. Brochure: Department of Tourist Activities (194?).

In the late twentieth century and early years of the twenty-first, national parks – at least those with conventionally Romantic landscapes – continued to evolve as explicit sites of romance for both married and unmarried couples. A 1973 publication about NSW national parks, *People in the parks,* featured on its cover a photograph of young lovers running happily through a park. Sydney author Ruth Park captured the attraction of national parks in her contribution to the book, 'Silence is a sound for lovers':

> Parks are running, jumping, laughing, loving, giving and taking places – places where the continuity of life and humanity is perceptible to both head and heart. Parks are for helping you to shut out the high, humming unreality of city existence, so that you can hear your own thoughts and those of your companion.[63]

This rather utopian allusion to national parks appears as an attempt to promote and perhaps modernise the notion of national parks for a 1970s audience. Offering the opportunity to indulge in a modern romance was one way of achieving that aim.

National parks increasingly became destinations where romantic couples could go to enrich their relationship. Emphasis began to rest heavily on the romantic benefit of national parks, which were embraced as great places for the romantic getaway; an opportunity to strengthen relationships, to reignite romance. Holiday accommodation in areas close to or within parks capitalised on this romantic attraction. Tree Tops Guest House in Bundanoon, where the 'wonders of the Morton National Park await', promoted itself as 'the perfect setting for a weekend of romance'.[64] A Barrington Tops visitors guide played on the romantic allure of its national park, enticing couples that may be 'quietly plotting a romantic getaway where you're not trapped with all the other romantic playmakers'.[65] The national park experience for young couples today is also more than a romantic interlude. One bushwalker who recently

---

63 Park (1973), 46.

64 'Tree Tops'. Advertising brochure.

65 Barrington Tops visitors guide. Sydney: NPWS (1988).

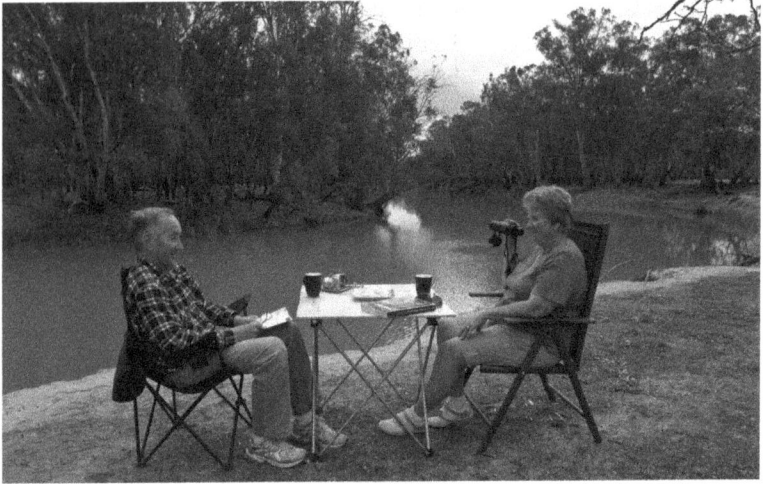

Fig 2.5. Romance never stops. National park campgrounds across the state are popular among 'grey nomads'. Woolshed camp, Yanga National Park 2009. Boris Hlavica / OEH.

spent a month travelling NSW national parks with his girlfriend explained his appreciation of national parks: 'getting out and walking has really cemented our relationship'.[66]

Some national parks continued to be appreciated for their remoteness and seclusion and the opportunity this provided for romantic and sexual encounters. Milo Dunphy (son of Myles Dunphy) is one well-known bushwalker who enjoyed the seclusion offered by national parks for romantic trysts. His biographer explained Milo's relationship with his lover Penny: 'Bushwalking was something they did a lot together. Out in the bush … their relationship became deeply companionable'.[67] In 1979 in Barrington Tops National Park, Milo's play for Penny is described as a 'well-tried tactic'. Penny explains that, upon Milo setting up the tent, 'it was quite obvious we were going to be

66 'Who I walk with', *The Fresh Air Magazine*, October–November 2007, 41.
67 Meredith (1999), 285.

sleeping together.[68] Today, the topic of sex in national parks invariably summons a laugh. 'We went for a walk up there, and there's a young couple having sex on the beach, we saw from a distance', laughed Dieter Meyering, telling of his experiences in Yuraygir National Park.[69] In the mid-1960s, one couple so engaged was interrupted by a whole school excursion of chortling teenage boys in the Royal National Park.[70]

'Feeling you are the only man and woman ever to enter this soft silence',[71] Ruth Park alluded to the silent solitude of national park environments, invoking Romantic sensibilities as well as a sense of romance. The Romanticism of local landscapes in NSW which contributed to the shaping of national parks as places of romance for lovers in the nineteenth century, continues to find expression today. Of the highlands in Kosciuszko National Park, one visitor described the environment as offering a type of 'spiritual alley' – whereby nature inspired a sense of elevation, a sensation akin to the Romantic sentiment,

> Of an early morning just driving through the high country and all the snow gums with the mist rising and the steep country going through the low range, with the motor ticking over, it's just absolutely stunning, you feel as though you're on an upper level, there's no doubt about that.[72]

This transcendent quality offered by national park landscapes finds expression in other ways. Some have argued that the environmental movement since the 1970s is a revived form of Romanticism in that they are made up of 'cults of nature' concerned entirely for the natural environment derived from a Romantic, individualistic discourse.[73] Alternatively, others have argued that the wilderness movement in 'no sense stands in a lineal relationship to nineteenth century Romanticism'.

---

68 Penny Figgis cited in Meredith (1999), 284.
69 Dieter Meyering. Interview, Wooli, 21 April 2008.
70 Richard White. Interview, 21 April 2008.
71 Park (1973), 46.
72 Carm & Ken. Interview, Wooli, 21 April 2008.
73 Daniels (1983), 4.

There is no connection between the two, argues Peter Hay, because the point of wilderness preservation is not the benefit of humankind but the right of the natural world to exist independently from its human use.[74] Yet romance continues to flourish. By the twenty-first century national parks had become widely popular locations for wedding ceremonies. A field officer in Yuraygir National Park estimates as many as 1000 weddings have been held in the park in the twenty years he has worked there.[75] Other areas popular for national park weddings, such as the Blue Mountains and Southern Highlands, offer extensive wedding information services, including wedding brochures and detailed websites.[76] The Office of Environment and Heritage website offers information and application forms for people who wish to hold wedding services in a park, verifying their popularity as wedding locations. A national park may be chosen as a wedding venue because it holds special significance for a couple but also because it suits the highly charged emotions of a wedding. The transcendent quality of the scenery offers an alternative spiritual setting to those who choose not to marry in the traditional spiritual arena of a church.

In 2008, two oral history respondents, a married couple who had retired to Wooli on the border of Yuraygir National Park, were asked, 'Do you think national parks are romantic places?' 'They're marvellous', replied the wife immediately. Her husband responded thoughtfully, 'Well, what do you mean by that?' 'Oh', she exclaimed, 'use your imagination!' We all laughed. His question was certainly not a silly one, but nor was her jibe. They continued to describe the elevated and transcendent emotion that national parks inspired in them as a couple. It was as if

---

74 Hay (1986/7), 12–13.

75 Dave McFarlane (cited) & Wayne Stevens, field officers at Yuraygir National Park. Interview, Grafton, 24 April 2008.

76 See Blue Mountains and Nepean Weddings, www.bluemountains-weddings. com.au, who also offer a free weddings publication; Tourism Southern Highlands offers an extensive range of information about wedding services in the Southern Highlands, (home to Morton National Park) [Online] Available: enquiries. southern-highlands.com.au/pages/weddings/ [Accessed November 2008].

'there's nobody else on the planet but us'.[77] This scenario confirms the correlation that continues to exist between an imagining of national parks according to the Romantic aesthetic and an understanding that they are appropriate settings for romance.

Conclusion

The importation of Romantic ideals to NSW landscapes in the nineteenth century, through art and literature, helped construct popular interpretations of national park landscapes. Representations of mountain landscapes in particular evoked the sublime and picturesque. The proliferation of rail and travel literature in the early twentieth century transmitted these aesthetic notions to a wider audience. The picturesque image continued to dominate tourist material while sublime representations were gradually reduced to travel clichés. Nevertheless, as has been demonstrated, the sublime and picturesque imagery that characterised national park landscapes contributed to shaping these locations as places of romance for lovers in the early twentieth century. Both the uplifting appeal of natural vistas and the intimate and secluded settings of the bush made national parks appropriate venues for romantic and sexual expression.

As fitting settings for romance, national parks thus became popular sites for romantic recreation. National parks had, by the mid twentieth century, come to be widely appreciated as romantic locations for lovers. Initially, parks acted as heterosocial spaces in which men and women could socialise with one another. Soon they became places where couples could escape to claim moments of privacy and intimacy. Bushwalking in national parks in particular encouraged romantic encounters which led to marriage on occasions. The popularity of national park locations as honeymoon destinations exemplified an appreciation of park landscapes as romantic places well and truly by the 1940s.

National parks have continued to be appreciated as locations of romance in more recent times. They are promoted as ideal areas for the romantic getaway, continuing to offer seclusion for the romantic

---

77 Carm & Ken. Interview, Wooli, 21 April 2008.

rendezvous. It is also apparent that an ideological lineage from the Romanticism of the nineteenth century continues to influence impressions of national parks today and the recreational experiences they accommodate. Their natural scenery continues to inspire elevated emotional responses and the spiritual context in which they are sometimes regarded can be seen as a revived Romanticism. It is important that national parks be recognised for the historical role they have played as places of romance since 1879, not only so that they can continue to fulfil this role, but also because individual personal associations with national parks are integral to existence and survival of these national assets.

References

Belbin, Phil & David Burke (1981). *Full steam ahead: across the Blue Mountains.* Sydney: Methuen Press.

Burke, Anne (1985). ' "Awesome cliffs, fairy dells" and lovers silhouetted in the sunset – a recreational history of the Blue Mountains, 1870–1939', in Peter Stanbury & Lydia Bushell (eds). *The Blue Mountains: grand adventure for all.* Sydney: Macleay Museum.

Butler, Dorothy (1991). *The barefoot bush walker: a remarkable story of adventure, courage and romance.* Sydney: Envirobook.

Butler, Dorothy (1987). 'The decade of getting together', in Ainslie Morris (ed.). *The Sydney bush walkers: the first sixty years.* Sydney: Sydney Bush Walkers.

Coghlan, TA (1906). *Picturesque New South Wales: an illustrated guide for settler and tourist.* Sydney: Government Printer.

Daniels, Kay (1983). 'Cults of nature, cults of history'. *Island Magazine*, 16(Spring).

Davidson, Jim & Peter Spearritt (2000). *Holiday business: tourism in Australia since 1870.* Melbourne: Miegunyah Press.

Dubinsky, Karen (1999). *The second greatest disappointment: honeymooning and tourism at Niagara Falls.* New Brunswick: Rutgers University Press.

Ford, Caroline (2005). 'Gazing, strolling, falling in love: culture and nature on the beach in nineteenth century Sydney'. *History Australia*, 3(1).

Fox, Brian (2006). *Blue Mountains geographical dictionary*. Bathurst: B. Fox.

Guide to the National Park and Port Hacking (1918). Sydney: Government Printer.

Gould, Nat (1896). *Town and bush: stray notes on Australia*. London: Routledge.

Hall, C Michael & John Shultis (1991). 'Railways, tourism and worthless lands: the establishment of national parks in Australia, Canada, New Zealand and the United States'. *Australian Canadian Studies*, 8(2).

Harper, Melissa (2007). *The ways of the bushwalker: on foot in Australia*. Sydney: UNSW Press.

Harper, Melissa (2000). 'Sensuality in sandshoes: representations of the bush in the walking and writing of John Le Gay Brereton and Percy Grainger'. *Australian Historical Studies*, 31(115).

Hay, PR (1986/7). 'The environmental movement: Romanticism reborn?' *Island Magazine*, 29(Summer).

Holiday resorts: a tourist guide to the railways of NSW (1916). Sydney: Government Printer.

Hotels, boarding houses etc. in the tourist districts: at or near railway stations (1898). Sydney: Government Printer.

Horne, Julia (2005). *The pursuit of wonder: how Australia's landscape was explored, nature discovered and tourism unleashed*. Melbourne: Miegunyah Press.

Johns, Elizabeth et al. (1998). *New worlds from old: 19th century Australian and American landscapes*. Canberra: National Gallery of Australia.

Kendall, Henry (1970). 'Twelve sonnets: a mountain spring c.1880', in Henry Kendall. *Leaves from Australian forests: poetical works of Henry Kendall*. Melbourne: Lloyd O'Neil.

Macquarie, Lachlan (1956). *Lachlan Macquarie, Governor of New South Wales. Journals of his tours in New South Wales and Van Diemen's Land 1810–1822: prospectus*. Sydney: Trustees of the Public Library of New South Wales.

McDougall, Garry (1992). *Heritage walks in New South Wales: heritage field guide*. Kenthurst: Kangaroo Press.

McKinsey, Elizabeth (1985). *Niagara Falls: icon of the American sublime.* Cambridge: Cambridge University Press.

Meredith, Peter (1999). *Myles and Milo.* Sydney: Allen & Unwin.

NSW Railway tourist guide, Illawarra Line (1889). Sydney: Government Printer.

Official guide to the National Park (1894). Sydney: Government Printer.

Official guide to the National Park (1914). Sydney: Government Printer.

Orwell, George (1941). 'The art of Donald McGill'. *The complete works of George Orwell.* [Online] Available: www.george-orwell.org/The_Art_of_Donald_ McGill/0.html [Accessed 10 November 2008].

Park, Ruth, (1973). 'Silence is a sound for lovers', in Dick Wordley. *People in the parks.* Sydney: Harbourtop of Australia.

Peiss, Kathy (1986). *Cheap amusements: working women and leisure in turn-of-the-century New York.* Philadelphia: Temple University Press.

Pleasant places convenient to the railways: a tourists' guide (1906). Sydney: Railway Commissioner.

Rossmanith, Kate (2008). 'On the edge'. *The Monthly*, August 17.

Smith, Jim et al. (1999). *Walking track heritage study, Blue Mountains district.* Sydney: NPWS

Speirs, Hugh (1981). *Landscape art and the Blue Mountains: the artistic, historical and environmental influences upon the landscape art of the Blue Mountains, New South Wales, Australia.* Sydney: Alternative Publishing.

Thompson, Patrick (1986). *Myles Dunphy: selected writings.* Sydney: Ballagirin.

White, Richard et al. (2005). *On holidays: a history of getting away in Australia.* Melbourne: Pluto Press.

Chapter 3

It's not all fun and games: rules, regulations and bad behaviour

Justine Greenwood

Where do regulations fit into a history of recreation in NSW national parks? After all, recreation is meant to be all about pleasure. And there are certainly numerous pleasures to be had in national parks: picnicking in the day or sitting around a campfire at night, rock climbing for the more adventurous and plenty of 'glens of exquisite loveliness' for the romantically inclined to while away the hours.[1] To those engaging in such pleasurable activities, any talk of regulations must seem out of place. However, if their thoughts did turn in that direction they may begin to notice that regulations are, and always have been, part of the very landscape of national parks.

For instance, in 1906 the trustees of the (Royal) National Park declared that visitors had no excuse for misbehaviour since 'large boards containing the by-laws [had] been erected in most conspicuous centres'.[2] Today, managers go out of their way to ensure visitors to national parks are not confronted by a list of dos and don'ts. Yet there are reminders that regulations are still there. Signs urge visitors not to feed the wildlife, markers delineate the size and number of campsites and notices at the entrance to the parks encourage people to 'be a considerate visitor'.[3]

---

1   *Official guide to the National Park* (1893).

2   Report of the National Park Trust, from 1 July 1904 to 13 June 1906, Parliamentary Papers, Second Session of 1906 (2): 807–09.

3   The Office of Environment and Heritage (OEH) website also provides a list of ways to 'be a considerate visitor'. [Online] Available: www.environment.nsw.gov. au/lookingafterparks/BeAConsiderateParkVisitor.htm [Accessed 2 Nov 2011].

Regulation needs to be understood as more than simply signposts dotting the park landscape. As Jeffrey E Frost and Stephen F McCool suggest, regulations 'are intended to circumvent undesirable behaviour by directly prescribing the behaviours that are not allowed'.[4] Yet if one looks over the entire history of regulation in national parks, it becomes clear that there is no fixed notion of what behaviours are undesirable. Some behaviours, such as littering, have consistently been prohibited. Others that were once considered improper may become acceptable. Acts that would hardly raise an eyebrow now, such as youths boating without their shirts on, once attracted the ire of national park rangers and the attention of the *Daily Telegraph* in 1939. The reverse can also occur: activities that were once allowed may be banned. A leap off the rocks into the lagoon at Wattamolla in Royal National Park was once considered a rite of passage for local children, but overcrowding, the risk of injury and the management's fears of possible litigation under public liability means that it is no longer permitted.[5] Changes in attitudes can be tinged with regret. One ranger recalled how:

> Once upon a time it was a tradition to pick a bunch of Christmas Bells and a bit of Christmas bush at Christmas. This has passed and something has been lost. It is strange that the cessation of an illegal act should diminish us.[6]

New developments in technology may mean that it is necessary to regulate behaviours that were not even thought of a few years earlier. The rise of car ownership in the 1950s and 1960s saw cars clog up picnic areas and race along roads in the parks. regulation of trail bike riding through the parks has had to be introduced in recent decades.[7]

---

4   Frost & McCool (1988), 5.

5   'Objection to bare chests', *Daily Telegraph*, 4 May, 1939; Victor Harnadi, Ranger. Interview, Royal National Park, 6 March 2008.

6   Senior (1976), 31–34.

7   Goldstein (1976), 30.

Fig. 3.1. Generations of children visiting Wattamolla in the Royal National Park have leaped from these rocks to the lagoon below, an activity that is no longer permitted due to safety concerns. State Records NSW.

Regulations are not simply confined to dictating what one cannot do, they also help to define what one can do. While there is no list provided as to what one should do in a national park, regulations, in expressly limiting behaviours that are seen as inappropriate, help shape what *is* considered appropriate. For instance, trail biking is restricted in most parks as it is perceived to be destructive to flora and fauna, while low-impact activities such as bushwalking or picnicking are tacitly encouraged through the provision of specific areas and designated walking tracks. Rowdy barbecues, a particular worry for Royal National Park rangers in the 1960s, may be watched closely but 'ordinary family picnickers' are perceived as posing little threat. Thus, regulations not only define appropriate activities but also characterise certain visitors as legitimate and others as 'nuisances'.[8]

---

8   Megan Levy (2004), 'Illegal trail bike riding targeted', *Illawarra Mercury*, 27 September, 9; Park Patrol Report, January 1968; State Records NSW: National Park Trust, 10727; Copies of minutes of Board of Trustees, 1950–1967.

As such, visitors whose behaviour falls into the nuisance category may find themselves excluded from that all-important group, 'the people', for whose benefit national parks were established. Attempts to be included with 'the people' or to exclude others from that group are a recurring feature of a history of regulations in national parks. Early annual reports of trustees congratulated the general public for providing 'every assistance in protecting that which, after all, is their own property' yet excluded from this public certain 'undesirable people' who had transgressed the by-laws. In the 1960s wildlife protection groups sought to differentiate 'the people' from 'the destroyers'. At the same time trail-bike riders argued that they had just as much right to be seen as 'legitimate users' of the parks as bushwalkers. More recently, park rangers and field officers at Yuraygir National Park slipped easily into defining 'the people' as encompassing families and couples and excluding those engaging in drunken behaviour.[9]

The above reveals two important points about regulation in national parks. Firstly, the fact that rangers, park management, visitors and wildlife groups are all involved in the process of defining 'the people' indicates that regulation is far from a simple one way process of a domineering authority imposing rules on a homogeneous public. Indeed, those in authority, such as rangers, may on occasion question the need for certain rules or even regret the disappearance of some illicit activities. Similarly, members of the public may take it upon themselves to request even stricter regulations.[10] Furthermore, regulations that restrict the activities of some users enhance the experience of others. What this demonstrates is that regulation is an ongoing and complex process of negotiation between a wide range of people involved in national parks, including park management, rangers, field officers, contractors, park users and locals.[11]

---

9   Wayne Stevens and Dave McFarlane, NPWS field officers. Interview, DECC Grafton Depot, 24 April 2008; Hitchcock (1972), 2–3; A Report of the National Park Trust, from 1 July 1904 to 13 June 1906, 807; McKenzie (1961), 8..

10 Senior (1976), 31–34; McKenzie (1961), 8.

11 Ian Hoskins suggests that regulations in urban parks should also be viewed in this way. See Hoskins (1996).

The second point is that what is being negotiated is often the very idea of what a national park should be. In attempting to define who is and who is not a part of the parks, people seek to define and hence control the concept of a national park. Multiple definitions are possible. A trail-bike rider may define a national park completely differently to a member of a bushwalking club. Park management may see its main priority as reducing the impact of visitors on the parks, while campers may envisage a national park as their traditional holiday spot. However, what is common to these and other negotiations is that their overall vision of a national park can be placed into one of two categories, either recreation or conservation. This ongoing tension, between the so-called competing aims of recreation and conservation, is what regulation seeks to reconcile.

In order to observe these aims in action this chapter will consider two moments in the history of NSW national parks, one from the earliest days of the Royal National Park in 1879, and another moment in Murramarang National Park nearly 130 years later. Before focusing on these two examples it is important to discuss the broad changes to regulations in national parks over that time which show how balancing the protection of nature with the rights of people to use the parks is a difficult task, one which has seen the pendulum swing back and forth between the two aims many times during NSW national parks' 130-year history.

Striking a balance

The earliest by-laws, those put in place in the National Park at Port Hacking in the late nineteenth century, had three aims. The trustees set out to provide an area for decent and healthy recreation, to protect flora and fauna and to prevent unauthorised commercial use of the park. However, the balance at this stage favoured recreation. The park trustees did not perceive a contradiction between preserving the natural features of the park and clearing areas for football and cricket fields, erecting cottages and planting ornamental gardens, although this perhaps has more to do with changing perceptions of what constitutes preservation and conservation than any deliberate rejection of conservationist principles on the part of the Trust.[12]

As developments in transport, in particular the mass ownership of cars, allowed the National Park and other newly proclaimed national parks to become more accessible, regulations began to reflect concerns about the impact of the numbers and class of visitors. Trustees feared that parks were being swamped by an ever growing public. Annual reports from the late 1930s to the 1960s complained about the large amounts of rubbish left in the parks by visitors, an increase in incidents of vandalism to park property and the natural environment, and rising numbers of wild parties.[13]

A sense that things were getting beyond the control of park authorities pervades the last reports of the Royal National Park Trust written in a tone of weary defeatism:

> The Trust welcomes rapidly increasing public use of the Park but joins with other sections of the community in deprecating the growing incidence of bad attitudes. The litter problem is worse than ever before ... Vandalism accounts for loss and damage. A recently constructed stone roadway sign has been used for a barbeque. Road signs have been knocked down and used for firewood.[14]

Such a feeling may have been shared by other parks trusts in NSW. In 1967 the various park trusts were disbanded and replaced by the National Parks and Wildlife Service (NPWS). All national parks in NSW now shared the joint aims of:

---

12 For an analysis of early understandings of preservation in Australia see Bonyhady (2000). For the development of a conservation consciousness specifically within national parks in Australia see Hall (1992); Report of the National Park Trust for the year ending 30 June 1908, Parliamentary Papers, Second Session of 1908, 2(2): 945–951; *Official guide to the National Park* (1893). 64–5.

13 National Park Trust: 10732, State Records NSW: Annual Reports of the National Park Trust, 1938–1967 [9/2194].

14 Annual Report of the National Park Trust, 1964.

Fig. 3.2. Standing near the edge of the Kanangra Walls, Oberon. State Records NSW.

> The encouragement and regulation of the appropriate use, understanding and enjoyment of the park by the public. The preservation of each national park in its natural condition, the protection of the special features of the park and the conservation of the wildlife therein.[15]

The NPWS held up recreation and conservation as its two key aims but there was a growing sense that conservation was the more vital goal. Regulations increasingly reflected that shift. Even before the advent of the NPWS, a brochure entitled 'What does a ranger do?' distributed by the Fauna Protection Panel which was then charged with the management of the state's wildlife, described the role of a ranger, including the enforcing of regulations, almost entirely in terms of conservation: 'A ranger must be a competent wildlife conservationist ... He talks wildlife conservation and tries to influence others to think in

---

15 *The National Parks and Wildlife Act* 1967. Cited in Smith (1998), 6.

terms of wildlife conservation'.[16] Interestingly, such brochures revealed another shift in national park policy, from simply forbidding certain practices to encouraging people to adopt conservation ideals and hence regulate their own behaviour and that of others. The staff newsletter of the NPWS, *Napawi*, facetiously referred to this approach to regulation in an article entitled 'Parks are for propaganda' by Jenny Fea, whose position was described as 'Royal A/V Screenwriter Extraordinaire'. She described the implementation of new visitor programs as a 'propaganda job [influencing] people's opinions about what a Good Time is'.[17] A good time was one that took into account the environmental impact on an area. That the balance had swung firmly towards conservation was confirmed in 1992 when restrictions were placed on four-wheel-drives in Yuraygir National Park. The director of NPWS, Bill Gillooly, announced, in relation to the competing demands of conservation and recreation, that 'conservation ultimately means more to me'.[18]

While the emphasis on conservation in national parks has continued in the twenty-first century, there has also been a subtle shift towards understanding that the way people have used and shaped national parks is also worthy of protection. Plans of management seek to preserve historic features of the park, while research into particular national parks focuses on the traditional uses of the parks by a range of user groups. Park managers must consider the needs, rights and demands of Aboriginal people to access and use parks, as distinct from recreational park users and conservation groups. Managers now acknowledge that persistent use of an area, including recreational use, creates attachments. Therefore before new regulations are put in place in an area, visitors to parks are consulted. As one NPWS ranger explains, it is 'really important to realise the history of use'. If regulations do need to be changed then the NPWS aims to 'do it slowly and talk, talk, talk and people come around'.[19]

---

16 'Information for the guidance of rangers'. Fauna Protection Panel, 1965, in Conroy (1991).

17 Fea (1979), 19.

18 Susskind (1992), 1.

19 See for instance OEH, Cultural landscapes: connecting history, heritage

Any history of recreation in national parks in NSW must recognise that it is, in a large part, the history of a constant balancing act of the aims of conservation and recreation. Park regulations provide a useful source for examining the ways the various parties involved in national parks – management, wildlife groups, holiday makers and so on – have sought to negotiate their way between these two aims or been excluded from the process. The next two sections provide the two historical moments that, despite being over a century apart, are linked by this common theme.

The first section explores the ways in which regulations are born out of particular social contexts, as in the case of the foundation of the first national park in NSW in 1879 and its links to the development of urban parks (parks in or close to the city). Urban parks provided a way for people to imagine how to behave in national parks. Ideas that stemmed from urban parks, their place in creating healthy people and an ordered society, were drawn on by national park management. Regulations were the practical expression of these ideas.

The second section adds the users of national parks to the picture. The focus shifts to Pretty Beach in Murramarang National Park, where campers have struggled to adapt to changes to Pretty Beach introduced by park management over the past decade. This section demonstrates that the image of a park held by management is not always compatible with the ways in which people desire to use the parks. When regulations seek to change these patterns of use, people's attachments to the parks are often threatened.

Read together, these two case studies demonstrate that finding a balance between recreation and conservation in national parks is an ongoing process. Creating regulations that cater for both is, as Bill Gillooly, then director of the NPWS, stated in 1992, 'like balancing on a knife's edge'.[20]

---

and reserve management. [Online] Available: www.environment.nsw.gov.au/chresearch/CulturalLandscapesProject.htm [Accessed 8 June 2008]; NPWS ranger. Interview, DECC Ulladulla Office, 23 January 2008.

20 Susskind (1992).

Regulating the bush

Australia had a national park before it was officially a nation. Dedicated on 26 April 1879 the National Park was 'national' in the sense that it was provided 'for the people'.[21] However, when the *Official guide to the National Park* spoke of who would use the park, 'the people' tended to be narrowed to 'the people of NSW' or even more specifically, 'the jaded citizen of Sydney'. Indeed, it was the Sydneysider caught up in the 'rush and turmoil of every-day life' that was envisaged as the primary visitor to the park, so it is useful to view the development of regulations within the National Park from the perspective of the city of Sydney.[22]

Regulation should not be understood as simply referring to a list of rules. The dos and don'ts grow out of a larger framework of ideas about what a national park is. Yet in 1879 the idea of a national park was a new one, so Sydneysiders sought to find pre-existing models that could serve as a guide to what a national park should be and what behaviour it should require. Although the world's first national park, Yellowstone in the United States, had been established in 1872, it is unlikely that it inspired Sydney's National Park. Yellowstone, 1600 km from any city of Sydney's size, could hardly be seen as a providing the concept for a park 22 km from the centre of Sydney.[23] Sydneysiders instead turned to the city to find a more appropriate model.

The period encompassing the foundation and early development of the National Park was a time of great change for Sydneysiders. In the years between 1880 and 1930 the people of Sydney experienced shifts in what Stephen Kern has broadly described as the essential framework of experience, time and space.[24] New modes of transport made it easier to travel longer distances, new forms of communication allowed for contact with far-flung places, and areas of the city were ordered and given specific uses. At the same time, a heightened consciousness of

---

21 For a discussion of how the idea of 'the people' justified the 'national' in 'national park' in NSW, see Chapter 1. Also see Harper & White (2008).

22 *Official guide to the National Park* (1893), 9, 64.

23 Goldstein (1976), 18.

24 Kern (1983).

time and time-measurement led to different hours, days and weeks being assigned particular activities. Sydney was in the process of becoming a modern city.[25]

An integral part of that process was the setting aside of green space for the purpose of rest and recreation. Sydney in 1879 already had green spaces in the form of Hyde Park, the Botanical Gardens and the Domain. Centennial Park, the people's park, was added to the city's lungs in 1888. It was in the context of ongoing debates about the need to provide more breathing spaces in the city that the 1893 *Official guide* could begin to outline the role of the National Park. Thus urban parks provided a way of imagining what a national park could be and the kinds of behaviours that could take place there.[26]

The first point of comparison between urban parks and the National Park was in their prescribed purpose. Ian Hoskins in his study of the modernisation of urban parks in Sydney explained that one of the key roles of the park in the modern city was to facilitate 'healthful recreation' for the population.[27] Cities were viewed as crowded, dirty and corrupting, polluting both the body and the mind. Parks were seen as cleansing the individual, both physically and psychologically. However, they did not just benefit the individual. 'The perfectly equipped municipal body', wrote journalist and urban reformer JD Fitzgerald in 1907, 'must create country conditions in the city, if it desires to preserve the stamina of the race'.[28] A concern with the overall health of society had already been expressed in relation to the establishment of the National Park, the *Official guide* describing both urban parks and the National Park as vital for ensuring 'a healthy and consequently vigorous and intelligent community'.[29]

---

25 For a description of elements of the Australian experience of modernity see Greenwood (2008); Matthews (2005); Waterhouse (1995) and Davison (1993).

26 Hoskins (1996), 9; *Official guide to the National Park* (1893), 7.

27 Hoskins (1996), 9.

28 Fitzgerald (1907), 196–201.

29 *Official guide to the National Park* (1893), 7. For a brief outline of the long history in the West of the notion of escaping the city for the benefit of one's health, see White (2005), 70–71. The idea of ensuring the 'stamina of the race' through

Fig. 3.3. Modern signage alerts visitors that they are entering national parks, and display park regulations. Michael Lauder/OEH.

From these remarks we can begin to build up a picture of the kind of visitors and the behaviour of these visitors that was seen as appropriate for a national park. The call to provide places for recreation for the entire 'race' suggested that the park was intended for all members of the community. Indeed it was. However, there was also a particular focus on the working class and urban poor. These members of society, living in the worst and most densely populated parts of the city, were seen as being most in danger of degeneration and most in need of escape from 'slums, foul air and pollution' to the purifying air of the park.[30] Early National Park reports noted that such people would not have the means

healthy activity within national parks continued for some time. For instance, in 1939 the NSW government set up the National Fitness and Physical Education Branch which had a similar aim. More generally, there is a growing body of research in the area of public health and the role of the state in creating a healthy populace. These histories analyse the relationship between national fitness and national identities. See, for example, Bashford & Strange (2007), 87–92.

30 White (2005), 70; Hoskins (1996), 11.

or ability to reach the park and the Trust very quickly sought to take advantage of the building of the Illawarra railway line with a branch line to National Park station, which opened in 1886. These reports recorded the Trust's delight in the growing number of visitors the park attracted every year and their hope to encourage more by extending the railway all the way to Audley, the park's most popular recreation area.[31]

While the trustees eagerly welcomed growing numbers of visitors, not all were seen as desirable. It was assumed that the working and urban poor, living as they did in the worst parts of the city, could not help but be exposed to the most dangerous of vices, resulting in bad behaviour that threatened the wellbeing of society. Healthful recreation offered a way to stem this threat. Thus, tied up with ideas about creating healthy people were notions of creating a better social order. Healthy bodies equalled a healthy and therefore orderly and cohesive society. Only visitors that participated in activities that could be seen as contributing to the creation of such a society were included in the trustees' welcome. It is in this light that we can read the following National Park by-law:

> 13. No person in a state of intoxication, or of reputed bad character, shall enter or remain within the Park; and no persons shall behave in a disorderly or offensive manner, or use any bad language, or commit any act of indecency therein.

Drinking, rowdy behaviour and bad language might not cause environmental damage, but it is easy to understand how such behaviour had no place in a national park that was meant to assist in the physical and mental improvement of the individual and of the society of which they were a part.[32]

The above by-law, read once again, seems somewhat ambiguous. It was clear that intoxication was prohibited, as was bad language, but terms such as disorderly, offensive and indecently were essentially left to be defined by the prosecuting authority. However, there were other ways

---

31 Goldstein (1976), 21; Report of the National Park Trust, from 1 July 1904 to 13 June 1906, 807.

32 Hoskins (1996), 66.

that park authorities could make clear what behaviour was acceptable. Terrence Young, writing about modern urban parks in the US, explains that from the 1880s, park planners believed that certain behaviours could be encouraged through physically segmenting the park and assigning each part a specialised use. Prior to this, parks had been used for a variety of activities, with no one area designated as being for a particular purpose. The working class and urban poor especially used parks for a variety of political, recreational and work-related activities. However, the modern psychology of the day saw disorder in the physical realm inevitably leading to disorder in the social realm.[33]

The ordering of Sydney's urban parks was evident as early as the 1850s. For instance, the trustees of Hyde Park 'attempted to turn the area into a well ordered civic space with extensive plantings and well defined pathways'. Hoskins notes that by 1907 'the infrastructure of respectability', lights, clean seats, kiosks and pathways, had become commonplace in most of Sydney's urban parks.[34] Likewise, from its very beginnings, the National Park was envisaged as an area that would be divided up into specialised sections. The trustees were empowered to 'set apart and use such portions of the Park' for ornamental gardens, zoological gardens, cricket or any other lawful game and so on. Audley, the main camp of the park, was also segmented. Sections included a clearing of five acres of land on the bank of the river for a horse paddock, two acres for a vegetable and fruit garden, premises that could sleep up to twenty-two guests, a clearing for the convenience of picnic parties and an aviary for Australian birds. On a larger scale, the entire park itself could be seen as being ordered into distinct areas. Audley was to be a pleasure ground reminiscent of an urban park, while the areas surrounding it were presented as 'primeval forests', to remain untouched for all time.[35]

---

33 Hoskins (1996), 53; Young (1995), 535–51.

34 Hoskins (1996), 28–29, 56.

35 State Records NSW: National Park Trust (Royal National Trust, Audley); 10724, Minute books of Board of the Board of Trustees, 1879–1958; Land Grant Register Book, vol. 821, fol. 755; *Official guide to the National Park* (1893), 14–16, 64.

Despite the similarities between the two spaces, it is in this division between modern pleasure ground and primeval bush, that the National Park starts to appear quite unlike an urban park. There are other indications that the National Park was conceived somewhat differently to an urban park. For instance, there was far more of an emphasis on passive and organised recreation in urban parks. Racing or games were not allowed in many of the city's parks. Centennial Park banned all sporting activities and only relented and permitted organised sports after intense pressuring by sporting clubs. Casual sporting activities continued to be discouraged in this and other parks. On the other hand, such regulations were never in place in the National Park. Indeed, the trustees encouraged games. An area of eighteen acres near Loftus was 'cleared, ploughed and sown with grasses for the purpose of making a cricket and football ground'. Other non-passive types of recreation were also encouraged. Bathing enclosures were established near Audley, rivers were cleared for boating, and picnic tables close to fire places and swings were provided.[36]

No conclusive statement can be made as to why these differences existed. As has been demonstrated above, the National Park and urban parks were often thought of in very similar terms. Certain understandings about healthy bodies and healthy societies provided a framework for what a national park was and what one was expected to do there. Indeed, something of this kind of thinking is still found in NSW national park literature of the new millennium – although, of course, the eugenics agenda no longer informs such policy making. The Office of Environment and Heritage website advertises the Healthy Parks Healthy People program which is described as 'a program of events and activities that highlight the benefits of a healthy park system and its contribution to the health of individuals and the community'.[37] Ultimately, urban parks were vital in providing a way for Sydneysiders to imagine something that was quite new – a park in the bush.

---

36 Hoskins (1996) 50–53; Report of the National Park Trust, from 1 July 1904 to 13 June 1906, 808.

37 Office of Environment and Heritage, Healthy Parks Healthy People. [Online] Available: www.environment.nsw.gov.au/HPHP/ [Accessed 20 May 2008].

It is in thinking about the bush, the primeval forests, that we can perhaps begin to understand why the National Park, and other national parks since, eventually came to be perceived and hence regulated quite differently to urban parks. An urban park was surrounded by the city, whereas Audley and the other main picnic grounds in the park were surrounded by what was imagined to be untamed wilderness. The activities provided in the built up areas of the National Park can perhaps be viewed as inducement to stay in the main camp area. Today's park managers try to ensure that camping grounds are designed in such a way that people are not enticed to venture into the surrounding bushland to camp. Areas are cleared, the trees are pushed back from the campsites and official walking tracks provide safe routes for those who must explore. The reason for this, as a Grafton field officer explained, is partly to do with limiting the impact on the environment and ensuring the safety of visitors. The bush can be a dangerous place for the uninitiated. Yet it is also because once a visitor enters the bush it is more difficult to restrict their activities. Having certain areas that are obviously meant for recreational use allows national parks staff to supervise visitors more easily, encouraging the ordinary pleasure-seeker to stay within a safely contained area while still allowing the more intrepid adventurer access to the bush.[38] It would appear that this kind of thinking has informed the regulation of national parks since the opening of the National Park in 1879.

However, the notion of supervision, even for safety's sake, does not sit well with the idea of a national park. Many Australians, indeed Westerners generally, are attached to the idea that wilderness should be free from the constraints of society. Today, campers and visitors to national parks echo this sentiment when they talk about relaxing in nature, away from everything and everyone. This suggests an underlying tension between the idea of the bush as a place which is free of rules and the regulations which are imposed on visitors to the parks. Certain circumstances may bring this tension to the surface. One such instance will now be explored.

---

38 Wayne Stevens & Dave McFarlane. Interview, 2008.

'Our site'

National parks, from their earliest days, have sought to provide recreation for the nation, conservation for the nation, or both. However, ask visitors why they appreciate national parks and their immediate answer is usually not related to these grand visions. Many will, of course, eventually speak of the importance of national parks in terms of the role they play in ensuring that the bush is safe from those who are 'willing to chop it down for small gains'.[39] Yet for many people a national park is, and has long been, first and foremost where they go for their holidays.

Not all visitors to national parks are there for a holiday. In national parks close to the main urban centres the majority of users are day-trippers, out to enjoy a bushwalk or a picnic in a natural setting. However, the coastal parks have long attracted visitors who camp for anything from one night to several weeks. Campers tend to distinguish themselves from day-trippers. Giselle Buller, camping at Pretty Beach in Murramarang National Park on the South Coast of NSW in January 2008, claimed not to mind sharing the park with day-trippers, but as she explained, 'Campers look after things because you like to come back and have that same sort of feeling and character. And so you look after things – pick up rubbish and bottles from the beach which day-trippers don't do'.[40] Giselle's comments display a strong sense of ownership of the camping area and surrounding beach. Indeed, regular campers are a particular group of users of national parks who tend to form very deep connections to a place based on years of returning there for their holidays. This connection can be disrupted by changes in rules and regulations.[41]

39 Julie & Roland Mangos, campers. Interview, Meroo National Park, 22 January 2008.

40 Giselle Buller. Interview, Murramarang National Park, 21 January 2008.

41 Sharon Monk & Giselle Buller, campers. Interview, Pretty Beach, Murramarang National Park, 21 January 2008; NPWS, Royal National Park, Heathcote National Park & Garawarra State Recreation Area – draft plan of management (August 1994), 1–75.

Jeffrey E Frost and Stephen F McCool have explained that most visitors to national parks expect a certain amount of regulation. In fact, they often see regulation, even to the extent of controlling numbers or banning various activities in a particular vicinity, as enhancing their overall experience. The Mangos family, who spent two weeks in the 2008 Christmas holidays camped at a 'natural' campsite (i.e. limited number of campsites, no running water or electricity and basic toilet facilities) at Termeil Point in Meroo National Park on the South Coast, felt that the restrictions placed on the use of the area, such as not being able to reach the campsite by car, were beneficial for their own camping experience. As Julie Mangos explained, 'One of the beauties of camping at Meroo is that those who want to set up their generators to run their fridge, boom boxes or whatever else aren't willing to carrying them in down here'. However, not all visitors respond to regulations in this positive way. As Frost and McCool have written, 'visitors who do view the restrictions as unacceptable may no longer visit an area, in a sense being displaced'[42] (Of course, there is always the argument to be made that if boom boxes were allowed visitors like the Mangos family would feel equally displaced).

Regulations are most likely to be viewed as unacceptable when they are changed after a long period of time, particularly for visitors who have been regular users of an area. Examples of such changes may include charging fees in an area that was originally free, restricting the use of electricity/water at a site that was originally powered, or banning campfires at grounds where they have been an integral part of the camping experience. One NPWS ranger recognised that 'people like continuity not change'. In the last decade NPWS has become increasingly aware of this and has sought to 'maintain the experience ... in order to ensure that people are able to have physical and emotional continuity at a site'.[43] However, as the experience of campers at Pretty Beach in Murramarang National Park shows, this has not always been possible.

---

42 Julie & Roland Mangos. Interview, 2008; Frost & McCool (1998), 5–9.
43 NPWS ranger. Interview, DECC Grafton Office, 23 April 2008.

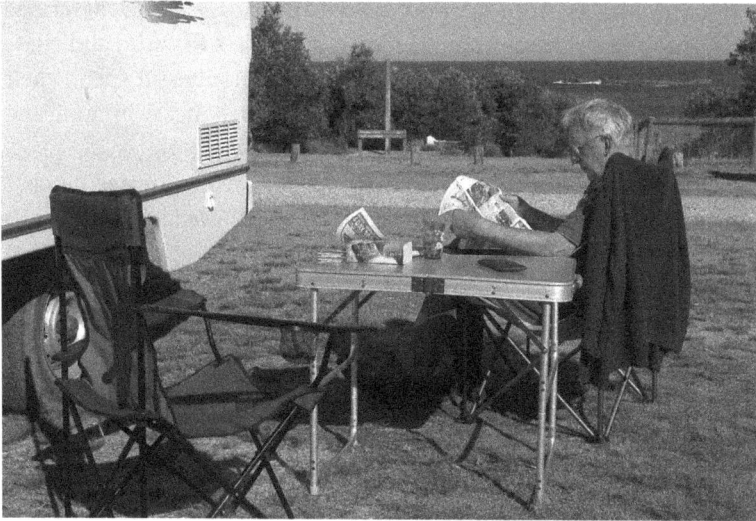

Fig. 3.4. Many regulars in coastal national park campgrounds have been returning annually for decades. Pretty Beach, 2006. Michael Van Ewijk / OEH.

Murramarang National Park, reserved in 1973, covers an area of approximately 1970 hectares on the south coast of NSW. The area is very popular with tourists and is within a few hours drive of Sydney, Wollongong and Canberra. Pretty Beach is situated in the northern section of the park. It more than deserves its name – the view from the headland looks out over a picture perfect beach. Holiday periods have always seen the beach full of families and the campsite packed to capacity.[44]

Many of the visitors to Pretty Beach have a special personal connection with the area. Two families in particular, the Mumfords and the Monks, have a long history at Pretty Beach. Both families have holidayed there, three weeks each Christmas, since the late 1960s. The oldest members of the families camped at Pretty Beach as children, and years later continue to bring their own children there to share in a style of holiday that has not really changed much in all those years. John

---

44 OEH. *Murramarang National Park*. [Online] Available: //www.environment. nsw.gov.au/NationalParks/parkCamping.aspx?id=N0025 [Accessed 8 June2008].

Mumford, who has been camping at Pretty Beach since 1968, described his early holidays there in simple terms: 'sun, sea, surf, swim and chase girls'. Forty years later, in 2008, John and his family still spend their days fishing, bike riding, playing beach cricket, walking, swimming and relaxing.[45]

In 2008 there were seventy sites at Pretty Beach. Caravans, camper trailers and camping beside a vehicle were allowed. The area was provided with drinking water, flush toilets, an amenities block, hot showers, picnic tables and rubbish bins. The camping ground, set a short distance back from the beach, provided no views of the ocean. However, this was not always the case. Up until 2007 the campsite extended further, parts looking right over the beach, giving those at the front uninterrupted views of the sea. These sites were coveted by all campers, but most went to families who had been coming to the ground for years. In 2008 this area was marked off for revegetation. The number of overall sites was also reduced, as was the number of sites with power. From 2003, campfires had been banned during the peak seasons of Christmas, Easter and long weekends.[46]

The 1997 *Plan of management* of Murramarang National Park signalled these changes to Pretty Beach. The plan noted that 'some recreation facilities in the park are over developed ... As opportunities arise, these will be re-designed and landscaped to create a more natural setting'. The plan drew on visitor surveys to support this stance. Users stated they were attracted to national parks for their 'quiet, restful atmosphere and scenic and natural qualities' and opposed 'increased sophistication of facilities'. Pretty Beach, which in 1997 was operated by a concessionaire and contained mostly privately owned permanent caravans, a small number of cabins and on-site vans, was placed as a high priority for redevelopment along more 'natural' lines.[47] One issue the NPWS needed to address was whether the preference given to regulars limited the access and experience of other potential users.

45 John & Alison Mumford, campers. Interview, Pretty Beach, Murramarang National Park, 21 January 2008.

46 *Murramarang National Park*; John & Alison Mumford. Interview, 2008.

47 NPWS (2002). *Murramarang National Park plan of management*, 24–30.

Overall, the redevelopment was not met favourably by many of the regulars. NPWS proceeded slowly with the changes – the plan was flagged in 1997 and was gradually implemented over the next ten years – and did so in consultation with park visitors. The changes themselves were not overly drastic. Even with the revegetation and cutting back of sites, the area, with its powered sites and flush toilets, could hardly be described as a 'natural' camping ground. Yet regular users still felt as if the changes were forced upon them. Sharon Monk, who has holidayed at Pretty Beach for twenty-seven years, stated that NPWS did not let them know that the summer of 2006–07 would be their last year 'up the front' (near the beach). Nor were they told about fee increases or that they would no longer be able to have a fire.[48]

The constant refrain of the regular campers was that the new regulations had 'changed the whole experience' at Pretty Beach. Restrictions on campfires meant that the families no longer had a nightly focal point where they could enjoy each other's company and a few drinks. John Mumford believed that this particular restriction encouraged the development of behaviours that had the potential to be far more dangerous. No campfires in the camping ground meant that young kids would venture unsupervised into the bush or down to the beach to light fires. Increased fees and restrictions on the number of sites were other factors that changed the whole experience. Low fees and a large number of sites allowed families who perhaps could not afford another type of holiday to return every year.[49] In doing so, families formed long lasting friendships. As Sharon Monk explained,

> When we first started camping here 27 years ago we didn't know anyone, we just came here with our family and then we got to know all the other families that came here as well and formed friends with them and then you just met up every year and became friends with their kids and grew up. And then you have your own kids and bring them here too.[50]

---

48 Sharon Monk & Giselle Buller. Interview, 2008.
49 John & Alison Mumford. Interview, 2008.
50 Sharon Monk & Giselle Buller. Interview, 2008.

For these families, the changes to Pretty Beach disrupted a vital experience in their lives, the all important annual family holiday. In order to understand their sense of loss, it is necessary to realise the huge significance of the kind of holiday experienced by campers at Pretty Beach and quite possibly at national parks all over NSW. As suggested by Richard White:

> In the very repetition of going to the same place year after year, seeing the same people, doing the same things, there was something ritualistic and fulfilling, an annual marking out of special time.[51]

For both the Mumfords and the Monks the annual holiday in the national park provided two important opportunities: the ability to spend time with their families and the ability to have this time in a beautiful and affordable setting. Giselle Buller, a member of the Monk contingent, explains that, 'holidays are all about quality time together … [they] keep families together and what better place to have a holiday than in the beautiful and natural environment'. John Mumford agreed: 'the experience of a national park is a family thing'.[52] Time with the family and the perception that the holiday destination remained unchanged from year to year, sustained people through 'a year of hard work'.[53]

One NPWS ranger commented on a similar situation in Yuraygir National Park, where a particular principle underlies people's experience of national parks. He described it as, 'Price is what you pay, value is what you get'.[54] The value of national parks for many visitors is found in the 'repetition of going to the same place every year' and in the continuity of experience that the parks provide. This explains why the introduction

---

51 White (2005), 132.

52 John & Alison Mumford. Interview, 2008; Sharon Monk & Giselle Buller. Interview, 2008.

53 John & Alison Mumford. Interview, 2008.

54 NPWS ranger. Interview, 2008. In early 2008 Yuraygir National Park raised fees at several campgrounds in the Park. This was met with great opposition from many of the users. See, for example, Kijas (2009); Miller (2008).

of regulations that alter this experience in order to meet conservation aims, as in the case of Pretty Beach, can be met with resistance. This should not be taken to mean that the Pretty Beach campers did not appreciate the natural environment. Indeed, as Giselle Monk and John Mumford made clear, one of the main reasons they holiday at Murramarang is that they value the natural beauty the camp provides. Rather, their resistance reveals the disconnect between what some park users may perceive as natural and what park managers, and perhaps other visitors, perceive as natural. For Giselle and John powered sites and campsites overlooking the beach were completely in accord with the natural environment. More than that, they were how things had always been.

Essentially, what the example of Pretty Beach shows is that breaking the continuity of experience that the parks provide, through the implementation of new regulations perceived as favouring conservation of the natural environment over the traditional use of a place, can leave those with long associations with a national park feeling dispossessed of both their special place and their special time with their families.

Conclusion

Rules matter. They matter especially in a history of recreation in national parks. All recreation sits in a framework of rules and regulations. And behind each by-law, each signpost dotting the landscape, there is an entire history. As we have seen, it can be a history of park authorities trying to find a way of imagining an entirely new concept – a park in the bush. It can also be a history of families struggling to come to terms with changing conceptions of the role of a national park.

What runs through these two case studies, and through the history of regulation in national parks in general, is the difficulty that park managers face in finding a balance between the aims of recreation and conservation. The fact that there is a wide range of people involved in national parks – from rangers to wildlife groups to a variety of different holidaymakers – means that the very notion of what constitutes conservation and recreation is hard to pin down. To further complicate matters, as the two case studies show, both concepts have changed and developed over time, as has their relative importance.

The National Park founders in 1879 prioritised recreation in order to create a healthy population. Regulations, both those written in the by-laws and mapped out on the very landscape of the park, reflected this aim. Yet conservation concerns, even if their methods hardly seem to fit the modern understanding of the term, still drove the park founders. After all, a 'healthy' population needed a natural environment and a natural environment needed protection.

The experience of campers at Pretty Beach highlights the unintended consequence that regulations, which seek to create a particular vision of a national park, can have on people's attachments to a national park. Once again, in the implementation and reaction to regulations we can see the difficulties of balancing conservation and recreation and of juggling access to the parks between competing groups. The value of looking at regulations, behind the by-laws, beyond the signposts, is that they reveal that the ability of people to use the parks for recreation must be, is, and always has been balanced with conservation concerns. However, the process of finding a way between the two aims is definitely not all fun and games.

References

Bashford, Alison & Carolyn Strange (2007). 'Thinking historically about public health'. *Medical Humanities*, 33.

Bonyhady, Tim (2000). *The colonial earth*. Melbourne: Miegunyah Press.

Conroy RJ (1991). Collection of Papers on the Role of the Ranger (NPWS).

Davison, Graeme (1993). *The unforgiving minute: how Australia learned to tell the time*. Melbourne: Oxford University Press.

Fea, Jenny (1979). 'Parks are for propaganda, or A/V programs, Royal National Park'. *Napawi*, 7(4).

Fitzgerald, JD (1907). 'Parks and open places'. *Lone Hand*, 1 June, 196–201.

Frost, Jeffrey E & Stephen F McCool (1988). 'Can visitor regulations enhance recreational experiences?' *Environmental Management*, 12(1).

Goldstein, Wendy (1976). *Royal National Park*, Sydney: Government Printer.

Greenwood, Justine (2008). 'The 1908 visit of the Great White Fleet: displaying modern Sydney'. *History Australia*, 5(3).

Hall, C Michael (1992). *Wasteland to World Heritage: preserving Australia's wilderness*. Melbourne: Melbourne University Press.

Harper, Melissa & Richard White (2008). 'The "nationalisms" of the first national parks: was the Australian model different?' Conference paper. Civilising nature: national parks in transnational historical perspective. Washington DC: German Historical Institute. 12–14 June.

Hitchcock, Peter (1972). '2 Wheels vs. 2 Legs'. *Napawi*, 1(9).

Hoskins, Ian (1996). Cultivating the citizen: cultural politics in the parks and gardens of Sydney, 1880–1930. PhD Thesis, University of Sydney.

Kern, Stephen (1983). *The culture of time and space, 1880–1918*. Cambridge: Harvard University Press.

Kijas, Johanna (2009). *There were always people here: a history of Yuraygir National Park*. Sydney: Department of Environment and Climate Change.

Matthews, Jill Julius (2005). *Dance hall and picture palace: Sydney's romance with modernity*. Sydney: Currency Press.

McKenzie, Ian (1961). 'Protecting our flora and fauna from people: the psychology of the destroyers of our natural reserves'. *The National Parks Journal*, 1(4).

Miller, Daniel (2008). 'Campers cry foul over national park fees'. *Daily Examiner*, 8 January.

Official guide to the National Park (1893). Sydney: Government Printer.

Senior, Harold (1976). 'A ranger's experience – Royal National Park'. In Wendy Goldstein (ed.). *Royal National Park*. Sydney: Government Printer.

Smith, Stewart (1998). *National Parks in NSW*, Briefing Paper No 22/98. NSW Parliamentary Library Research Service.

Susskind, Anne (1992). 'Conservation comes first'. *The Sydney Morning Herald*, 23 September.

Young, Terence (1995). 'Modern urban parks'. *Geographical Review*, 85(4).

Waterhouse, Richard (1995). *Private pleasures, public leisure: a history of Australian popular culture since 1788*. Melbourne: Longman.

White, Richard et al. (2005). *On holidays: a history of getting away in Australia*. Melbourne: Pluto Press.

Chapter 4

Playing with fire: the place of campfires in nature tourism

Julia Bowes

Since the creation of the first national park in NSW in 1879, the campfire has been among the most popular and cherished recreational pastimes of park users. The use of fire has been regarded as essential to the camping experience, enabling campers to cook, stay warm and socialise after dark. The value of fire in national parks, however, has always extended beyond its sheer practical necessity. The ritual of campfires within the parks has endowed the activity with cultural resonances that have connected park users with both national myths and the primitive history of fire. The connective force of fire has long fostered a sense of belonging and nostalgia for those who gather around the campfire, connecting them not only with each other, but with family, local, national and universal traditions.

The meanings attributed to the campfire and the enjoyment derived from it are neither universal nor static. At some points, the campfire has been valorised as the quintessential activity of the Australian bushman, a symbol of colonisation and of a distinctive national identity. At other times, the value of fire has been viewed as primitive and universal, evidenced by Indigenous Australian's use of fire. The primitive appeal of fire positions the activity as a phenomenon so fundamentally human that it is almost an ahistorical practice. Although there are undoubtedly innumerable other personal meanings attributed to the campfire, those recorded in historical sources can mostly be encompassed within these two broad categories of meaning.

This chapter first investigates the nationalistic and then the universal value of the campfire. I will argue that a commonality exists between these divergent meanings. In both cases the campfire was an exercise in escapism, deriving its meaning and value against what it was not. The power of fire to conjure up a sense of culture and tradition has led regular national parks users to become zealously attached to this practice. In this context, the National Parks and Wildlife Service (NPWS), as the responsible authority for increasing numbers of traditional camping grounds in national parks, accordingly had control for fire regulation within them. The final section of this chapter considers the interaction between the NPWS and campground users in negotiating the use of fire as a recreational pursuit within NSW national parks.

National legends and national recreation around the campfire

The popular construction of the campfire experience at the turn of the twentieth century was consciously Australian in flavour. The campfire regularly figured as the backdrop to the tales and stories of Australia's literary nationalists such as Banjo Paterson and Henry Lawson. Though campfires were a feature of camping scenes globally, Paterson and Lawson made efforts to particularise the campfire experience to an Australian context, employing Australian vernacular to describe the 'bush' experience, of a 'swagman' with his 'mates' who sat around 'billabongs' with their 'billies' telling 'yarns' about 'one-eyed bogans'. Their works painted the campfire experience in a distinctly 'Australian' light, attaching a national significance to the activity.

The popularity of Paterson and Lawson's works at the turn of the twentieth century points to the widespread propagation of the notion that the billy over the campfire was a cultural emblem for the burgeoning Australian identity. Indeed, Paterson used the 'jolly swagman' who 'waited till his billy boiled' as the protagonist in his famed 'Waltzing Matilda', believed to have been written in 1895. The song was popularised when it was used to advertise Billy Tea from 1903, becoming an unofficial national anthem later in the century.[1] Similarly,

---

1   Harper (2009), 88. Some debate persists over the exact date of authorship, and whether the work was wholly original. For a discussion of this issue see: National

Henry Lawson evoked the billy as a cultural emblem in his first major short story collection *While the billy boils*, published in 1896.[2] These stories, widely circulated in the 1890s in the *Bulletin* and other magazines, disseminated the notion that the campfire was a site where national stories were told to the backdrop of the Australian bush.[3]

Early recollections of camping experiences recorded in the popular *Sydney Bushwalker* magazine reveal that campers drew on this bush vernacular to describe their own experiences. One bushwalker at Barrington Tops recounted that 'returning to our camp we heard a voice hailing us and found a couple of timber getters at our fire boiling their billies. They were jolly fellows and we heard many a yarn.'[4] Echoes of Paterson and Lawson's popular poems and stories could be heard in another camper's description of how his 'mates ... sang, yarned, played games, laughed, dozed, burnt, shivered and chuckled around the campfire' until the wee hours.[5]

The popularity of this conception of Australian recreation occurring around the billy fire gave rise to an industry of song and story books designed to be used around the campfire. Books such as Clifford Evan's *Stories told around the camp fire* (1881), Harry John White's *Round the fire* (1893) and John Mystery's popular *Camp fire hour* (1938) all fuelled the idea that the camp fire was at the heart of bush nationalism.[6]

The content of these books encouraged patriotism. In rousing voices, readers were encouraged to:

Library of Australia, 'Waltzing Matilda'. [Online] Available: www.nla.gov.au/epubs/waltzingmatilda/index.php?p=c1-intro [9 May 2012].

2   Lawson (2004).

3   Lawson (2004), 3.

4   *Sydney Bush Walker,* 1934, 20, 2. Barrington Tops officially became a National Park in 1969.

5   *Sydney Bush Walker,* 1932, 8: 4.

6   Mystery (1938); *Sydney Bush Walker,* 1932, 7: 14; HJ White (1893); Evans (1881).

102 • Playing in the bush

> raise, raise high your voices Australians and sing
>
> In praise of the bright sunny land
>
> Of your birth.[7]

Through song and story, Australians were encouraged to celebrate their nation around the campfire. Books such as these forged a strong relationship between campfire recreation and patriotism. Of course, this bush nationalism was quite contrived. Although campfire song and storybooks may have emerged to satisfy consumer demands, they were the self-conscious byproducts of the national literature created by the likes of Paterson and Lawson. The campfire books provide a pertinent example of the 'national obsession' Richard White has argued Australians have held with forging a national identity, with Paterson and Lawson being early producers in the 'industry of image makers' that told Australians what they were.[8]

The ill fit of the bushman identity for the majority of Australians reveals the contrived nature of this myth. Russel Ward contended that the national self-image of the 'typical Australian' was focused on the 'minority of bush-dwellers' because they 'differed most graphically from the average Briton and so were seen as identifiably Australian'. Therefore, while Australia has been a predominantly urban country, the national-self image has been an 'idealized image of bush workers' with which urban Australians identify.[9] Richard White concurs that the national culture was a product of 'the city-dweller's image of the bush'.[10]

National parks formed an essential bridge between urban Australians and their self-image. National parks provided Sydney residents with an opportunity to participate in this national narrative. The very first national parks in NSW, the National Park at Port Hacking to Sydney's south and Ku-ring-gai Chase in the north, reserved bushland bordering Australia's largest urban centre to allow city-dwellers to make daytrips that connected their lives with a supposedly authentic Australian bush

---

7   HJ White (1893), 3.

8   R White (1981), viii.

9   Ward (1978), 10–11.

10 R White (1981), 85.

experience. Campfire experiences spawned evocative articles in bush walking magazines such as 'Embers' and 'Campfire chatter' as campers enthusiastically recorded their memories of singalongs by the campfire.[11] Lighting campfires within national parks established a connection with the national self-image of the swagman by the billy fire. The extension of national parks across the twentieth century preserved increasing amounts of natural habitat where New South Welshmen could connect to this national myth. Their campfires and the enjoyment they derived from them were defined against their modern, predominantly urbanised lives. By 1916, DE Hutchins could term billy tea the 'national drug'.[12]

Throughout the twentieth century, and more than a century after Paterson popularised the term, the traditional billy fire still enjoyed popularity amongst Australian campers. In 1958, the Royal National Park's annual report noted a growing demand for fireplaces.[13] In 2007, *Great Walks* magazine reviewed portable kettles, but still appraised the billy as 'best way to prepare food and hot drinks out in the sticks … the old-fashioned way, over a campfire'.[14] Even though the author acknowledged it was 'probably the least practical and time-efficient', the 'smokiness of the eucalypt coals' made it the 'most satisfying way to boil two cups of water … if you're an incurable romantic'.[15] A 1999 survey of northern NSW Parks revealed that both day-visitors and overnight campers at national parks shared this nostalgic attachment to the campfire, with a 'significantly strong' preference for wood fireplaces over gas and electric barbecues.[16] This romanticisation of the campfire remains a focus for national nostalgia.

---

11 'Campfire Chatter'. *Sydney Bush Walker Magazine*, 1983, 38: 10; (1959); 'Embers' *Y.H.A.C.C. NSW*, 1:10.

12 Hutchins (1916), 24.

13 NSW National Park Trust (1958). 78th annual report for the Royal National Park Trust. Sydney: Thomas Henry Tennant, Government Printer, 2.

14 'Walk smart: camp fire cooking from caveman to superman'. *Great Walks*, 2007, October/November, 63.

15 'Walk Smart' (2007), 63.

16 Griffin & Archer (2001), 89.

Fig. 4.1. A campfire provides warmth, deters insects, heats food and water and becomes the 'bush TV'. NPWS.

The billy and the campfire became symbols of a nationalist movement that celebrated the distinctiveness of Australia through its landscape. One extreme view was expressed by PR Stephensen, the ultra-nationalist founder of the Australia First movement. Stephensen claimed that 'Australian culture will diverge from the purely local colour of the British Islands to the precise extent that our environment differs from that of Britain'.[17] The physical distinctiveness of Australia made the country unique, and it followed that the encounters of Australians with that landscape helped to define a burgeoning Australian identity.[18] Most frequently, urban Australians encountered the distinctive bushland on picnics and camping trips in parts of Australia that were increasingly preserved as national parks. Campers in Barrington Tops in 1934, in land that would be officially reserved as national parkland in 1969, wrote glowing recollections of the shadows cast by their campfire upon

17 PR Stephensen cited in Robin (2007), 4.

18 Stephen Pyne makes a similar point about how Australians integrated their locality into their identity in the celebration of the Bushman. See Pyne (1991), 301.

'blue gum forests', remarking on the smell of eucalypt.[19] It was during these trips, in this distinct landscape, that the billy fire developed such cultural resonance.

Yet the affinity Australians held for their natural surroundings was complicated by the tough, harsh and perilous relationship the land demanded. The original European colonisers had struggled to survive in the unfamiliar landscape, and thus another strand of the national narrative came to celebrate those who overcame the natural challenges of Australia to survive and build a prosperous nation. The emergence of this narrative is evident in the early histories of Australia. Historian Ernest Favenc asked in 1893 if we can 'look for an instance of greater bravery in the exploration of any other portion of the globe?'[20] Adam Jamrozik has argued that the accepted history of Australia came to be 'the history of pioneers who ventured into the vast open spaces, harnessed the harsh and unwelcoming terrain and made the country productive'.[21] It was white Australia pitted against their new homeland, and Jamrozik highlights the aim of colonisers 'to *conquer and control* the land, not to *cultivate* it'. In this regard, nature was 'seen as the enemy that had to be harnessed'.[22]

Bushfires are a prime example of the ever-threatening natural conditions of Australia, making fire an enemy that needs to be controlled. Stephen Pyne, in his discussion of Australia as a fire continent, has argued convincingly that bushfires have 'even inspired a kind of liturgical calendar of environmental horror, the great fires named of the days of the week – Ash Wednesday; Red Thursday; and Black Sunday, Monday, Thursday, Friday and Saturday'.[23] Indeed, Australia's only Nobel laureate writer, Patrick White, drew on the Australian fear of the bushfire in his first international success, *The tree of man*, deploying the bushfire as a metaphor for all that is alien, unassimilable and threatening about

---

19 Taylor (1934), 2.

20 Favenc (1888), 398.

21 Jamrozik (2004), 9.

22 Jamrozik (2004), 130. Emphasis original.

23 Pyne (1995), 35.

Australia.[24] In addition to these popular literary representations of bushfires, recurrent media articles documenting the threat and human devastation of bushfires consolidate this fear.[25] These real and imagined depictions of bushfires served as reminders of the inherent dangers of fire, and of the risks assumed by all who used fire as a tool to a range of ends.

The exercise of building a campfire gave Australians an opportunity to enact the national myth of man overcoming nature. In the same way that the pioneers overcame the harshness of the Australian landscape by developing survival skills and bushcraft, campers and bushwalkers often remarked on their triumphs over the dangers of fire as they harnessed and domesticated it to serve their own purposes.[26] Indeed, a story and song book from 1893 entitled *Round the campfire* was dedicated to the 'toilers of Australia'.[27] This no doubt fuelled the self-perception of campers who believed they were enacting the legend of the true blue Aussie bushman, roughing it in the harsh and unforgiving Australian bush, or at least demonstrating their bushcraft.

By the mid twentieth century, camping literature came to promote the idea that fire should be controlled and contained, and a persuasive metaphor of a master and servant relationship gained currency. In 1976, Ted Foster noted that it was 'fashionable' in the introduction of books regarding fire to 'remark that fire is a good servant but a bad master'.[28] The linguistic concept of a master/servant dichotomy was also made explicit by the Bush Fire Advisory Council when they released a poster in the 1960s instructing the public to 'Make fire your servant and not your master'. A campfire in the foreground of the poster, it suggested, had led to the house in the background being enveloped in flames. Another poster published around the same time, 'Prevent Bushfires', showed six potential scenarios in which fire could spread. Each image

24 P White (1961); Pyne (1995), 36.

25 See for example Pakula (1998), 1.

26 Pyne argues that 'humans domesticated fire' and that 'the quest for fire is a quest for power'. See Pyne (1999), 79–80.

27 HJ White (1893), 4.

28 Foster (1976), 8.

Fig. 4.2. Anti-bushfire campaigns have long targeted campers, warning
of the importance of controlling campfires. Mitchell Library, State Library NSW.
© State of New South Wales through the Department of Attorney General and
Justice and reproduced with the approval of the State Library of New South Wales.

was dominated by a masculine hand which represented the control
needed to domesticate fire.[29]

29 NSW Bush Fire Committee (1978). Collection of posters promoting bush fire
prevention. Held by the Mitchell Library, Sydney. Posters 1605/1; 1605/2; 1605/3;
1605/4.

Despite the concerns expressed by camping books and the Bush Fire Advisory Council, bushfires were rarely caused by the failure to control campfires. A 1971 report into the causes of bushfire revealed that only one fire that season was caused by campers, a statistically insignificant figure.[30] Similarly, a report into the causes of bushfires in NSW national parks in southern NSW between 1989 and 1994 reveals that only two out of the fifty-nine fires recorded during the period were caused by camping or cooking.[31] Reports into the causes of fire repeatedly cited intentional arson as the most common cause of bushfire.[32] Thus, it was rarely the failure of humans to make fire their servant that led to bushfires. It is possible that the Bush Fire Council and the parks association exaggerated the link between bush fires and campfires as it was one of the few controllable causes of bushfires: arson was difficult to deter through criminal sanction and the weather was difficult to predict. Nonetheless, the result of these public awareness campaigns was to play into the myth that man could master nature and that those engaged in lighting campfires were asserting that mastery.

The primitive pull of the campfire

Across the twentieth century, there were competing cultural narratives concerning the campfire. Many campers were aware of and indeed drawn to the cultural connotations surrounding the campfire that pre-dated colonisation, and saw the campfire as linking them with many of the oldest civilisations on earth. One example was the 1961 edition of the *Herald caravanning guide*, which made references to traditional Indigenous uses of fire in a section entitled 'Camping's the life!' It instructed would-be campers how to build the 'black-fellow' type of fire, which it claimed was 'unequalled for winter camping'.[33]

---

30 Report cited in Foster (1976), 11.

31 NPWS (1998). *Living with fire: bushfire management, the environment and the community*. Sydney: NPWS. 12.

32 Foster (1976), 11.

33 'Camping's the life!' (1961). In *Herald caravanning guide*. Melbourne: Herald Touring Clubs, 7.

Not only did this demonstrate an appreciation of how other cultures and communities had come to domesticate fire, but it linked twentieth-century camping practices to the longstanding traditions of Australia's Aboriginal population. The recognition of Indigenous uses of fire, however, was by no means an effort to incorporate Aboriginal Australians into the national narrative. This is evident in the way in which the Herald Touring Group referred to the Indigenous populations of Australia and North America as if both held equal relevance to the Australian context. While the 'black-fellow' fire was for winter camping, the 'Red Indian' fire was described as 'better suited to summer camping'.[34] Another author believed it was incumbent to 'learn to live with nature as the Australian Aborigines and American Indians did'.[35]

Rather, the valorisation of Indigenous Australian uses of fire was dependent on the association of Indigenous peoples generally with primitivism. The notion of living with nature, as distinct from living in modern civilised cities, encouraged campers to fashion themselves on what they imagined to be primitive people. In an era when Aboriginal people were closely associated with their pre-contact ancestors, identification with Indigenous fire practices reflected a more general desire to escape the modern.

National parks were established as a respite from the conditions of a modern existence. The 1902 *Official guide to the National Park* explained that the park was designed to provide an escape from the 'crowded and *artificial* conditions of city life', while the 1914 edition explained that parks would 'ensure the sound health and vigour of the community'.[36] As with the national park, much of the appeal of the campfire lay in its simplicity, juxtaposed against an increasingly complicated technological existence in cities where a concoction of electricity, gas and iron ovens assumed the role the fire had once functionally played.

---

34 'Camping's the life!', 7.

35 Foster (1976), 8.

36 *Official guide to the National Park* (1902). Emphasis added; *Official guide to the National Park* (1914), 13.

The desire to set up a campfire was an expression of nostalgia for the lost simplicity of the past, a phenomenon Marianna Torgovnick, an art historian, terms primitivism. As Victor Li argues, in a modern existence, 'the primitive is valorised, *in order to save us*, its radical heterogeneity all too predictably serving our desire for a way out of modern civilisation'.[37] Paddy Pallin, a renowned Australian camper, explained this primitive attraction of camping in similar terms: the pretence of urban life was lost when you 'cast off this skin that you put round yourself in town and become the *real* person that you are meant to be in the bush'.[38] The notion of self-actualisation occurring in the primitive conditions of the bush gave a personal dimension to the appeal of the campfire.

In the same manner that the nationalistic overtones of the billy fire were defined against the British identity, the primitive pull of fire was defined against the modern. A regular camper at Illaroo National Park encapsulated this paradox perfectly when he described the attraction of the campfire as the 'bush TV', defining it as an alternative to the sources of recreation in modern society.[39] Ironically, the primitive that was so valorised by campers was a construction of modernity; the desire to escape the modern was defined against the modern civilisation, and thus was itself a product of modernity. In its ability to extend the day beyond the naturally defined setting of the sun, the campfire represented one of humanity's first triumphs over nature.

Regulating the campfire

The campfire could not escape modern hierarchies. Despite the supposed simplicity and rawness of the campfire there was a right and wrong way to approach it. Bushcraft was something that had to be learned. The average camper was described as thoughtless if 'he' began his fire with the gathering of the nearest wood and kept it going by 'piling anything on'.[40] The so-called 'expert builds the foundations of his

---

37 Li (2006), 30. Emphasis original.
38 Paddy Pallin cited in Harper (2003), 381.
39 Camper at Illaroo. Interview, Yuraygir National Park, 23 April 2008.
40 'Camping's the life!', 15.

Fig. 4.3. The distinctive haze of campfire smoke over a national park camping site.
A Fox / NPWS.

fire carefully, eliminates the use of damp or wet wood and keeps the fire
going throughout the night by using back stakes on which are carried
logs in tiers so that as the lowest log burns another drops down into
its place'.[41] Mirroring the conditions of modern life, those with more
knowledge positioned themselves as superior to campers who were less
equipped to build a proper fire.

Information about how to light a fire correctly was disseminated
through detailed descriptions in camping magazines and pictorial
representations in the posters of the Bush Fire Advisory Council.
Proficiency in bushcraft became a social obligation. Fire-making could
be seen as a test of manhood or patriotism. Failure to complete the test
could be viewed as a grave social transgression with potentially dire
consequences. As *The bush boy's book* advised in 1930, fire was not an
element to be used for your 'own convenience'. Campers had to consider
the 'comfort, safety, and fortunes of other people'.[42] Ted Foster asks how

41 'Camping's the life!', 15.
42 McDonald (1930), 1.

potential transgressions of campers should be addressed: 'how do we detect the small proportion which is careless, apathetic, ignorant or immature. Should we attempt to punish people like this, educate them or expose them to public ridicule?'[43]

In practice, misuse or reckless use of fire was regulated by criminal sanction with fines and the threat of imprisonment for those who left open campfires unattended or lit fires in a 'bush fire danger period.'[44] These sanctions changed in form over time, from the *Careless Use of Fire Act 1912–1946*, the *Bush Fires Act 1949* and the *Rural Fires Act 1997*.[45] However, the substance and purpose of these laws remained relatively unchanged. The regulation and rules that typified modern society persisted around the campfire with bushcraft customs and laws, meaning campers were never completely free from the restrictions of modern society that they sought to escape.

The vigilance that accompanied the drive for fire education was also a defensive expression of the importance of fire among campers. Fire-lovers did not want to see those who were 'careless, apathetic, ignorant or immature' misuse fire in a fashion that provoked a permanent fire ban, thus depriving them of their own enjoyment.[46] This prompted a wealth of literature calling for the self-regulation of the recreational use of fire by such interest groups as bushwalking clubs and the National Parks Association.

The zealous attachment to campfires became more pronounced once the NSW National Parks and Wildlife Service was established and assumed control over an increasing number of traditional camping grounds, because the management of fire in parks became more coordinated and visible. In 1949, each Australian state had agreed on a unified and cohesive national plan to manage bushfires.[47] This plan

43 Foster (1976) , 99–101.

44 NSW Bush Fire Committee (1959). Manual of instruction for Fire Patrol Officers, issued by the Bush Fire Committee. Sydney: Government Printers, 7–10.

45 NSW Bush Fire Committee (1959), 10; National Parks Association of NSW (1980). Fire policy. Sydney: NPANSW, 2.

46 Foster (1976), 78.

47 *The Bush Fires Act* which became law in December, 1949, replaced the *Careless*

included granting certain bodies the discretionary power to implement full and partial fire bans where appropriate. Prior to this point, the implementation of fire bans had been ad hoc and inconsistent. In NSW, this power was vested in the NPWS upon its formation in 1967.

The objectives of national parks were articulated under the *National Parks and Wildlife Act* of 1974. Fire policies have been developed over time to support these objectives. The primary aims of the NPWS Fire Policy Manual, the policies of which were enacted by each national park through fire management plans, are to protect life, property and community assets, to coordinate fire management and cooperate with other fire authorities and the community, to manage fire regimes to maintain and enhance biodiversity, and to protect Aboriginal sites and other places of cultural significance.[48] To achieve these aims, the NPWS has restricted the areas in which fires can be lit in national parks and entrusted staff with the discretion to declare a full fire ban if weather conditions are highly conducive to bushfires.

Managing community attitudes around fire regulation has proven to be nearly as arduous a task as fire management itself. Campers interviewed at Murramarang National Park on the NSW south coast in 2008 were unsure of the motivations behind NPWS regulation of the use of fire, commenting that 'we used to be allowed to have fires on but now that it's a national park, or strictly a national park or something, they changed it so that's a bit of a blow out'.[49] A family tried to explain what had happened to fire in their regular camping spot at Murramarang:

> No Fires! No fires in this park ... as opposed to other places
> where you're allowed to have fire but just for some reason not

---

Use of Fire Act 1912–1946, and the *Bush Fires Act 1930*. It marked a big step forward in the prevention, suppression and control of bush fires. For the first time in the history of the state an attempt had been made to deal with this national menace on a full and unified basis. See NSW Bush Fire Committee (1959), 5.

48 NPWS, 'Fire management policy'. [Online] Available: www.environment.nsw. gov.au/fire/TheNPWSfiremanagementmanual.htm [Accessed 2 June 2011].

49 Campers at Pretty Beach. Interview, Murramarang National Park, 21 January 2008.

here. But, in winter you're allowed to have fires here, just not in summer, for some reason.[50]

Similarly, an editor of *Great Walks* magazine lamented the regulations restricting fires in national parks when 'you can't light fires willy-nilly these days, and even if you are allowed a fire, time and environmental factors such as wind and rain can limit what you can do and how you can do it.'[51]

In a 1980 Fire Policy Report, the National Parks Association of NSW argued it was 'not surprising' that 'some may regard the concept of management with suspicion as management and meddling have in the past tended to be indistinguishable. Mismanagement is almost a synonym for history'. The report called for better management, noting the need for scientific expertise but also seeking input from intelligent and concerned laymen. Acknowledging the high degree of overview for management policies from the advisory council and the minister, the report stated that the guiding principle for fire management was to 'manipulate sparingly'. The report, however, also acknowledged that public education was a major need as 'there is some validity in the claim [that] progress towards better fire control is limited by community attitudes'.[52]

The NPWS itself has recognised the cultural and recreational value of the campfire. At a conference on fire management held in 1970, Ku-ring-gai Chase National Park representatives acknowledged that most campers 'have an inbuilt urge to "boil the billy" with traditional vigour' and appreciated that it is 'difficult to suppress that rather satisfying feeling of starting a fire and standing around!'[53] Similarly, a ranger at Yuragyir National Park explained in 2008 that the campfire was

50 Monk family. Interview at Depot Beach. Murramarang National Park, 22 January 2008.

51 'Walk Smart', 63.

52 NPA (1980), 7.

53 NPWS (1970). 'F.A.O Fire Study Tour Conference Report'. Conference held at Ku-ring-gai Chase National Park, 25 February 1970. State Records A92, 2.

'something that we as a region want, we want to perpetuate fire because we think it's really important'.

The 1970 conference, however, also highlighted the difficulty of managing this popular pastime. The NPWS noted that they were balancing an environment that would quickly spread fire should it occur, and an influx of visitors 'most determined to light' fires in the worst time and place – that is, during the warmer months and close to water which is the ground position most conducive to maximum fire.[54] The NPWS was also increasingly aware of the ecological impact that the collecting of firewood was having in areas around campsites. Not only did the loss of dead and decaying wood affect habitat, but some park users even chopped down trees, sometimes to leave for future use. The challenges of communicating the reasons behind its fire management policies were exacerbated by the sense shared by many park users that national parks offer the chance to escape petty authority and that they have a 'right' or 'entitlement' to fire. The National Parks Association acknowledged this in their 1980 report, highlighting the need to 'correct the traditional attitude' held by park users and country landholders that they have a 'virtually automatic right to burn and light fires'.[55]

The assertion of an entitlement to fire in the face of efforts to manage the use of fire in national parks reflects a growing sentimentality attached to the campfire. A family at Murramarang National Park explained how a fire ban had interrupted their family tradition, stating 'it's very annoying considering we've grown up with fires for all our lives'. The attraction of fire to this family was simple: it was 'a great Aussie tradition'.[56] While some campers have drawn on national and family tradition to justify their claim to fire, NPWS restrictions have also led some campers to claim they have a natural right to fire. By painting fire as a primitive, tribal practice and a historical constant, campers legitimate their claim to fire. One surfer, reflecting on his twenty-five years of campfires at Yuraygir National Park, claimed that 'it was almost

---

54 NPWS (1970), 2.

55 NPA (1980), 7.

56 Sharon Monk. Interview at Depot Beach. Murramarang National Park, 22 January 2008.

a tribal gathering'.[57] The notion that fire is a natural and universal primitive expression implicitly challenges the authority of the NPWS to regulate it. This sentimentalisation of the campfire has led to some camp users asserting their sense of entitlement by continuing to light fires in restricted areas. Campers at Pretty Beach even argued that the fire bans were actually counterproductive because 'they make it more dangerous because we kind of have to go up into the bush more [to light them]. If they just let us do it, it would be much more safe'.[58]

For some users, however, the NPWS is simply arbitrating the use of fire in accordance with the knowledge hierarchies discussed earlier. David Redhill, who began camping at Angourie in 1974 and remains a regular visitor, commented:

> I know very few people with the knowledge and experience to
> use fire in the open Australian landscape. When I used to camp
> in the outback with my parents they taught me to use fire safely.
> I wouldn't trust 95 percent of people.[59]

Echoing these sentiments, a camper at Minnie Waters expressed his support for the restrictions, explaining that it was 'safer from a bushfire point of view' because 'the trouble is you get a lot of people who are not aware of the risks so it is probably better not to have it'. He qualified this by stating 'I wouldn't like to be told I couldn't have a safe campfire because I know I can, but yeah there are lots of people you shouldn't be trusting'.[60] That some campers distrust their fellow campers demonstrates the way in which modern knowledge hierarchies are continually reconstructed around the campfire and how perceptions of the park authorities are central to these debates.

The strong cultural resonances of the campfire, and perhaps in some part a defensive mentality on the part of campers in parks fearing

---

57 David Redhill. Interview at Angourie Point. Yuraygir National Park, 21 April 2008.

58 Campers at Pretty Beach. Interview, 2008.

59 David Redhill. Interview, 2008.

60 Camper at Minnie Waters. Interview, 23 April 2008.

Fig. 4.4. National parks are popular settings for company and school picnics. Staff of Imperial Chemical Industries of Australia and New Zealand socialised somewhat awkwardly in Lane Cove National Park at the company's annual barbecue, 1968. Anna Clements. Mitchell Library, State Library NSW.

fire was under threat, has prompted a spirited interest in preserving the campfire in national parks. From 1967 onwards, the NPWS provided electricity generators and gas barbecues as alternatives to campfires in a significant proportion of camping grounds. A 1999 survey in northern NSW parks revealed that park users preferred upgraded facilities, especially toilets and showers, rather than embracing nature in its untouched form. Yet even though fifty-nine percent of park users made use of the barbecues provided, the survey showed a significantly strong preference for wood fires over gas and electric barbecues. Along with a preference for natural walking tracks over paved ones, open fireplaces stood out as an exception to the general trend of patrons wanting an upgrade of facilities.[61]

While many campers, such as David Redhill, will state that the attraction of national parks lies in the idea that they are 'left in their absolutely natural state', the majority seem to be selective in how far they extend the principle.[62] The fact that campers prefer the traditional campfire over its technological counterparts indicates that there is something specific to the pull of the campfire that has ensured its continued popularity. Although campers used the barbecues provided, their overwhelming preference remained the campfire. Similarly, in *Great Walks* magazine's review of portable kettles, the author acknowledged that though the billy was 'probably the least practical and time-efficient' method of boiling water, it was still the 'most satisfying'.[63] The campfire has outlived its sheer functional necessity in national parks. Its persistence reflects the enjoyment derived from lighting a campfire as a recreational activity in its own right.

The preference of park users for an open campfire has led the NPWS to find innovative ways to protect this cultural practice while attending to safety and environmental concerns. Instead of replacing the open fire, the NPWS have made the practice safer in Guy Fawkes National Park by building a contraption for suspending a billy and cooking utensils. In a number of national parks the NPWS has begun to provide firewood imported to protect the natural cycle of wood decay around campsites. These modern adaptations of the billy acknowledge the continuing national and primitive appeals of the campfire tradition.

Conclusion

Although the element of fire has been a historical constant, the campfire derives its cultural significance from its context. From European

61 Griffin & Archer (2001), 88–89.
62 David Redhill. Interview, 2008.
63 'Walk Smart', 63.

settlement onwards, the campfire not only served the practical needs of campers but allowed them to colonise the harsh bushland around them. This practice became part of the national narrative as the billy came to assume iconic cultural status. Building a campfire allowed Australians to participate in their embryonic national story and it was around the campfire that they exchanged yarns and songs. The physical context of the campfire, along with the natural beauty of NSW that the first two national parks aimed to preserve, imparted a specific nationalist resonance as the landscape served as a point of contrast between the colonies and England.

The meaning of the campfire was constantly evolving, however, with changing conditions in modern society. As the world outside national parks became increasingly urbanised and modernised, campers also came to fetishise the primitive appeal of the campfire. The simplicity, universality and longevity of the camping experience epitomised by the campfire provided reprieve from the complicated, technological and often changing circumstances of urban life.

The national resonance of the campfire coincided with the modernising forces of nationalism. In contrast, the primitivism of the campfire, while also a response to modernity, was universal in its appeal. On the surface, these two dominant meanings appeared at odds. Yet two constants bound these different meanings. First, both were defined in opposition to an externality – with the outdoor Australian campfire juxtaposed against the traditional British hearth, and the primitive fire, the bush TV, juxtaposed against the modern fixation on technology. Second, both provided respite from modern life. The billy fire provided an opportunity to participate in an Australian bush nationalism from which many urban Australians felt alienated. The primitive fire provided a ritualistic and tribal experience, allowing campers to shed the strictures and pressures of modern civilisation.

The nationalistic resonance of the campfire took hold in the early part of the twentieth century, coinciding with the popularity of bush nationalism. The decline of nationalism and the rise of technological progress in the latter part of the twentieth century saw more campers relishing the primitive pull of the campfire. Yet the third commonality in these two cultural resonances was longevity, both outlasting the sheer functional necessity of fire to the camping experience. Despite the existence of alternatives for cooking provided both by the NPWS itself and by an increasingly elaborate consumer market for camping equipment, the practice of lighting one's own campfire has remained a very popular recreational activity. This popularity, coupled with the sense of tradition, ensured that park users were zealously sentimental about the campfire and often defensive in the face of efforts of NPWS to regulate its use. The NPWS has recognised the cultural value of the campfire and aimed to facilitate open fires wherever they have deemed it possible to do so. The preservation of campfire sites within NSW national parks underlines the contested but enduring cultural resonance of this recreational pursuit.

References

Evans, Clifford (1881). *Stories told around the camp fire*. Melbourne: Sandhurst.

Favenc, Ernest (1888). *The history of Australian exploration from 1788-1888*. Sydney: Turner & Henderson.

Foster, Ted (1976). *Bushfire history, prevention and control*. Sydney: A.H. & A.W. Reed.

Griffin, Tony & David Archer (2001). *Sustainable tourism: visitor survey 1999-2000 of northern NSW national parks*. Sydney: School of Leisure, Sport and Tourism, Faculty of Business, University of Technology, Sydney.

Harper, Melissa (2009). 'Billy'. In Melissa Harper & Richard White (eds). *Symbols of Australia*. Canberra: UNSW Press and National Museum of Australia.

Harper, Melissa (2002). The ways of the bushwalker: bushwalking in Australian 1788-1949. PhD thesis, Department of History, The University of Sydney.

Hutchins, DE (1916). *A discussion of Australian forestry*. Perth: Government Printers.

Jamrozik, Adam (2004). *The chains of colonial inheritance: searching for identity in a subservient nation*. Sydney: UNSW Press.

Lawson, Henry (2004).*While the billy boils*. Sydney: Sydney University Press.

Li, Victor (2006). *The neo-primitivist turn: critical reflections on alterity, culture and modernity*. Toronto: University of Toronto Press.

McDonald, Donald (1930). *The bush boy's book*. Sydney: Angus & Robertson.

Mystery, John (1938). *Camp fire hour*. Sydney: Publicity Press.

Official guide to the National Park (1914). Sydney: Government Printer.

Official guide to the National Park (1902). Sydney: Government Printer.

Pakula, Karen (1998). 'Park fire that trapped 100 under control'. *Sydney Morning Herald*, 10 October, 1.

Pyne, Stephen (1999). 'Consumed by either fire or fire: a prolegomenon to anthropogenic fire', in Jill Ker Conway, Kenneth Keniston and Leo Marx (eds). *Earth, air, fire, water: humanistic studies of the environment*. Boston: University of Massachusetts Press.

Pyne, Stephen (1995). *World fire: the culture of fire on earth*. New York: Holt.

Pyne, Stephen (1991). *Burning bush: a fire history of Australia*. Sydney: Allen & Unwin.

Robin, Libby (2007). *How a continent created a nation*. Sydney: UNSW Press.

Taylor, GM (1934) 'Barrington Tops', *Sydney Bushwalker Magazine*, 1.

Ward, Russel (1978). *The Australian legend*. Sydney: Oxford University Press.

White, Harry John (1893). *Round the campfire*. Port Augusta: D. Drysdale.

White, Patrick (1961). *The tree of man*. Ringwood: Penguin Books.

White, Richard (1981). *Inventing Australia: images and identity 1688–1980*. Sydney: George Allen & Unwin.

Plate 1. The establishment of national parks followed the creation by artists of images of the Australian landscape influenced by European Romanticism. Eugene von Guérard, *North-east view from the northern top of Mount Kosciusko* (1863), oil on canvas, 66.5 x 116.8 cm. National Gallery of Australia, Canberra, purchased 1973.

Plate 2. National parks were part of a concerted effort to develop an appreciation of the Australian environment, as this NPWS publication makes clear. NPWS.

Plate 3. Boiling the billy has been an Australian ritual since at least the mid nineteenth century. Paul Mathews / OEH.

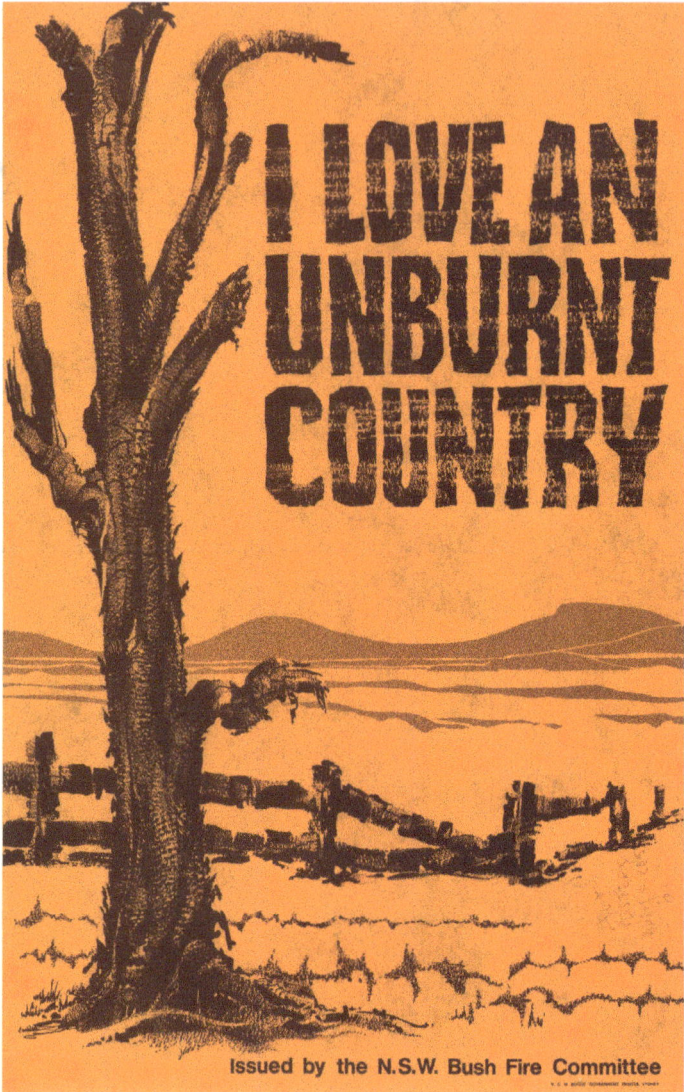

Plate 4. Campfires have been a relatively rare cause of bushfires in national parks. NSW Bushfire Committee. Mitchell Library, State Library NSW. © State of New South Wales through the Department of Attorney General and Justice and reproduced with the approval of the State Library of New South Wales.

Plate 5. Picnic facilities were often set into natural features such as caves in early national parks, immersing the visitors in nature. Mitchell Library, State Library NSW.

Plate 6. The Georges River National Park is popular with fishers from the suburbs of south-western Sydney. Claire Farrugia.

Plate 7. Abseiling became increasingly popular in the late twentieth century at places such as the Big Hole, Deua National Park (2009). Patrick Mickan.

Plate 8. Enjoying the view at Pretty Beach camping area, in Murramarang National Park. Richard White.

Plate 9. The campsites at the front of Pretty Beach camping area, in Murramarang National Park, were highly prized. The NPWS has vegetated the area and opened it to casual visitors. Michael Jarman / OEH.

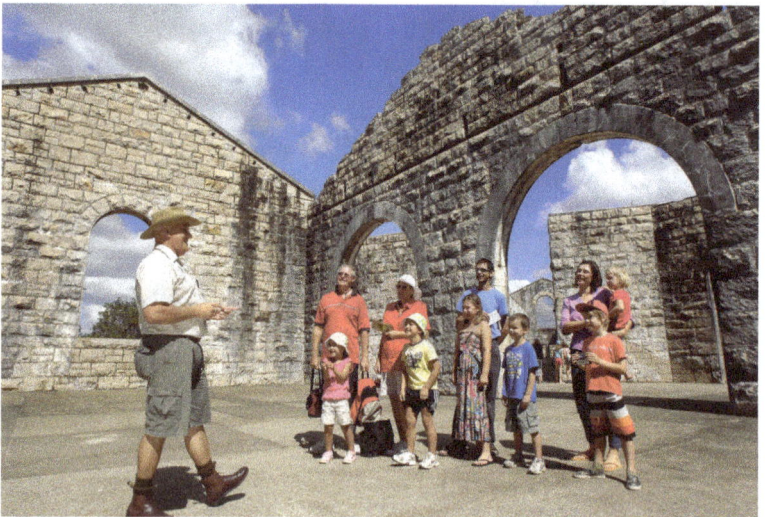

Plate 10. Tour guides at Trial Bay Gaol bring the past to life for visitors. Warren Crozier / OEH.

Plate 11. Hartley Historic Site protects one of the first rural settlements west of the Blue Mountains. Tourists come to see an intact 1830s village. Sonia Limeburner / OEH.

Plate 12. In 1985, Hill End celebrated the centenary of Bernhardt Holtermann's death with a historical re-enactment. Recreating the past for the visitor is one of the challenges for the NPWS. OEH.

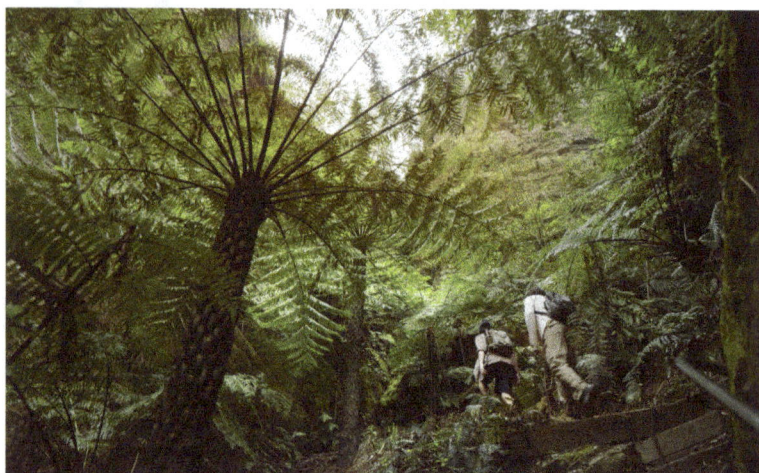

Plate 13. The sense of entering and being surrounded by nature remains one of the attractions of national parks: bushwalkers in Fern Gully, Blue Mountains National Park 2009. OEH.

Plate 14. Allambie House, Royal National Park, now demolished, provided accommodation and was particularly popular with honeymooners. State Records NSW.

Chapter 5

The comforts of nature: a history of recreational facilities

Fiona Howie

Recreational facilities occupy an ambiguous position in national parks. Additions such as picnic shelters, toilet blocks, dressing sheds and kiosks represent an attempt to improve parks and campsites by providing the visitor with an additional level of comfort. Yet such improvements can also detract from the natural experience sought by visitors in national parks. What types of recreational facilities are appropriate for national parks? Where should they be located? What designs are most suitable? These are questions that have always faced park managers and have as many different answers as there are visitors to national parks. This chapter will situate these debates within a historical framework by exploring the development of recreational facilities in national parks in NSW. In particular, it will examine the tension between the pressure to improve and modernise recreational facilities, and ideals of continuity – the attachment of users to things as they are – in national parks. A better understanding of past developments may assist in reconciling these two conflicting pressures.

The analysis in this chapter is based upon recreational facilities viewed in a sample of national parks in NSW, including the Royal, Lane Cove, Blue Mountains, Yuraygir, Murramarang and Meroo national parks. Photographic evidence provided information on earlier historic facilities, whilst written sources such as park management documents, official reports and newspaper articles provided valuable information on historic changes in recreational facilities and managerial policy in national parks.

This chapter will examine four particular influences upon the development of national park facilities: Romanticism, the demand for pleasure grounds for the Sydney populace, principles of conservation and, finally, changing attitudes towards cultural heritage.

The 1880s and 1890s were loosely characterised by an emphasis on Romantic facilities in places like national parks. The Romantic movement had a profound influence upon the way nature was depicted in art and literature. Romanticism grew as a counter-movement to the Enlightenment, rejecting views of nature as subordinate to man. Romantics viewed the fall from Eden as the separation of man and nature, and believed that the only way to achieve salvation was through the reunification of the two – closeness between man and nature was a Romantic ideal. In her chapter on romance in NSW national parks, Ella Barnett discusses the application of a Romantic aesthetic to the Australian landscape in the nineteenth century, which she defines as emphasising qualities of both the sublime (elevated, lofty landscapes evoking a sense of awe) and the picturesque (charming or striking landscapes with qualities that are pleasing to the eye). As Barnett observes, the picturesque, fostered by travel and tourist literature, was particularly influential in shaping the ideal Romantic experience sought by visitors to national parks. Fern gullies, waterfalls, caves and rivers were viewed as picturesque or Romantic locations and, particularly in the early years of national parks, this profoundly affected the location and style of recreational facilities, which were expected to complement their Romantic surroundings.

The second influence upon the development of national park facilities was the popularity of pleasure grounds, areas set aside for outdoor recreational activities such as picnicking, boating and dancing. Popular from the mid nineteenth to the mid twentieth century, pleasure grounds frequently contained an array of facilities to cater for these kinds of activities. The original vision of the trustees of the National Park (now the Royal National Park) was that certain areas of the park would be transformed into recreational grounds for the urban populace through the development of a sophisticated series of facilities. This vision was challenged in the 1930s and 1940s, when the trustees of the National

Park sought to further develop the recreational facilities at Audley, an increasingly popular part of the park. At Sydney's northern national park, Ku-ring-gai Chase, park facilities remained more modest. The trustees of Ku-ring-gai Chase were occasionally criticised for locking the park up by their refusal to develop it as extensively for recreation. On the other hand, when the trustees of the first National Park sought to implement the original vision, its suitability for these kinds of recreational facilities was strongly contested, reflecting an alternative vision of national parks as natural spaces where sophisticated levels of facilities were intrusive and inappropriate.

This contradiction reflected the fact that some Sydneysiders had come to value their parks as natural spaces and did not want to see them tampered with: their vision of what a national park ought to be was what they already had. But these views also foreshadowed the growing influence of conservation principles on the location and design of facilities from the mid 1960s onwards. A new style of park management was introduced in 1967, when the trustee system was replaced by a centralised National Parks and Wildlife Service (NPWS). Under the new management, a greater emphasis was placed on maintaining national parks in, or restoring them to, a pristine condition, leading to new notions of appropriate locations, design and materials for national parks facilities. For the first time, the NPWS also wanted a uniform style in national park facilities, which meant that what was considered acceptable became more strictly defined.

In the 1990s, the fourth influence on attitudes towards the treatment of recreational facilities in national parks became apparent. This was the increase in the importance of cultural heritage. During the 1970s and 1980s, many old facilities had been removed from the national parks because they did not conform to contemporary ideals of national park facilities. However, under the growing influence of cultural history and the heritage movement in the 1990s, historic recreational structures were accorded increased significance as items of cultural interest. By the late 1990s, old recreational facilities in national parks were recognised as possessing value, and an effort was made to preserve them. This pressure to conserve recreational facilities has often conflicted with other national park objectives, such as nature conservation.

The first part of this chapter discusses historical changes in the types of facilities considered suitable for a natural setting. The second examines the location of these facilities, and how this reflects transformations in the relationship between visitors and nature. The final part of the chapter addresses the question of design and the way definitions of suitable naturalness have changed over time.

What recreational facilities do national parks need?

Attitudes toward recreational facilities in national parks evolved considerably in the century after 1879. Conflicting attitudes came to a head in the 1930s in a series of debates concerning the provision of facilities, reflecting different visions of what constituted the ideal national park. In 1938, the trustees of the National Park boldly announced their plan to transform the park into 'the greatest playground in Australia'. As part of this vision, they planned to install a dance hall, a golf course, an Olympic swimming pool, bowling greens, tennis courts and croquet lawns. Golf and tennis were catered for because of their general popularity, whilst the bowling facilities had been requested by visitors to the park.[1] Most of the proposed facilities were to be concentrated at Audley, already a popular pleasure ground for the people of Sydney. However, not everyone wanted these kinds of facilities in the park. The *Sydney Morning Herald* responded angrily to the announcement of the instalment of these facilities by launching a sustained campaign against the trustees of the National Park. Critics argued that recreational facilities on this scale were inappropriate and threatened the natural values of the park.[2]

The facilities being proposed were in fact part of the original vision for the National Park. The original Deed of Grant permitted the trustees to manage the park for uses including ornamental plantations, lawns and gardens, zoological gardens, a race course, cricket and other lawful games, rifle butts or artillery ranges, the exercise or encampment of

---

1   *The Sun*, 18 May 1938.

2   'Preserving our parks'. *Sydney Morning Herald*, 21 May 1938.

Fig. 5.1 Early national park amenities were designed to enhance the visitor experience by their aesthetic appearance. Mitchell Library, State Library NSW.

military or naval forces, bathing places and any public amusement.[3] The impetus for the first national parks was the desire to provide spaces for the healthy recreation of the metropolitan populace.[4] One of the most important roles of the trustees was to meet the recreational needs of users. By providing sporting and entertainment facilities, the trustees sought to attract a broader range of visitors to the park as well as generate revenue. The other role of national park trustees was to conserve natural resources in the park for the future enjoyment of the public. The trustees of Ku-ring-gai Chase expressed their consciousness of this dual role in their description of the responsibilities of their employees, which included: 'the carrying out of improvement work, and second, equally important, that of acting as caretakers of the property and custodians

3   Conservation management plan for Bobbin Head, Ku-ring-gai Chase National Park Sydney: NPWS, 2006, 42–43.
4   Harper & White (2012).

of the natural beauties and natural resources of the Chase'.[5] The trustees of the National Park were also responsible for fulfilling both these roles, although they placed greater emphasis on the recreational development of the National Park than did the trustees of Ku-ring-gai Chase.

An important question raised in the debates of the 1930s was whether the trustees could legitimately balance recreational use of the National Park with the conservation of natural resources. The chairman of the trustees, Horace W Whiddon, argued that 'the trustees felt it was their duty to provide for the recreation of the people, and that this was in no way inconsistent with their duty to preserve the natural beauties of such a wonderful park'.[6] Opponents to the developments believed that these two aims were incompatible. Robert Tompsitt condemned the authorities for 'despoiling the National Park', and asked: 'is this area to be a sanctuary for wild life, as originally intended, or a national playground for the populace of Sydney? It cannot be both'.[7] Accusations of despoliation had a longer history. In 1922 the trustees caused a controversy by allowing commercial timber cutting within the park. Following a public outcry, Crown law authorities ended the practice, ruling that the trustees had no legal power to enter into a lease with a sawmilling company.

Historically, park managers viewed additions to the way of national park facilities as a form of progress. This was expressed in the language used to describe recreational facilities, which were referred to as improvements from the late nineteenth century. Improvements were recorded meticulously by the trustees of both the National Park and Ku-ring-gai Chase in their minute books and annual reports to the Minister for Lands, evidence of the trustees' commitment to providing recreational opportunities. In 1909 for example, the trustees of Ku-ring-gai Chase reported: 'the needs of campers have been recognised in improving the supplies of fresh water [at Cowan Creek, Bobbin

---

5   Trustees of Ku-ring-gai Chase (1903). 'Retrenchment'. Minutes of the meetings of the Trustees. 18 December, 1–4.

6   'National Park: Trustees' aims, improvements defended by Chairman'. *Sydney Morning Herald*, 2 June 1938.

7   Robert Tompsitt, 'National Park'. *Sydney Morning Herald*, 13 May 1938.

Head] ... and also by cementing the floors of some of the most spacious caves of that Inlet'. They noted that swimming areas had been enclosed with netting, and dressing sheds erected at Appletree Bay to provide for bathers (within access of the railway), whilst picnickers had been provided with additional shelter sheds, including the conversion of a large cave into a shelter.[8] This suggests that the trustees sought to meet the requirements of several different user groups, including both campers and day visitors. Providing recreational facilities was an important expression of their duty to the public, and they recorded increases in visitor numbers as a measure of success.

Audley was the most developed and popular area of the National Park, and as a result the trustees viewed it as their greatest triumph. In 1893, the *Official guide to the National Park* reported that in Audley and its environs 'the most pronounced proof of progress is visible, and it is here, if anywhere in the domain, that improvements effected have been fully justified'. By this time, recreational facilities already included a picnicking pavilion, accommodation, boat sheds and other conveniences.[9]

But not everyone viewed the recreational facilities proposed in 1938 as improvements. Letters published in the *Sydney Morning Herald* questioned the term, substituting 'so-called improvements' or 'official vandalism'.[10] Most writers agreed that some development was desirable, but did not want these types of recreational facilities in a national park. An editorial in the *Sydney Morning Herald* distinguished 'artificial' improvements of the kind proposed by the Trust from 'genuine' improvements, those 'needed in the way of better facilities and conveniences for enjoying the natural beauties, such as boats and bridle tracks'.[11] Other types of facilities, including those designed for

---

8   Minute books of the Board of Trustees [National Park Trust] 1879–1975. State Records NSW: NRS10724, Minutes of the meetings [Ku-ring-gai Chase Trust] 1894–1966. SRNSW: NRS 10704.

9   Elwell (1893).

10   For example, see *Sydney Morning Herald*, 13 May 1938, 3 June 1938 and 21 May 1938.

11   'Preserving our parks'. *Sydney Morning Herald*, 21 May 1938.

sport and entertainment, were viewed as artificial, and, by implication, inappropriate for a natural setting. According to this argument, the purpose of facilities in national parks was to improve visitor access to nature rather than to introduce other types of recreation to the park which could readily be developed elsewhere. This view was in direct conflict with the trustees' vision of improving the National Park by providing recreational facilities of varying types to attract greater numbers of visitors to the park.

The foremost conservation strategy employed by the trustees of the National Park seems to have been the deliberate concentration of visitors in particular areas of the park. Recreational facilities were focused on Audley, enabling the majority of the park to remain in what was considered to be a pristine state. To counter criticisms in 1938, the trustees pledged that 36 000 acres of the 36 320 acres of the park would remain in a virgin state, and most importantly, that no new roads would be opened up.[12] Their policy was to 'provide for a maximum amount of recreation at the cost of a minimum of space'.[13] A similar strategy was employed at Ku-ring-gai Chase National Park. In 1925, recreational facilities at the Chase included ten wharves and jetties, four boat sheds, eight shelter sheds, three bathing enclosures with sheds, one houseboat, eight boats, one punt, and two motor launches. Of the 38 000 acres of the Chase, only seven and a half miles of driving road and twenty-five miles of tracks existed.[14] The types of facilities available and relatively low percentage of vehicular road in the Chase suggest that visitor access was primarily restricted to areas close to the water.

In July 1938, the trustees of the National Park invited a party to inspect works in the park in an attempt to gain support for the proposed facilities. The party included AH Edmonds, a representative of the Town Planning Association of NSW. Edmonds reported that accepted town planning principles were being adhered to in what he viewed as the 'legitimate development of the Park for the healthy recreation of

12 'National Park: Trust's reply to critics – 36,000 acres will not be touched'. *Sydney Morning Herald*, 31 May 1938.
13 'Park Administration'. *The Australian*, December 1938.
14 Conservation management plan for Bobbin Head (2006), 42–43.

Fig. 5.2. Skiers outside Hotel Kosciuszko in the 1920s. State
Records NSW.

the public with due regard to the preservation of natural amenities.[15]
However, the critics were not silenced.

Related to the debate over facilities was the question of who the
park was intended for. Some visitors feared that the erection of sporting
and entertainment facilities would destroy the natural experience
that they sought. Eric Pockley, a representative of the Pioneers' Club,
argued that the proposed improvements would cause the National Park
to 'lose its appeal and value for the *type it was meant for*'.[16] Although
Pockley did not define exactly who it was 'meant for', his statement
implied that some members of the public had a greater claim to the
National Park than others. Presumably he was referring to those

15 AH Edmonds to the President of the Town Planning Association of NSW, 'The
National Park Trust: report on its work and policy' (1938). State Records NSW.
10732/9/2194.

16 Eric Pockley, 'National Park'. *Sydney Morning Herald*, 26 May 1938. Emphasis
added.

members of the public who sought a more natural experience of the bush. Another correspondent, Roy Reidy, wrote that 'marauding mobs' would destroy the park for those 'people [who] go to a National Park to swim or to admire our own birds, trees, animals, and flowers in the only place in which they are reasonably safe'. Reidy expressed the view that national parks were not national playgrounds.[17] The opinions of Pockley and Reidy suggest that much of the criticism came from people who visited the National Park to experience nature and who regarded alternative types of recreation as intrusive. Nature enthusiasts such as Reidy identified their own activities as a less damaging and hence more appropriate use of the park than sporting and social activities.

In the end, only some of the proposed facilities were erected in 1939. These included the tennis courts, a bowling green and a putting green, and the dance hall was eventually built. Recreational developments in the National Park never reached the scale envisaged by the trustees, partly because a new vision of national parks gained pace in the 1950s and 1960s.

By the middle of the century, a greater number of sporting and recreational facilities were available within the city, removing the need for city-dwellers to go further afield in search of these types of entertainment. Nature-based activities such as camping, picnicking and bushwalking meanwhile continued to attract visitors to the parks. National parks were no longer viewed as pleasure grounds, but rather as spaces where visitors came to pursue nature-based recreation.

By the 1960s, the next generation of park managers viewed the kind of sporting and entertainment facilities proposed in the 1930s as unsuitable. In the 1970s, NPWS management began removing facilities from historical pleasure grounds, including the tennis courts and bowling green at Audley that had been the subject of so much controversy. The kiosks, cottages, dressing sheds, swimming enclosures and a concrete lookout were also removed.[18] Similar facilities were demolished in Ku-ring-gai Chase National Park and the Warrumbungle National Park in central NSW, reflecting the broader policy of the NPWS to restore

17 *Sydney Morning Herald*, 12 May 1938.

18 Conservation management plan for Bobbin Head (2006), 42–43.

national parks as far as possible to a pristine state. Caroline Ford argues that it was not until the early 1990s that 'the cultural value of retaining these heritage sites replaced the policy of automatic demolition'.[19]

The removal of facilities reflected the increasing weight that park managers gave to the notion that national parks should be preserved as pristine spaces. Yet other types of recreational facilities continued to be installed by the NPWS, including shelters, tables, seats and fireplaces. What determined the endurance of these particular facilities? Firstly, such facilities supported the continuance of traditional recreational activities in national parks, including picnicking and camping, which were seen as compatible with a conservation ethos. These facilities also played an important part in managing visitor behaviour. As town planner AH Edmonds observed in 1938, 'lack of these amenities would tend to drive the public into primitive areas with harmful results to flora and fauna'.[20] By providing such facilities, park managers discouraged visitors from straying from allocated recreational areas and creating their own. This limited potentially harmful impacts on the environment.

History has shown Edmonds' fear to be justified, for in cases where these facilities have not been available, visitors have tended to produce their own. For example, when the Red Rock and Angourie National Parks were gazetted in 1975,[21] the NPWS discovered the site to be littered with mounds of rubbish, car seats and makeshift fireplaces constructed from drums. These were gradually removed and replaced with more formal facilities, including picnic shelters, fireplaces, toilets and rubbish receptacles. One park ranger explained that this was part of a conscious effort to improve the 'presentation' of the site and make it 'look like someone owns it'.[22] The symbolic replacement of the disorder of the makeshift with a uniform and ordered set of facilities was calculated to produce orderly behaviour within the park and discourage

19 Ford (2009).

20 AH Edmonds to the President of the Town Planning Association of NSW (1938).

21 These two parks were amalgamated to create Yuraygir National Park in 1980. See Kijas (2009).

22 NPWS ranger. Interview, DECC Grafton Office, 23 April 2008.

SOUTH-WEST ARM.

Fig 5.3. The 1893 *Official guide to the National Park* attempted to lure visitors to the park with romantic descriptions and photographs of the scenery at Lady Carrington Road, Audley, and the Port Hacking River. National Park Trust. *Official guide to the National Park* (1893).

a sense of private ownership. By providing cooking and eating facilities, park managers sought to discourage visitors from making their own modifications to the natural environment. The aim was also to confine activities such as cooking and eating to particular areas of the park to minimise damage to the wider natural environment. Similarly, the installation of rubbish receptacles encouraged the visitor to dispose of their litter thoughtfully rather than leaving it strewn throughout the park.

Following the creation of the NPWS, new types of facilities were gradually introduced throughout NSW national parks. Visitor centres

and interpretative shelters and signs reflected an increased focus on
the education of the visitor. Yet these signs, in their own way, detracted
from the natural experience. An example is the signs that have been
erected along the Angourie walking track in Yuraygir National Park,
which provide information on the devastating effects of the *bitou* weed
in the area and attempts by park managers to control it. The concept
of expanding environmental concerns to a dialogue with the public
through the use of facilities signalled a desire to both educate the visitor
and manage their behaviour.

The role of interpretation in managing national park visitors had
been recognised since at least the 1970s, when DF McMichael observed
that:

> the most important method of managing our Australian
> National Park resources is to implement a well-designed
> interpretation program, which seeks to inform the visitor of
> the values of the park and of nature conservation, not by direct
> teaching but by experience.[23]

By the 1990s, these ideas had gained credence. In 1993, Simon
McArthur and C Michael Hall argued that:

> Conventional heritage management has focused on the
> conservation of the resource, sometimes at the expense of
> the experience. Instead, we advocate an approach which
> emphasises the use of interpretation and education to maximise
> visitor experience while conserving the resource. Therefore,
> interpretation is a tool to manage both experience and impact.[24]

The erection of interpretative facilities in national parks was thus not
just a means of managing the behaviour of the visitor, but increasingly
also their experience. At Audley, these new attitudes were ultimately
symbolised by the transformation of part of the old dance hall into a
visitor centre under the management of the NPWS.

---

23 DF McMichaels (1972). 'Management of people and facilities for recreation'.
Cited in McArthur & Hall (1993), 26.

24 McArthur & Hall (1993), 18–40.

Locating the visitor: placing recreational facilities in national parks

The second part of this chapter will explore how the location of recreational facilities in national parks changed from 1879 to the early twenty-first century. I will argue that these shifts reflect an ideological transformation of the relationship between the visitor and nature, with the emphasis swinging from bringing visitors closer to nature to expecting them to display greater reverence for nature.

The earliest park managers sought to please park visitors by locating facilities in the areas they thought they would most want to use – often in areas promoted as possessing attractive or Romantic qualities. Managers even adapted some natural features for human use. The growth of ecological awareness in the 1950s and 1960s meant that protecting sensitive natural features from the impact of the visitor became a greater priority.

In the late nineteenth century, park managers sought to provide visitors with a Romantic experience of nature by locating facilities in the midst of scenic natural surroundings. Aesthetic perceptions of nature were strongly influenced by Romanticism and the ideal settings for recreational facilities were those that were considered to possess Romantic or sublime properties, such as waterfalls and rainforest gullies. Exotic vegetation was also considered desirable and some areas were planted with imported species to spice up the Australian bush. Tim Bonyhady has shown that ferns were also highly popular in the mid to late nineteenth century.[25] Picnic facilities were often located in ferny areas, encouraging visitors to literally immerse themselves in the beauty of nature in accordance with Romantic ideals which emphasised the spiritual connection between man and nature.

The Romantic picnic was promoted in the *Official guide to the National Park*, published in 1893. Figtree Flat, one of the most popular picnicking areas in the National Park, was described as 'a "bank whereon the wild flowers blow," sheltered by a widespreading figtree, around whose trunk bush seats and tables have been placed [in] ... a charming

---

25 Bonyhady (2000), 101–27.

situation, effectually shaded'.[26] The flowery Romantic language of the description – borrowed from Shakespeare – was typical of the *Official guide*. The incorporation of the fig tree into the design was important, as it reflected a managerial attempt to bring the visitor closer to nature whilst improving their comfort through the addition of seating.

Despite of the influence of Romanticism, park managers possessed a distinctly utilitarian attitude toward nature. Nature in national parks existed to meet the recreational needs of the public, rather than to be preserved for its own sake. Nature was protected, but it was also exploited. Aside from natural beauty, the three most important criteria of picnicking sites in the late nineteenth century were accessibility, proximity to drinking water and adequate shelter from the elements. Sometimes these criteria were met using natural sources. In the National Park, boats were initially the most common form of transport, and as a result most early picnicking sites were clustered around riverbanks. Shelter could be provided by natural features such as caves or trees, whilst creeks and streams supplied a natural source of drinking water. In other cases, conveniences were provided artificially through the construction of facilities such as roads, picnic shelters (originally known as shelter sheds) and water pipes. Most often, facilities combined natural resources and artificial enhancements. The most popular picnicking areas in the National Park in the late nineteenth century possessed these characteristics as well as natural beauty. The *Official guide to the National Park* reported that at Audley:

> the choice of the main camp was a happy one indeed, for, taking all the circumstances and calculations into consideration, especially the natural beauty of the position and its propinquity to the railway line a better site for preliminary operations and permanent convenience could not have been selected.[27]

A utilitarian outlook was also expressed in decisions to incorporate natural features such as caves into the design of recreational facilities.

---

26 *Official guide to the National Park* (1893), 34.

27 *Official guide to the National Park* (1893), 14.

Rest caves consisting of natural caves with artificial modifications were popular from the 1880s until at least the 1930s in NSW. Typical improvements included the levelling (and occasionally the cementing) of the floor of the cave, and the addition of chairs, tables and even fireplaces in order to make it more comfortable. The novel adventure of eating inside a cave may have appealed to the Romantic sensibilities of visitors seeking a natural experience, but park managers believed that the experience was enhanced with an additional level of comfort. This exploitative attitude of park managers toward nature saw caves modified in numerous locations in the National Park and Ku-ring-gai Chase, as well as other non-national park areas. At Kanangra in the Blue Mountains, a sophisticated 'dance floor cave' was created by the Oberon community in 1891 and remained in use for several decades by local families.[28]

In the first half of the twentieth century, recreational facilities continued to be located in picturesque locations such as caves and riverbanks. Under growing pressure from conservationists, the trustees began to justify recreational developments by arguing that the areas in which they were located were expendable. For example, in response to the negative media publicity of 1938, it was argued that river flats in the National Park had been cleared of useless undergrowth to provide additional picnic areas, and that the contentious bowling green had been constructed on hitherto swampy land. Golf links were to be laid out at a site previously used as an illegal rubbish dump.[29] The trustees sought to justify the impact of recreational facilities on the environment by locating them on land they considered less valuable. By later standards, however, many of these areas would be considered too ecologically sensitive for development, reflecting a shift away from utilitarian conceptions of the landscape.

By the 1960s, human development of national parks, particularly in especially picturesque areas, was subject to greater scrutiny. Facilities were removed from scenic areas, reflecting the emergence

---

28 'Dance Floor Cave', Item ID 1441, Historic Heritage Information Management System, Office of Environment and Heritage. Accessed 28 May 2008.

29 *The Open Road*, 14 July 1938.

Fig. 5.4. As well as adapting caves as romantic picnic shelters, free-form concrete caves were also built. These ones in the Blue Mountains now have heritage value. Fiona Howie.

of a conservation ethos governed by a sense of the fragility of nature. The most beautiful areas of national parks were no longer the first to be developed for human recreation. Instead they were preserved for posterity. In 1962, HJ Stanley, the Administrator for Parks and Reserves of NSW, advocated a 'middle course policy' in regard to the construction of facilities in national parks, acknowledging both the 'paramount duty to ensure the preservation of the landscape and the wilderness for future generations' and the conviction that the 'present day population is also entitled to use its national parks and to be provided with reasonable facilities for the purpose'. Warrumbungle National Park was upheld as a model of recreational development. Stanley wrote that 'an example of good forethought and planning is evident in the Warrumbungle National Park where basic facilities for visitors have been confined to a relatively unattractive area of the park, leaving the landscape and wilderness completely unspoiled'.[30] In 1963, the trustees of the National Park proposed the declaration of a series of primitive reserves, reflecting the increasingly vocal calls of conservationists. The South West arm, a 'very attractive portion of the park', was designated a primitive reserve, as was the 'singularly unique' Jibbon Point, a stunning stretch of coastline which also contains engravings by the Indigenous Dharawal people.[31]

Recreation remained an important aspect of national parks but greater attention was paid to the long-term impact of visitors upon the landscape of national parks. The removal of facilities from ecologically sensitive areas was an attempt to control environmental damage and hence preserve attractive areas for the enjoyment of future generations. These actions had some precedent in the US. During the 1950s, it was feared that rising numbers of visitors to national parks in the US would destroy the natural values of the parks if preventative action was not taken. The US Park Service had been established in 1916 and in 1956, looking forward to its fiftieth anniversary, a ten-year program known as Mission 66 was implemented to protect scenic areas of national parks for the enjoyment of future generations.[32] An important aspect of the program was the relocation of recreational facilities to less attractive areas of national parks. With the creations of the NPWS to oversee NSW's national parks in 1967, the style of centralised management displayed the influence of the US Park Service, even down to the uniforms of park officers. The NPWS adopted the US Park Service's policy of removing facilities located in attractive areas, including at Ku-ring-gai Chase and the Royal National Park. This was partly due to fears that the increasing concentration of visitors in areas with high natural value would have an adverse impact on the natural environment.

Adherence to these policies intensified in the 1990s and 2000s, with facilities increasingly located on the periphery of parks, rather than at a central base camp. The *Blue Mountains heritage walking tracks heritage assessment* reported in 1998 that:

---

30 Stanley (1962), 7–8.

31 Annual Report of the National Park Trust, vol. 83, 1963, 2, SRNSW: NRS 10732 [9/2194].

32 Stanley (1962).

> In accordance with current Service policy, picnic facilities now
> tend to be located in less sensitive environmental areas such as
> at track heads and adjacent to vehicular access points, whereas,
> in the past, such facilities were often provided in areas such as
> rainforest gullies … It was common practice until quite recently
> for visitors to 'boil the billy' or have a barbecue in natural
> environments which are now regarded as too sensitive.[33]

Traditions such as boiling the billy or having barbecues could be
damaging to the natural environment. Tramping around foraging for
firewood, lighting fires, pulling branches from trees, clearing a space
for a fire and littering could result in erosion, damage to vegetation and
a reduction in shelter for animals. As Melissa Harper has observed, the
billy was an Australian symbol – and part of the bushland experience.[34]
By restricting facilities to less scenic, more accessible areas such as track
heads and vehicular access points, the damage to the environment
could be limited to areas which were already exposed to high levels of
human visitation, preserving attractive areas of the national park in a
more pristine state.

The effects of these policies were also apparent in coastal national
parks of NSW. For example, between 2002 and 2008 a series of changes
occurred in the facilities provided at Murramarang National Park on
the South Coast of New South Wales. The 2002 conservation *Plan of
management* for Murramarang National Park identified damage to
the park from 'a high level of recreational use over a long period' as a
particular problem.[35] Regeneration and protection works were suggested
as an appropriate solution. As a result, a popular camping ground at
Pretty Beach was significantly reduced over a six-year period, to the
dismay of some regular campers.[36] Campsites closest to the coastline

---

33 NPWS (1998). Blue Mountains heritage walking tracks heritage assessment,
64.

34 Harper (2010), 83–91.

35 NPWS (2002). *Murramarang National Park, Brush Island Nature Reserve, and
Tollgate Islands Nature Reserve plan of management,* 3.

36 Giselle Buller, Sharon & Rod Monk. Interview at Pretty Beach, Murramarang

Fig. 5.5. Modern national park amenities, such as this toilet block in Yuraygir National Park, are designed to be functional and environmentally friendly. The emphasis has shifted from blending in with to having minimum impact on the natural surroundings. Fiona Howie.

were removed, a picnic shelter was erected, and the remainder of the area was dedicated to regeneration.

The changing location of recreational facilities reveals the ideological transformation of the national park experience. Recreational facilities were originally placed in Romantically attractive areas such as rainforest gullies and caves in order to enhance the visitor's experience. Over the course of the twentieth century, growing awareness of the sensitivity of these areas led to the relocation of facilities to areas further away, such as track heads or lookouts, where the visitor could observe beautiful scenery from a less intrusive distance. By the mid 1990s, however, the preservation of cultural heritage became an increasing consideration

National Park, 21 January 2008.

and was often at odds with the removal of old recreational facilities for environmental reasons.[37] The emphasis on the value of historic sites in national parks increased throughout the 1990s and 2000s, reflecting the expanded role of the NPWS as a custodian of historic, cultural and Indigenous heritage as well as the environment.

Harmonising with nature: the design of recreational facilities

Throughout the history of national parks, managers sought to design recreational facilities that were in harmony with their natural surroundings. However, notions of what harmonised with nature has changed considerably over time. In the 1890s, rustic design was viewed as the most appropriate. In the 1940s, modern materials such as concrete were increasingly used to create a new series of designs. In the 1960s, recreational facilities were increasingly standardised across all national parks, and emphasis was placed upon reducing the visibility of facilities in keeping with ideals of national parks as pristine spaces. By the 1990s, the emphasis upon disguising facilities with their natural surroundings was replaced by a stronger focus upon using building materials that were low-impact and ecologically sustainable. The design of national park facilities has also, at times, competed with a desire to preserve historic facilities that retain a sense of continuity with the past and came to be seen as having cultural value.

Ideals of continuity are central to the establishment of national parks. The original National Park was proclaimed as a place that would 'retain its natural characteristics for all time'.[38] Visitors to national parks have often expressed a belief in the value of continuity in national parks. Some regular campers at Pretty Beach in Murramarang National Park, for example, have been visiting the camping ground since childhood, continuing to return decades later with children of their own. They believe that their recreational uses of the park has remained essentially 'the same', and hope that their children will continue the tradition.[39]

37 For a more in depth discussion of these tensions, see Ford (2009).

38 *Official guide to the National Park* (1893), 16.

39 Giselle Buller & Sharon & Rod Monk. Interview, 29 January 2008.

Many park users have reacted negatively to managerial changes that they perceived as threatening their traditional activities in the park. Yet park managers have often viewed the recreational development of national parks as a process of change for the better. New recreational facilities have been described as improvements. Designs, materials and locations considered suitable for recreational facilities in one era have often become quickly outdated. Given that continuity is an important feature of national parks, how can it be reconciled with historical changes in conceptions of appropriate facilities in national parks?

The most obvious example of the pressure to modernise and improve facilities in national parks is found in the humble history of toilet designs. Toilet blocks have always been the most frequently modernised (and most frequently damaged) facilities in national parks, and park managers have often expressed a degree of pride in providing up-to-date toilet facilities. Definitions of what constitutes an acceptable toilet have changed as a result of the increasing sophistication of waste management systems, and park managers have sometimes felt pressured to provide the newest and latest technologies. Some of this pressure has come from recreational visitors themselves. In 1945, the trustees of the National Park were 'repeatedly congratulated' by visitors upon the installation of 'modern' septic toilets at Reid's Flat and were 'approached with requests for similar amenities at other favoured picnic resorts in the Park'.[40] Competition with surrounding areas has also influenced the modernisation of toilet design in national parks. In 1928, the President of the Trustees of Ku-ring-gai Chase reported that the nearby Warringah Shire had installed septic tanks on the 'Windmill System' from Manly to Palm Beach. He directed that a similar toilet be erected within the Chase within the next two months as he believed such toilets to be 'more of an ornament than an eyesore and … wonderfully effective'.[41]

By the 1990s, toilets were expected to be environmentally sustainable.[42] In the first decade of the twenty-first century, hybrid toilets

40 National Park Trust Annual Report, No. 65, 1945, SRNSW.

41 Minutes of the Meetings of the Trustees of Ku-ring-gai Chase. 8 November 1928: 4. SRNSW: NRS10704 [11/14308-18].

42 Gorrell (1994).

were installed at Yuraygir National Park in order to replace existing pit toilet systems that were considered to be outdated and damaging to the environment, and therefore 'incompatible with NPWS management objectives'. One of the objectives of improvement was to 'bring Yuraygir in line with surrounding community upgrades of sewerage management services', reflecting the real or imagined pressure felt by park managers to remain up-to-date in waste management.[43]

The pressure to be up-to-date can also be seen in the design of picnicking facilities, which has changed according to ideas of what harmonised with nature. In the 1890s, rustic design was viewed as the most appropriate. Rusticism may be defined as a style that sought to maintain an affiliation with the past and with nature, and in the latter sense was closely linked to Romanticism. The characteristics of rusticism included the use of natural materials such as stone and wood. Simple pastoral designs reflect a nostalgia for a pre-industrial imagined past. The resistance to modernisation was calculated to appeal to urban visitors seeking an escape back to nature, or as a writer in the *Sydney Morning Herald* put it:

> City-dwellers, it was hoped, could leave behind the nerve-racking hubbub of 'civilisation', to find beauty, rest, and happiness in an unspoilt domain of nature. The human spirit, shaking off the shackles of a mechanised urban life, could return to refreshing earth, drinking again for a brief moment at the wells of wonder and freedom.[44]

The *Official guide to the National Park* advertised the tables and seats around the fig tree in the Figtree Flat picnic area at Audley as suitably 'bush' or rustic. By the 1890s, the bush culture of old Australia was seen as something that was passing away.

In the early twentieth century, rustic design retained its status as an appropriate style for picnic facilities. In 1938, the trustees of the National Park removed older sheds and replaced them with rustic shelters covered

43 'Yuraygir National Park: Illaroo toilets'. DECC Official Record. 19 May 2005. Accessed in the DECC Grafton Office.

44 'Preserving our Parks'. *Sydney Morning Herald*, 21 May 1938.

with green tiles that were said to harmonise with the background. Shrubs were also planted to 'screen the public conveniences' in picnic areas.[45] The aim was to provide additional comfort to picnickers and other recreational visitors, whilst preserving the vestiges of a natural experience. While the continued use of rustic design expressed a desire to retain a connection with the past, its paradoxical modernity meant that many older recreational facilities were viewed as outdated. In 1938, Horace W Whiddon, chairman of the trustees of the National Park, described the old boatshed at Audley as an 'eyesore' and announced a plan to replace it with a new boatshed which would be 'one of the finest in the Southern Hemisphere'.[46]

In the middle of the century, more modern design came to be favoured, and new materials and technologies were introduced to the construction of facilities. Facilities no longer had to be rustic to be considered to be in harmony with the natural surroundings. In 1944, the trustees of the National Park reported with excitement the purchase of concrete block machines, and noted that 'experiments have indicated that, with the use of these machines an attractive and cheap construction can be obtained giving us buildings of a unique design and fully in keeping with the surroundings'.[47] The idea that modern materials could be used to create attractive facilities that remained 'in keeping with the surroundings' conflicted with the notion that rustic design was most appropriate for a national park setting. As late as 1963, attractive concrete tables and seats were installed at Audley and Willow Tree Flat in the Royal National Park.[48] Less concern appears to have given to disguising the facilities, as the designs themselves became a feature of the park.

---

45 Edmonds (1938).

46 'National Park: Trustees' aims, improvements defended by chairman'. *Sydney Morning Herald*, 2 June 1938, 10.

47 Annual report of the National Park Trust (1944), 64, SRNSW: NRS 10732 [9/2194].

48 Annual report of the National Park Trust (1963), 83: SRNSW: NRS 10732 [9/2194].

In the late 1960s, older recreational facilities were generally viewed to be no longer appropriate. It was thought that they failed to integrate not only with the natural environment, but also with each other. At a seminar on the practical problems of national parks in 1966, Russell Smith argued that:

> too often in the past, in a well meaning attempt to provide necessary amenities, piecemeal development has taken place – development which ... becomes clearly apparent as a waste of money or a blunder of ill considered siting.

Smith suggested the introduction of a higher level of organisational planning: 'introduced elements must be of such a nature that the alterations to the natural environment, both real and apparent, constitute an extension of the theme'.[49] The replacement of the various individual trusts by the NPWS led to a mass introduction of a series of national park facilities inspired by US Park Service models. The Royal National Park's trustees had already used a US Park Service design in erecting a stone toilet block at Audley in the early 1950s. From 1967, the NPWS attempted to standardise facilities in NSW national parks, attempting to avoid the 'piecemeal development' described by Smith.

During the first decades of the NPWS, the desire to present national parks as pristine spaces was paramount. This profoundly affected the design of facilities which were no longer imagined as a potential improvement upon the natural surroundings. Every effort was now taken to ensure the visual impact of park facilities on their surroundings was minimal. In the 1930s, the trustees of the National Park had experimented with colour and location to disguise some facilities including lavatories. These techniques were applied in a more considered manner by the NPWS, which in 1971 published its first *Park furniture manual* as a guide to the erection of facilities.

Particular attention was paid to the materials used in construction. In the 1950s and early 1960s, managers at Audley had considered concrete to be an aesthetically attractive material to use in the construction

---

49 Smith (1966), 77–82.

of recreational facilities such as tables and seats.[50] The *Park furniture manual* warned that concrete was a 'much less sympathetic material in the natural scene than stone'. Similarly, steel could 'appear aggressively conspicuous unless very well sited', although the manual admitted it was convenient for mass production. The best solution to the problem of aesthetically siting fireplace structures was to incorporate them into a bank or wall.[51] Like the trustees, the NPWS also sought to camouflage facilities by painting them in natural colours such as green and brown.

Subsequent sets of guidelines for facilities demonstrate that notions of appropriate design continued to evolve. The avoidance of what were viewed as past mistakes continued to be a major theme in the *Guidelines for park facilities* published by the NPWS in 1994. Greater focus was placed upon the environmental sustainability of materials used. According to the *Guidelines,* the use of rainforest timbers (local or imported) was no longer appropriate. Bush rock was also not to be used without knowledge that its source was 'appropriate' (environmentally sustainable), and it was observed that whilst there was a strong tradition of using local rock from disturbed areas within parks, care was to be taken to 'avoid robbing stream beds or other sensitive areas'.[52] These policies contrasted with attitudes in the 1930s when the construction of recreational facilities from local stone was used to disguise them. For example, in the late 1930s, picnicking furniture at Lane Cove National Park was built from stone quarried at the park as part of a series of works organised during the Depression. The use of local materials could have a camouflaging effect. Whilst the NPWS remained concerned with minimising the visual impact of facilities upon their surroundings, by the late twentieth century, environmentally sustainable practice was the highest priority.

Given the status of these parks as national, it is worth asking whether the design of recreational facilities has reflected shifts in Australian nationalism? The *Official guide to the National Park* promoted furniture at Figtree Flat picnic ground as 'rustic' or 'bush', evoking the bush

---

50 Annual Report of the National Park Trust (1963).

51 NPWS (1971). *Park furniture manual.* Sydney: NPWS.

52 Gorrell (1994).

legend popularised in the 1890s.[53] Yet at the same time, the introduction of exotic species to NSW national parks during their first sixty years suggests that European Australians may have had an ambiguous relationship to their natural landscape. National parks were reserved as places where visitors could enjoy the natural scenery, but they were also modified to fit conventional contemporary ideas of natural beauty and thus appear less native, reflecting a belief that Australian bushland was not sufficiently attractive in itself to beautify a pleasure ground.

In the new millennium, a further transformation occurred in the design of picnic facilities, and could be seen in a new *Park facilities manual* released in 2007. This manual contained a series of new designs inspired by a self-consciously Australian architecture. They combined traditional Australian building materials such as stone and corrugated metal, with contemporary forms. These designs reconciled the contrasting principles of providing updated recreational facilities and retaining continuity with structures of the past. Many of the designs featured corrugated metal, a material praised by the *Park facilities manual* for its association with Australian identity. Architect Glenn Murcutt was well known for his use of corrugated metals to create a uniquely Australian style of architecture. In 2007, a new style of picnic shelter installed at Pretty Beach featured a slanted roof made of corrugated metal and made no attempt to disguise its presence. Other facilities in the new style can also be found at Bedlam Bay Regional Park, Rouse Hill Regional Park and Belair National Park in South Australia.[54]

The sophistication of these designs suggest the re-emergence of a notion that recreational facilities can be attractive in their own right, and do not necessarily have to be subordinate to natural surroundings. For example, the emergence (or re-emergence) of steel as an 'appropriate' building material for park facilities contrasted with previous policies of disguising facilities, reflected in the 1971 *Park furniture manual*, which listed the conspicuousness of concrete as one of its drawbacks.[55]

---

53 *Official guide to the National Park* (1893), 16.

54 *Park facilities manual* (2007). Sydney: Department of Environment and Climate Change, 293.

55 NPWS (1971).

Whether this style will become ubiquitous in the national parks of NSW remains to be seen. Considering the varied history of recreational facilities in national parks, it seems likely that managerial perceptions of suitable recreational design will continue to evolve.

The history of the design of recreational facilities in national parks suggests that park managers have striven to meet a similar series of goals, including the desire to provide up-to-date amenities, the creation of a sense of continuity in national parks and harmonisation with the natural surroundings. These competing goals have been variously expressed in the use of rustic design, camouflage, modern materials and environmentally sustainable approaches. At the same time, park managers have consistently sought to improve and modernise recreational facilities, leading to the alternate introduction and removal of different styles, technologies and guides to the construction of recreational facilities. This raises the question of whether recreational development is truly a process of improvement or simply one of change that belies attempts to retain a sense of continuity in national parks.

Conclusion

The history of recreational facilities demonstrates the changing attitudes of park managers toward nature and recreation in national parks. In the late nineteenth century, the appeal of nature was interpreted in Romantic terms. The design of facilities was deliberately rustic, offering the urban visitor an escape to a pre-modern world. The ideal visitors came to the national park to express their appreciation for the beauty of nature by immersing themselves in it. Recreational facilities were located in areas of the park considered the most scenic. National parks offered both spiritual and physical rejuvenation for the tired labourer and healthy recreation in national parks was believed to offer positive benefits to society. But the beauty of nature was valued only according to what it could offer the visitor. As a result, nature was also exploited. Natural features such as caves were transformed into recreational facilities, and the most beautiful riverside areas were dramatically modified and transformed into picnicking grounds.

During the early twentieth century, park managers sought to improve recreational opportunities in national parks through the introduction of increasingly sophisticated facilities. But as the debates of the 1930s have demonstrated, not everyone believed that these types of facilities were suitable for a natural setting. Critics argued that they threatened the unique value of national parks as places where nature could be preserved. These arguments reflected the contemporary emergence of a competing vision of national parks as spaces of nature conservation. Although the provision of specifically designated and designed recreational spaces remained an important priority of the trustees, less emphasis was placed on opening up new areas for recreational development. Instead, recreational facilities were primarily concentrated on previously developed areas in the National Park (and constructed more sparingly at Ku-ring-gai Chase), expressing the desire of park managers to maintain national parks in a relatively natural state. Recreational facilities continued to be placed in sensitive areas, but greater emphasis was also placed upon concentrating recreational facilities in areas of the park that were considered to be less attractive, including swampy areas. The trustees of the National Park also experimented with disguising facilities by painting them green. Rusticism continued to be viewed as an appropriately natural design, but emphasis was also placed on providing increasingly modern types of facilities.

The 1940s and 1950s was a period of transition and modernisation. The visitor was increasingly distanced from nature as the trustees sought to manage larger numbers using national parks. It was no longer usual for natural features such as caves to be adapted for recreational use. Instead, artificial facilities proliferated in an attempt to cope with greater numbers. Traditional construction materials such as stone and wood were replaced with modern substitutes such as concrete, enabling facilities to be constructed faster and more cheaply. These materials were now considered to be aesthetically pleasing, reflecting the abandonment of Romantic ideals of national parks as pre-modern spaces. Arguably, the loss of Romantic conceptions of nature during this period made it possible for the radical managerial changes of the 1960s to occur.

From the mid to late 1960s, park managers displayed a greater awareness of the fragility of nature. In the late nineteenth century, visitors were encouraged to immerse themselves in the beauty of nature. A century later, the ideal visitor was supposed to admire nature's beauty from a more respectful distance. Recreational visitors were viewed as a potential threat to the natural values of national parks. Park managers consciously sought to distance the visitor from nature in a bid to conserve important ecosystems and protect it for the enjoyment of future generations. Recreational facilities were removed from scenic environmental areas and relocated in less sensitive areas of national parks. Increased attention was paid to the role of facilities in managing the behaviour of the visitor and greater importance was given to the education of visitors, in particular the cultivation of ecological awareness.

Managerial changes of the 1960s were also reflected in the introduction of a new style of recreational facilities, as under the NPWS, park managers aimed to create a more uniform style of park facilities. These designs were subsequently revised and updated over the next half century, reflecting an enduring notion that recreational facilities of the past do not sufficiently meet the needs of the present.

The history of national parks facilities demonstrates that the pressure to modernise has existed uneasily alongside ideals of continuity in national parks. Changing managerial conceptions of the visitor's relationship to nature, the purpose of national parks, and definitions of the natural have all influenced the provision of recreational facilities in national parks. At the same time, both visitors and park managers have often expressed a desire for continuity in national parks, most explicitly in the recognition of the cultural heritage values of the older facilities. Can these two competing pressures be reconciled? And how will future changes in managerial conceptions of the relationship of the visitor to nature affect the provision of facilities? Whilst a recreational history of national parks may not provide answers to such questions, this chapter has sought to demonstrate that it is a worthwhile subject for future research.

References

Bonyhady, Tim (2000). *The colonial earth*. Melbourne: Melbourne University Press.

Official guide to the National Park (1893). Sydney: Government Printer.

Ford, Caroline (2009). *Challenges in the landscape: memories of conserving historic heritage in the NSW park system 1967–2000*. Sydney: Department of Environment, Climate Change and Water.

Gorrell, Stephen (1994). *Guidelines for park facilities*. Sydney: NPWS.

Harper, Melissa (2010). 'Billy', in Richard White & Melissa Harper (eds). *Symbols of Australia*. Sydney: UNSW Press.

Harper, Melissa & Richard White (2012), 'How transnational were the first national parks? Comparative perspectives from the British settler societies', in Bernhard Gissibl, Sabine Höhler, Patrick Kupper (eds). *Civilising nature: national parks in global historical perspective*. Munich: Berghahn Books.

Kijas, Johanna (2009). *There were always people here: a history of Yuraygir National Park*. Sydney: DECC.

McArthur, Simon & C Michael Hall (1993). 'Visitor management and interpretation at heritage sites', in McArthur and Hall (eds). *Heritage management in New Zealand and Australia: visitor management, interpretation, and marketing*. Auckland: Oxford University Press.

Smith, Russell C (1966) 'The architectural aspects of national parks'. Practical problems of national parks. Proceedings of the seminar held at the University of New England.

Stanley, HJ (1962). 'Should national parks be developed?' *The National Parks Journal*, 1(6).

Chapter 6

'The adventurer's playground': courting danger in national parks

Isobelle Barrett Meyering

The Blue Mountains National Park is an 'adventurer's playground', promises New South Wales Tourism's pocket guide to the region.[1] An array of sports, from horse riding and abseiling to canyoning and mountain biking, are available to the modern-day thrill-seeker. Similar activities can be found in national parks across the state. Favourite sites among rock climbers include the sandstone cliffs of Sydney Harbour, while white-water rafters take on the river rapids of the Nymboi-Binderay and backcountry skiers head to the slopes of Kosciuszko.

Since the 1970s, visitor demand for these activities has increased and the term 'adventure recreation' has gradually crept into the NPWS vocabulary.[2] The increased demand for these activities has in turn prompted vigorous debate over the role of the NPWS in regulating park usage. This chapter seeks to bring greater clarity to this often heated debate by placing adventure recreation in its historical context. In doing so, it emphasises the paradoxical role of national parks in both enabling and constraining the experience of danger sought by adventure recreationists. It also unpacks some of the assumptions behind adventure recreationists' hostile responses to regulation.

---

1   New South Wales Tourism (2008). *Pocket guide 2008: Blue Mountains, Lithgow and Oberon*, 11.

2   Adventure recreation is now a standard section in park management plans, and also features in the facilities and activities section on the Office of Environment and Heritage website for some parks. Available: www.environment. new.gov.au/nationalparks [Accessed 19 December 2008].

Fig. 6.1. Skiers at 'The Chalet', Mt Kosciuszko. Skiing was one of the earliest adventure sports to be enjoyed in Australia and also posed problems for the management of national parks. State Records NSW.

This chapter is divided into two sections. The first section outlines the longstanding attraction of national parks as a site of adventure recreation. The second focuses on debates between adventure recreationists and park authorities over questions of public safety and conservation. This chapter deals with a range of different adventure activities, using rock climbing, one of the oldest forms of adventure recreation in national parks, as the main case study. However, before exploring the history of adventure recreation in national parks, it is important to be clear about how the category has typically been defined, as well as the limitations of that definition.

In the broader academic literature, the term 'adventure recreation' is used to refer to activities which 'contain structural components of real or perceived danger' and 'involve a natural environmental setting'.[3] In this respect, there is an important distinction between adventure recreation and extreme sports. Adventure recreation applies exclusively to activities which take place in a natural or wilderness setting, whereas

3   Ewert & Hollenhorst (1997), 21.

extreme sports is an umbrella term which includes adventure recreation as well as activities which take place in an urban environment, such as skateboarding or indoor rock climbing. One of the most obvious problems with this definition of adventure recreation is the imprecise nature of danger encompassed under its banner. A brief perusal of the NSW Office of Environment and Heritage (OEH) website is all it takes to realise that adventure recreation is a nebulous term. It is used to cover a wide range of activities, from stargazing and rock climbing at Warrumbungle National Park through to canyoning and caving at Deua National Park.[4] The adoption of this terminology is itself significant, as it implies that these activities fall into a unified category and thus require the same policy response.

To a certain extent, such a response is warranted given adventure recreationists' own representations of themselves as a single community. To the outside observer, it might seem absurd to place bushwalking and ice climbing in the same category, given the different levels of risk involved. Yet those claiming to represent adventure recreationists have typically sought to gloss over these differences. *Wild* magazine (originally *Australian Wild*), for example, seeks to represent bushwalkers, ski tourers, canoeists and climbers. Introducing the inaugural edition in 1981, founder and editor Chris Baxter was adamant that these groups shared a common understanding and that 'a ready rapport comes naturally wherever they meet'.[5] That participants across these sports encounter different levels of risk seemed to be irrelevant to Baxter: no doubt he had an interest in ensuring a broad market for the magazine. However, the commercial success of *Wild* suggests there is a loyal readership that and the loyalty of his readers suggests that the reading public shares Baxter's view.

Despite optimistic pronouncements about participants' ready rapport, one does not have to dig deep to uncover the fractures within the adventure recreation community. There are, and always have been, points of division among adventure recreationists, not least in their

---

4   Available: www.environment.nsw.gov.au/nationalparks [Accessed 19 December 2008].
5   Baxter (1981), 3.

attitudes towards national park management. As this chapter endeavours to demonstrate, understanding what constitutes danger and attitudes towards the natural environment vary significantly. In examining the history of adventure recreation in national parks, we need to keep this diversity in mind. Similarly, any attempts to regulate the behaviour of adventure recreationists needs to address the range of belief systems and interests at play.

National parks as adventure destinations

Adventure recreation is by no means a new phenomenon in NSW national parks. At the beginning of the twentieth century, Freda du Faur was exploring the ridges and valleys of Ku-ring-gai Chase, learning to 'scale a face that had little more texture to it than sandpaper'.[6] Du Faur's father had been the prime advocate of the park's gazetting as a national park. Du Faur would become internationally renowned as a mountaineer. In the 1930s, climbers Dr Eric Dark and Dot Butler were making 'intrepid' ascents at Bungonia Gorge and the Warrumbungles.[7] Indeed, adventure recreation preceded the creation of most national parks. Melissa Harper describes the development of a 'bushwalking-conservation nexus' from the 1920s. Bushwalking clubs, led by figures such as Myles Dunphy and Marie Byles, were key proponents of the expansion of national parks.[8]

What was new was the scale on which park users were participating in adventure recreation by the late twentieth century. For most of the century, adventure recreation in parks was confined to 'relatively small cliques of enthusiasts with tight networks'.[9] However, activities which were once the preserve of an exclusive few became increasingly mainstream. Park visitors' activities began to change noticeably in the 1970s, leading NPWS staff member Gary Steer to comment in 1979 that they 'seem to be getting out, getting away from their cars,

6   Irwin (2000), 62.
7   Williams (1988), 38.
8   Harper (2007), 257, 259.
9   Brown (1997), 44.

going bushwalking, cross country skiing, cycling, canoeing, caving or rock climbing.[10] The commercialisation of adventure recreation also first became evident during this period, with tour companies offering guided trips for the inexperienced. The adventure recreation industry in the Blue Mountains, for example, dates from the early 1980s.

While the massive changes of the past three decades make it tempting to focus on the recent history of adventure recreation, the long-standing attraction of national parks as a site of adventure recreation also needs to be explained. In this respect, two questions are pertinent. First, what is the general appeal of adventure recreation? Second, how have national parks catered for this?

The popularisation of adventure recreation across the Western world since the 1970s has generated significant interest among academics from a range of fields, from sociology to psychology.[11] In accounting for its appeal, researchers have tended to emphasise the allure of risk. Sociologist Deborah Lupton, for example, is typical in arguing that the principal attraction of adventure recreation lies in the 'courting of danger', the testing of human endurance of fear.[12] She is also typical in linking the popularisation of extreme sports to the rise of neoliberalism and the increasing acceptability of other forms of risk-taking, such as share-trading.[13]

While this focus on risk is not in itself misplaced, it is all too easy to generalise about the appeal of adventure recreation, whilst ignoring the particular locations in which it takes place. None of the existing explanations directly accounts for the appeal of national parks as a site of adventure recreation. This reflects the general lack of geographic focus in recent studies and their subsequent failure to recognise the historic importance of particular sites to adventure recreationists.[14]

---

10 Steer (1979).

11 The rise of adventure recreation is documented in a range of studies, including Wheaton (2004), 1–28; Palmer (2002), 323–36; Kan (2000/1), 32–33.

12 Lupton (1999), 149.

13 The relationship between neoliberalism and extreme sports is explored in Kusz (2004) 197–213; Tulloch & Lupton (2003); Simon (2002), 177–208; Lupton (1999).

14 Those studies which do incorporate a geographic angle tend to centre on the

Furthermore, the argument that adventure tourism is a product of the rise of neoliberalism is ahistorical, ignoring the much longer and continuing popularity of activities such as mountaineering, cross-country skiing and hunting.

In contrast, new themes emerge when we explore the history of adventure recreation in national parks, enabling us to become more precise about the nature of danger sought by participants. Given that adventure recreation, unlike other extreme sports, depends on a setting in a relatively natural environment, we need to closely examine how the wilderness enhances the adventure recreationist's experience. In doing so, it is important to recognise that there is no such thing as true wilderness in Australia – that is, land in a completely natural state – as all land has been used and transformed by people over many thousands of years. Nonetheless, as 'areas of land protected for their unspoiled landscapes, outstanding or representative ecosystems, native plant and animal species, and natural or cultural significance', national parks perhaps come closest to representing what is popularly thought of as the Australian wilderness.[15]

The attraction of the wilderness is an important part of adventure recreation discourse. Indeed, when asked what he thought appealed most to clients about adventure recreation, High 'n' Wild Mountain Adventures manager Darren Trew acknowledged that the 'thrill' was 'a large part of it', but suggested that 'the beauty of the canyons', the 'stunning geography' and the 'incredible biodiversity of plants and animals' were equally important.[16] The title of Australia's leading adventure recreation magazine, *Wild*, would appear to prove his point.

---

world's adventure capitals such as Mount Everest (Nepal), Interlaken (Switzerland) and Queenstown (New Zealand), while neglecting lower-profile destinations. Rosen (2007), 147–68; Bell & Lyall (2002), 21–37; Kan (2000/1), 32–33.

15 'National parks'. [Online] Available: www.environment.nsw.gov.au/nationalparks [Accessed 19 December 2008]. The concept of wilderness is itself debated. On the intellectual history of wilderness, see Miller (1995), 38–40; Nash (1982).

16 Darren Trew, High 'n' Wild Mountain Adventures. Interview, Katoomba, 18 May 2008.

Yet it is misleading to see the thrill of adventure recreation and the appeal of the wilderness as entirely separate factors behind the attraction of such activities. The two are in fact interdependent. The thrill of adventure recreation derives not just from the activities themselves, but the setting in which they occur. For adventure recreationists, the wilderness is not just an aesthetic backdrop to their activities but one of their key sources of danger. The sense of danger associated with the unpredictability and untrustworthiness of the natural elements, for example, is captured in Brian Walters' description of his ice climbing trip to Blue Lake in Kosciuszko National Park:

> most of all I will remember overcoming the surge of fear that convulses my stomach as I trust myself to ice axe and crampons. A grip on ice seems tenuous at best, and the ice a shifting, untrustworthy medium that separates me from the firm rock beneath.[17]

It is also the scale of the wilderness which enhances the thrill of adventure recreation. In their analysis of bungee jumping in New Zealand, Claudia Bell and John Lyall suggest that 'the mystification and glorification of the experience depends greatly on the environment in which it takes place'. Adventure recreation presents 'an invitation to engage with the landscape on an heroic scale: to be daring, to be reckless'.[18] Adventure recreation photography, for example, reflects the way in which the vastness of the Australian wilderness evokes a sense of danger. Photographs tend to fall into two broad categories. The first category consists of close ups, shots highlighting the taut muscles and intense concentration of rock climbers, or the skilled manoeuvres of surfers. The second category consists of wide-angle shots: photographs of white-water rafters plummeting down waterfalls, and shots capturing the grandeur of the cliff faces and valleys below rock climbers, who dangle precariously from cliff overhangs.[19] Insofar as they are intended

---

17 Walters (1983), 36.

18 Bell & Lyall (2002), 27.

19 'Figure-in-a-landscape' is a specific category on the website of rock climbing

Fig. 6.2. The rivers and waterways that run through national parks, such as the Guy Fawkes River, provide opportunities for water-based adventure recreation. Greg Steer / NPWS.

to evoke a feeling of awe at the immensity of nature, there is a distinctly Romantic quality to these latter images, a sense of the sublime.

As the above examples demonstrate, adventure recreationists' experiences of danger are at least partially dependent on their access to a wilderness setting. The opposite is also true. Adventure recreationists see danger not only as a desirable, but as a necessary component of an authentic wilderness experience. They think of their activities as maximising the authenticity of their wilderness experience in a number of ways.

Part of the appeal of adventure activities is that they often require participants to go to rarely visited sites, and thus lay claim to a more exclusive wilderness experience. The manager of High 'n' Wild

photographer Simon Carter. Simon Carter, Onsight Photography website. [Online] Available: www.onsight.com.au [Accessed 4 June 2008].

Mountain Adventures noted that 'you can experience the beauty of the Blue Mountains just by going for a walk' and that the virtue of canyoning is that you will visit sites that are 'really rare and unspoilt'.[20] Similarly, for rock climbers, one of the satisfying aspects of first ascents is the sense of discovery. This feeing is captured by Russell Kippax in his description of the first ascent of the Breadknife in the Warrumbungle National Parks in 1954: 'Very few climbers had visited the region … It seemed as though we had, before us, the magic pudding'.[21] Adventure recreationists thus measure the authenticity of their experience in relation to its exclusiveness.

Fundamentally, adventure recreationists measure the authenticity of their wilderness experience in relation to the apparent levels of risk associated with it. The underlying claim of adventure recreationists is that their activities, by virtue of the dangers involved, bring them closer to nature. To experience danger is to experience the 'real' wild, in its most pristine and pure form. The justification of twenty-year-old Wendy Butler's death as the cost of 'priceless experiences' of nature is a prime example of this attitude. When Wendy (the daughter of Dot Butler) died in November 1966, *Thrutch* urged people not to be deterred from adventure recreation. Butler drowned when her foot became jammed in a crevice while cascading in the Kowmung River, which flows through the Blue Mountains and Kanangra-Boyd National Parks. The obituary in *Thrutch* portrayed her as an exemplary conservationist whose 'love of nature dominated her personality'. While her death was tragic, the writer insisted that it was simply 'the price we pay for these priceless experiences' of nature:

> To the parents who worry every time their sons and daughters go climbing or walking, I ask you to remember that you have never seen the grandeur and splendour of mountain scenery; nor heard the roar of waterfalls; nor swum between the mossy walls of a canyon; nor felt the thrill of exposure on a rockclimb

---

20 Darren Trew. Interview, 2008.
21 Russell Kippax, 'Five climbs'. *Thrutch,* 50th anniversary edition, 9.

> … Risk of life and chance of limb is the price we pay for these
> priceless experiences, so refreshing in a world of artificiality.[22]

The implication is that only those willing to risk life and limb are
truly able to access an authentic experience of nature. The wording of
the obituary also highlights the deeply nostalgic nature of adventure
recreationists' attitudes. Here, the authenticity of the wilderness is held
up against the artificiality of the modern world. This is a typical trope
in the writings of adventure recreationists, who present their activities
as a reaction against 'our materialistic way of life' and as an attempt to
reinsert a sense of hardship, of 'elemental simplicity', into their daily
existence.[23] This trope can also be found in academic literature on
adventure recreation. In the *Journal of Popular Culture*, Elizabeth Rosen
explains the attraction of mountaineering at Mount Everest in terms of
the lack of risk in ordinary life: 'modern civilization, with its urbanity, is
so safe compared with life centuries ago'.[24]

However, the different ways in which adventure recreationists
engage with national parks exposes a tension within this discourse.
In particular, the notion that adventure recreation is an escape from
materialism is inconsistent with participants' increasing reliance on
modern equipment to minimise the risks involved in their pursuits.
For this reason, the use of technology is a consistent source of division
amongst adventure recreationists. This tension is at the heart of recent
debate over whether it is appropriate to include four-wheel driving and
trail bike riding under the banner of adventure recreation.[25] However,

---

22 'Obituary'. *Thrutch*, December 1966, 16.

23 Walters (1983), 36.

24 Rosen (2007), 152.

25 Ian Brown includes four-wheel driving and trail bike riding under the banner
of adventure recreation. Brown acknowledges this is somewhat tenuous given
their reliance on machine-based power, but argues that they 'share many common
characteristics with the conventional suite of adventure recreations'. Melissa
Harper has also identified the parallels between the rhetoric of four-wheel drivers
and bushwalkers in so far as they see themselves as 'self-reliant adventurers'. See
Harper (2007), 283; Brown (1997), 6.

the issue is by no means new. Similar questions have, for example, divided rock climbers since the 1960s, when artificial aids started to become more readily available. The debate over the comparative virtues of adventure climbing where participants restrict themselves to natural forms of protection and assistance (such as cliff cracks) to complete a climb and aided climbing, is worth considering in more detail as it provides useful insight into the divisions within the adventure recreation community and their implications for national parks.[26]

The rise of aided climbing began in the 1960s due to 'quantum leaps' in climbing equipment.[27] Significant technical advances occurred during this period, when hemp rope, steel karabiners, pitons, expansion bolts and, most importantly, the hand-held electric drill, were added to the rock climbers' kits. In contrast, previous climbing kits 'consisted of a pair of Dunlop sandshoes, a 1-inch sisal rope, makeshift slings and pebbles for use as chocks!'[28] A backlash against aided climbing quickly followed. In the 1970s, bolts were removed from climbs where they were regarded as unsafe, not well placed or where natural protection was readily available.[29] However, the issue is far from resolved and the debate over bolting continues to rage in climber magazines and online forums.

Part of what is at stake in this debate is the reputation of climbers who make the first ascent of a climb. Keith Royce, a leading developer of climbs in the Wolgan Valley in the Blue Mountains National Park, made the first ascent of Sod ('Shit, Oh Dear!') with Les Ormand and Dave Massam in June 1969, but it was retro-bolted and renamed 'Deathbed Confessions' by Andrew Penny in 1985.[30] When Royce returned to the climb in the late 1990s and noticed the change, he was deeply concerned:

26 Donnelly (2003), 292–93.

27 Wade Stevens, 'The master's cave'. *Thrutch*, 50th anniversary edition, 12.

28 Rachel Gleeso, '50 years of the Sydney Rockclimbing Club'. *Thrutch*, 50th anniversary edition, 1.

29 Warwick Williams, 'My perspective: the 1970s'. *Thrutch*, 50th anniversary edition, 15.

30 Stevens (2000).

> I don't really mind that the climb I put up and called Sod has
> been bolted, but I do mind that the prized first ascent of an
> outstanding Wolgan wall has been claimed by someone who can
> drill a heap of holes.[31]

Also at play here is the conservationist argument concerned with
the environmental degradation caused by bolting. Warwick Williams,
a member of Sydney Rockclimbing Club (SRC), reassured *Thrutch*
readers that Australian climbers have never 'gone berserk in large
numbers and "raped" the cliffs with pegs and bolts'.[32] However, damage
to cliff faces by bolting became an issue prompting intervention from
NPWS management, a subject discussed later in this chapter.

The issues of reputation and environmental degradation are
ultimately secondary arguments in the debate over the comparative
merits of adventure climbing and aided climbing. At the core of this
debate is a disagreement over how the danger in rock climbing should
be managed. For adventure climbers, the answer is that the limitations
of a climb should be imposed by the cliffs themselves – that is, by nature.
Thus, sociologist Neil Lewis asserts that in adventure climbing, 'nature
facilitates and becomes a co-participator in the leisure experience'.[33] In
contrast, aided climbers are more likely to see themselves as setting the
limits of the climb and are happy to use artificial devices to undertake
what would otherwise be an impossible route. The division among
rock climbers lies in the debate over whether or not it is desirable to
use technology to control nature. That both sides see a relationship to
nature as being central to the experience makes it an important issue for
those charged with protecting natural environments such as national
park managers.

Conflict among rock climbers over the comparative merits of
adventure climbing and aided climbing offers a useful reminder that
adventure recreationists are far from a homogeneous group. Their

---

31 Quoted in Stevens (2000).

32 Warwick Williams, 'My perspective: the 1970s'. *Thrutch*, 50th anniversary
edition, 15.

33 N Lewis (2004), 83–84.

understandings of what constitutes danger and their attitudes to the wilderness vary not only across different adventure activities but within individual sports. Yet, as we will see, such nuances are frequently lost in the debate over NPWS regulation. Instead, debate over regulation tends to be reduced to a contest between adventure recreationists and park authorities, and deep-seated conflicts within groups of adventure recreationists are glossed over.

Managing adventure recreation

The question of how adventure recreation should be managed has been passionately contested since the mid 1980s. Where adventure recreationists were previously left to their own devices, their rising numbers and the increasingly commercialised nature of adventure recreation eventually prompted greater regulation. This responsibility increasingly fell to the NPWS. NPWS intervention has reflected two main concerns: the safety of visitors and environmental damage. Both forms of intervention have been perceived by adventure recreationists as impeding their particular national park experience. Using a number of historical examples, this section demonstrates how adventure recreationists' hostile responses to NPWS regulation were tied to their perceptions of themselves as model park visitors.

The most obvious management challenge posed by adventure recreation is that of public liability. Two major liability cases were successfully brought against Australian park agencies in the 1990s, resulting in substantial awards of damages.[34] The first involved a man who became a quadriplegic after diving into a natural swimming pool and striking his head on a submerged rock. The second involved a sixteen-year-old girl falling 6.5 metres from the top of a cliff at Casuarina Beach, Darwin, causing high level paraplegia. Neither of these cases involved adventure activities. Nonetheless, they highlighted park authorities' responsibility to protect the safety of visitors.

---

34 *Nagle v Rottnest Island Authority* (1993) 177 CLR 423; *Romeo v Conservation Commission of the Northern Territory* (1998) 151 ALR 263. Although neither of these cases involved New South Wales national parks, they set precedents for subsequent liability cases. Buckley, Witting & Guest (2001), ii–iii.

Due to the high-risk nature of adventure activities, park authorities have understandably become concerned about their susceptibility to future litigation. However, NPWS intervention has not always followed a predictable course. Regulations relating to adventure recreation have been tightened: under section twenty-one of the National Parks and Wildlife Regulation, 2002, a person may not 'engage in any activity or recreational pursuit that involves risking the safety of the person or the safety of other persons or damaging the environment' without the consent of a park authority. However park authorities have taken a more flexible approach to the management of these pursuits. The most recent *Blue Mountains National Park plan of management*, for example, recognises that 'it is neither desirable nor appropriate for specific consent to be required for every instance of persons undertaking these activities. Instead, the plan allows abseiling, rock climbing, canyoning and river activities in approved areas. Any other activities require permission from the Regional Manager, while bungee jumping, base jumping and hang-gliding are specifically prohibited.[35] The plan thus establishes a hierarchy of activities, with relaxed regulation of those perceived to be less risky (such as abseiling) but tough regulation of those considered to be more dangerous (such as base jumping). It should be noted that risk is not the only factor being considered here. More rigorous regulation also applies to activities that involve more equipment, pose more environmental threat, affect other users or involve higher levels of commercialisation.

Given the regulatory context, this response represents a relatively hands off approach to adventure recreation – one which we might expect adventure recreationists to welcome. The problem is that although many adventure activities were not directly restricted by the NPWS, participants took issue with the Service's broader policy on bush safety. In their eyes, the threat lay not so much in efforts to regulate their activities but in efforts to regulate the safety of other park users. The majority of duty of care claims faced by park authorities related to general safety issues such as falls from heights, and falls and slips on paths. The type of care which courts may expect of a park manager

---

35 NPWS (2001). *Blue Mountains National Park plan of management*, 79–80.

Fig. 6.3. Life on the edge: the safety of visitors is an increasing concern for national park managers at a time when adventure tourism is increasingly popular. NPWS.

include warnings, exclusions and fencing.[36] However, such measures are typically perceived by adventure recreationists as undermining the wilderness setting they savour. Surfer David Redhill, for example, worried that if national parks were made safer they would turn into theme parks:

> I don't think that national parks should be like theme parks. I think they should left absolutely in their natural state. Maybe some markings so people don't get lost, some warning signs on critical issues or hidden dangers and some rubbish bins but once you start regulating trying to make it safer you stop it being a natural park.[37]

---

36 Brown (1999), 16–17, 33.

37 David Redhill. Interview at Angourie Point, Yuraygir National Park, 21 April 2008.

What initially appears to be a straightforward issue of public safety is thus complicated by a philosophical debate over what is the appropriate balance between precaution and risk in national parks. Within this debate adventure recreationists have typically presented themselves as model park visitors pitched against power-hungry park authorities. The writings of Chris Baxter, editor of *Australian Wild* during the 1980s, are a good example of this attitude. While he initially promised that the magazine would not 'become obsessed by the politics of the wilderness', Baxter regularly used his monthly column to weigh into the debate on bush safety.[38] His primary objection to regulation was that it would 'inevitably debase' the wilderness experience.[39] The 'bush administration', he claimed, 'is apparently hell-bent on completely "sanitising" outdoor adventure'.[40] Instead, Baxter advocated 'personal *choice* and responsibility'. He cast self-regulation in terms of maintaining an authentic wilderness experience, of respecting rather than controlling wilderness: 'Rather than attempt to tame wilderness we have a responsibility to ensure that all who enter it know the risks they may face'.[41] In this sense he did carry some of the rhetoric of neoliberalism over into the debate on adventure tourism.

Yet the position of both groups has always been far more complex than Baxter's simple dichotomy suggests. Among park authorities, there has never been a single position over what level of comfort and security should be provided to visitors. The early trustees of the now Royal National Park prided themselves on having made the visitor's experience as effortless as possible, boasting in 1914 that 'the present-day visitor ... motors in comfort or strolls at ease along the well-ordered roads and paths which lead easily to all the points of interest'.[42] While the desire to cater for less intrepid park visitors has continued to inform NPWS policy-making into the twenty-first century – a prime example being the installation of facilities such as picnic tables and toilets at

---

38 Baxter (1981), 3.

39 Baxter (1986a), 3.

40 Baxter (1986b), 3.

41 Baxter (1984), 3.

42 *Official guide to the National Park* (1914), 18.

camping sites, as Fiona Howie discusses in this volume – the Service has also retained a strong emphasis on adventure recreation, which continues to feature prominently in its advertising material.[43]

Equally, Baxter's fellow adventure recreationists are not entirely innocent themselves. In their purist approach to risk and individual responsibility, adventure recreationists have tended to overlook the ways in which their own activities can detract from the wilderness and scenic qualities of national parks. Gary Steer worried in the late 1970s that hang-gliders might constitute a form of 'visual pollution' which intrudes on other users' sense of being in wilderness. Steer asks: 'Are they a "peeping Tom of the air" detracting from other people's sense of being alone or at least away from crowds of people?'[44] Similarly, rock climbing on the Three Sisters has increasingly come to be seen as detracting from thier scenic appeal while some visitors appreciated it as a form of entertainment.[45]

Furthermore, adventure recreationists' assumptions that they are beyond external regulation are often fuelled by their prejudices against other park users. Adventure recreationists frequently stereotype the public as cowering with fear before the natural hazards of national parks, caught up in 'anguish – even hysteria' about flies, mosquitos and leeches.[46] In turn, they see their own valiant confrontations with danger as grounds for special treatment. Such stereotypes are largely unwarranted. In reality, all visitors seem to accept these dangers as an inevitable part of their visit. For example, in interviews carried out in Yuraygir National Park in April 2008, visitors expressed concerns about snakes and spiders but rationalised these fears in accordance with a conservation ethic.

---

43 Of particular note is a recent addition to the OEH website, 'Where to go if you're looking for adventure', which outlines the top destinations for adventure recreation in New South Wales parks. [Online] Available: www.environment.nsw. gov.au/parks/Adventure.htm [Accessed 4 December 2009].

44 Steer (1979), 77.

45 NPWS (2001). *Blue Mountains National Park plan of management*, 79.

46 Bardwell (1982), 13.

Fig. 6.4. Climbing the Three Sisters at Katoomba became an iconic challenge for adventure tourists and raised new problems when it came under NPWS management. A member of the Sydney Rockclimbing Club makes the ascent of one of the Three Sisters in1952, just a year after the club was formed. W Brindle. NAA A1200, L14963.

More often than not, debates over the role of the NPWS in managing public safety seems to have been driven by a false dichotomy between adventure recreationists and park authorities. As a result, opportunities to recognise the shared interests of adventure recreationists and the NPWS in promoting better safety education have frequently been missed. Similar problems are at the heart of conflict between adventure recreationists and park authorities over the other main area of NPWS regulation: the issue of conservation.

The popularisation of adventure recreation in the second half of the twentieth century coincided with a shift in the objectives of the conservation movement. Within this period, there was a paradigm shift from viewing wilderness in anthropocentric terms, where nature is seen as providing experiential benefits to visitors, to viewing wilderness in biocentric terms, where nature is valued for its biodiversity.[47] The privileging of environmental protection over recreation has created a dilemma for current participants that did not exist for previous generations. Traditionally, adventure recreationists have been a key constituency of the conservation movement. As discussed earlier, bushwalkers had a vested interest in promoting the expansion of national parks in the first half of the twentieth century. Even in the 1960s, rock climbers viewed the wilderness largely in terms of the direct benefits that they could derive from it. 'The "wilderness" was there for us to use just as with any other natural resource' reflected SRC member Warwick Williams. 'The wilderness was envisaged as boundless.'[48]

Support for conservation remains strong within the adventure recreation community, who recognise their 'duty to support the responsible preservation of distressingly scarce wild places.'[49] However, contemporary adventure recreationists sometimes find themselves in a compromising position. Adventure recreation now has to be reconciled with a growing awareness of the environmental degradation caused by

---

47 Lesslie & Taylor (1985), 311.

48 Warwick Williams, 'My perspective: the 1970s'. *Thrutch*, 50th anniversary edition, 15.

49 Baxter (1981), 3.

these activities.[50] How have adventure recreationists negotiated this dilemma?

One way of justifying adventure recreation is in terms of its educative aims. The manager of High 'n' Wild summed up this position, highlighting the role of guides in 'interpreting nature' for customers to help them 'respect it'. He described the 'wear and tear' caused by activities as a 'good trade off' for this education.[51] This justification is by no means unique to the adventure recreation community. It is part of the ethos behind recreation in national parks more generally.

The second form of justification taken up by adventure recreationists is more specific. Just as adventure recreationists have argued for the self-regulation of safety, they have also argued for self-regulation of environmental impact. Rock climbers have formulated their own codes of conduct and at times positioned themselves as more concerned and knowledgeable about the environment than others. Accordingly, the perceived failure of governments to protect wilderness areas. Writing in 1986, Baxter accused governments of being 'notoriously fickle on environment matters', and encouraged adventure recreationists to 'set an example for bush protection'.[52] These comments were made in the context of the Franklin Dam dispute in Tasmania and prior to the expansion of national parks in NSW.

Today, such attitudes remain pervasive but for slightly different reasons and in a significantly different political context. Due to their pioneering efforts in promoting conservation, adventure recreationists argue that they can be trusted by national parks to approach the bush in a respectful manner.[53] Adventure recreationists see themselves as

---

50 For example, the most recent Blue Mountains management plan noted that canyoning, abseiling and rock climbing were having a damaging impact on the environment, causing vegetation disturbance, erosion, tracking, water pollution, damage to rock features and installation of rock bolts. NPWS (2001). *Blue Mountains National Park plan of management*, 78.

51 Darren Trew. Interview, 2008.

52 Baxter (1986), 3.

53 Bushwalkers, for example, have seen themselves 'as responsible users and

stakeholders to be consulted on conservation issues rather than passive followers of NPWS decisions. The position statement of Cliffcare, a Blue Mountains climbing group which operated between the early 1980s and early 2000s, reflected this attitude. The statement emphasised cooperation and mutual agreement with the NPWS, deeming regulation of climbing practices as acceptable 'only if it follows from discussions and agreement between local climbers and land managers.'[54] As in the debate over bush safety, adventure recreationists' hostility to NPWS regulation of their activities on the grounds of conservation ultimately lies in the fact that they see themselves as model park visitors and thus above external scrutiny.

Since the 1980s, safety and conservation concerns have driven conflict between adventure recreationists, other park visitors and NPWS management. The case of rock climbing is instructive in demonstrating the impact NPWS regulations have had on certain adventure recreationists. Early generations of rock climbers gave little consideration to the issue of access to sites. In the 1960s, due to the small number of climbers, 'access issues did not rate a single thought.'[55] However in the 1980s, the NPWS began to take a more active role in regulating climbers' access to sites under its jurisdiction. In most cases, NPWS regulation has been relatively minor, ranging from restrictions on the use of bolts and chalk to the imposition of maximum party size numbers and the introduction of formal permit systems. In several cases, however, the NPWS concluded that more drastic action was required. To the horror of the climbing community, it began to implement climbing bans at key locations.

One recent battle between climbers and park authorities was played out over the Three Sisters in the Blue Mountains National Park. Due to

---

as pioneering conservationists' and thus 'viewed themselves as above reproach'. Harper (2007), 292.

54 Blue Mountains Cliffcare, 'Policy'. [Online] Available: cliffcare.org.au/ [Accessed 25 May 2008].

55 Warwick Williams, 'My perspective: the 1970s'. *Thrutch*, 50th anniversary edition, 15.

its close association with the history of the sport, the Three Sisters is one of the most iconic sites for Australian climbers. It has been described as the birthplace of the Sydney Rockclimbing Club which was formed after Russell Kippax, Neville Wilson, Ken McLeod and Dave Rostron successfully traversed the Three Sisters in 1951.[56] The Three Sisters is also tied to the personal histories of individual climbers. In his biography of Greg Mortimer, Lincoln Hall reveals that it was at the Three Sisters that Mortimer, as a young teenager, first became 'spellbound' watching climbers.[57] Climbers' reactions to climbing bans at this iconic site tell us much about their relationship with the NPWS.

In 2000 the NPWS imposed a five-year moratorium on climbing on the Three Sisters, citing environmental and cultural concerns. The 2001 *Blue Mountains National Park plan of management* stated that climbing is considered 'to be inconsistent with environmental sustainability and the feature's status as an internationally recognised natural icon and tourist attraction of the Blue Mountains'.[58] When the ban was reviewed in 2005, additional concerns regarding Aboriginal heritage values of the site were raised. The site is part of the Gundungurra people's Muggadah or 'Seven Sisters Dreaming'. The Gundungurra Tribal Council was opposed to climbing on the site.[59]

This was not the first time that climbing on the Three Sisters had been banned. In 1983, the Blue Mountains City Council (BMCC) prohibited climbing on the western side of the Three Sisters (the BMCC has since handed over control of the western side to the NPWS). The reason provided for the ban was public safety. It was argued that rocks were falling on spectators below, endangering other visitors. Climbers were quick to object and suggest that the tracks should simply be re-routed.[60] After a public campaign, with TV appearances from the SRC President Russell Taylor, a compromise was reached. Climbers agreed to

56 Rachel Gleeson, '50 years of the Sydney Rockclimbing Club'. *Thrutch*, 50th anniversary edition, 1.

57 Hall (1996), 7.

58 NPWS (2001). *Blue Mountains National Park plan of management*, 79.

59 D Lewis (2005).

60 'Wild information' (1984). *Australian Wild*, 4 (1): 5.

stick to one traverse line on the eastern face and to erect official BMCC signs delineating this restriction.[61]

Overall, climbers have been far more accepting of the recent ban than the 1983 ban. However, as a discussion forum on the Australian Rockclimbing Association's website between 28 February 2006 and 3 February 2007 demonstrated, there is still significant anxiety within some sections of the climbing community over the ban.[62] 'Macciza' described the situation as 'a horrible grey limbo', while 'rodw' expressed frustration with NPWS 'mismanagement': 'I cant believe NPWS didn't follow through with their stated aims … thats so unlike them … NOT!!!' The forum also highlighted the divisions within the climbing community over the appropriateness of climbing bans, and the paranoia of some climbers that others will disobey regulations. 'Mjw' urged fellow climbers to respect the ban: 'Please, lets make sure that nothing we do as climbers affect access of crags. In the grand scheme of things, the loss of the 'West Wall' isnt the end of the world'. 'Hangdog', the initiator of the forum, responded defensively 'hey take a "chill pill"', reassuring 'Mjw' that it had never been their intention to challenge NPWS authority.

This final comment goes to the heart of what is at stake in the debate not only over climbing bans but regulation in general. The success of regulation ultimately hinges on the ability of the NPWS to convince adventure recreationists that they should respect NPWS authority. What makes this so difficult to achieve is the fact that adventure recreationists have long assumed that their activities make them model park visitors and thus above external regulation. Park authorities will continue to confront this issue and negotiate adventure recreationists' cooperation. Some forms of recreation will always prove to be more difficult to negotiate than others.

---

61 Russell Taylor, '80s – time of changes'. *Thrutch*, 50th anniversary edition, 23.

62 Australian Climbing Association, 'Can we climb on the 3 sisters yet?', online forum, created 28 February 2006. [Online] Available: climb.org.au/index. php?page_id=6&action=view&uid=788#788 [Accessed 25 May 2008].

Conclusion

The role of national parks in the popularisation of adventure recreation is paradoxical. On the one hand, national parks enable adventure recreation by providing the requisite wilderness setting and facilitating participants' experience of danger. On the other hand, national parks have also served to constrain adventure recreation, with NPWS safety measures frequently perceived as lessening the sense of danger coveted by adventure recreationists.

As a result, the relationship between adventure recreationists and the NPWS has not always been a cooperative one. Since the early 1980s NPWS regulation of adventure recreation has been a battleground for ideas about what constitutes proper park usage. Adventure activities are perceived by the NPWS as a potential source of public liability, and as a source of interference with other park users and environment damage, making them less than ideal. Meanwhile, adventure recreationists are inclined to see themselves as model national park users, both more self-reliant and more appreciative of the wilderness than other visitors.

Adventure recreationists have also proven themselves to be ready to compromise rather than risk losing access to national park sites altogether. Moreover, negotiations with the NPWS have brought to light conflicts within the adventure recreation community itself, in much the same way that debates over the use of artificial aids divided rock climbers in the 1960s and 1970s.

From a NPWS perspective, the history of adventure recreation in national parks demonstrates the importance of reconciling the needs of diverse park users, whether they are picnickers, wildlife enthusiasts or thrillseeking adventure recreationists. The sport's future will depend on the adventure recreation community's ability and willingness to negotiate access with park authorities.

References

Bardwell, Sandra (1982). 'Getting started: bushwalking'. *Australian Wild*, 2(3).

Baxter, Chris (1986a). 'Death in the hills'. *Australian Wild*, 6(1).

Baxter, Chris (1986b). 'Going our own way'. *Australian Wild*, 6(4).

Baxter, Chris (1984). 'Bush Safety: How much can we take?' *Australian Wild*, 4(2).

Baxter, Chris (1981). 'The wild idea'. *Australian Wild*, 1(1).

Bell, Claudia & John Lyall (2002). 'The accelerated sublime: thrill-seeking adventure heroes in the commodified landscape', in Simon Coleman & Mike Crang (eds). *Tourism: between place and performance*. New York: Berghahn Books.

Brown, Ian D (1997). Adventure recreation demand in protected areas of New South Wales. Draft report to NPWS Tourism Project.

Brown, Kate (1999). Public liability risk for park managers. Master of Laws thesis, University of Melbourne.

Buckley, Ralf, Natasha Witting & Michaela Guest (2001). *Managing people in Australian parks*. Gold Coast: Sustainable Tourism Cooperative Research Centre.

Donnelly, Peter (2003). 'The great divide: sport climbing v. adventure climbing', in Robert E Rinehart & Synthia Sydnor (eds). *To the extreme: alternative sports, inside and out*. Albany: State University of New York Press.

Ewert, Alan W & Steven J Hollenhorst (1997). 'Adventure recreation and its implications for wilderness'. *International Journal of Wilderness*, 3(2).

Hall, Lincoln (1996). *First ascent: the life and climbs of Greg Mortimer*. Sydney: Simon & Schuster.

Harper, Melissa (2007). *The ways of the bushwalker: on foot in Australia*. Sydney: UNSW Press.

Irwin, Sally (2000). *Between heaven and earth: the life of a mountaineer, Freda du Faur 1882–1935*. Hawthorn: White Crane Press.

Kan, Graeme (2000/1). 'Danger zone'. *Australian Leisure Management* (Dec 2000–Jan 2001).

Kusz, Kyle (2004). 'Extreme America: the cultural politics of extreme sports in 1990s America', in Belinda Wheaton (ed.). *Understanding lifestyle sports: consumption, identity and difference*. New York: Routledge.

Lewis, Neil (2004). 'Sustainable adventure: embodied experiences and ecological practices within British climbing', in Belinda Wheaton (ed.). *Understanding lifestyle sports: consumption, identity and difference*. New York: Routledge.

Lewis, Daniel (2005). 'Once were seven – now we must protect the last sisters'. *Sydney Morning Herald*, 29 August.

Lesslie, RG & SG Taylor (1985). 'The wilderness continuum concept and its implications for Australian wilderness preservation policy'. *Biological Conservation*, 32(4).

Lupton, Deborah (1999). *Risk*. New York: Routledge.

Miller, Jonathan (1995). 'Australian approaches to wilderness'. *International Journal of Wilderness*, 1(2).

Nash, Roderick (1982). *Wilderness and the American mind*. New Haven: Yale University Press.

Official guide to the National Park (1914). Sydney: Government Printer.

Palmer, Catherine (2002). ' "Shit happens": the selling of risk in extreme sport'. *The Australian Journal of Anthropology*, 13(3).

Rosen, Elizabeth (2007). 'Somalis don't climb mountains: the commercialization of Mount Everest'. *Journal of Popular Culture*, 40(1).

Simon, Jonathan (2002). 'Taking risks: extreme sports and the embrace of risk in advanced liberal societies', in Tom Baker & Jonathan Simon (eds). *Embracing risk: the changing culture of insurance and responsibility*. Chicago: University of Chicago Press.

Steer, Gary (1979). 'Parks for recreation', in Wendy Goldstein (ed.). *Australia's 100 years of national parks*. Sydney: NPWS.

Tulloch, John and Deborah Lupton (2003). *Risk and everyday life*. London: Sage.

Walters, Brian (1983). 'The main range in winter'. *Australian Wild*, 3(2).

Wheaton, Belinda (2004) 'Introduction: mapping the lifestyle sport-scape', in Belinda Wheaton (ed.). *Understanding lifestyle sports: consumption, identity and difference*. New York: Routledge.

Williams, Tom (1988). 'Blue Mountains rock climbing'. *Australian Wild*, 8(1).

Chapter 7

Teaching citizenship: education and the nation in urban national parks[1]

Claire Farrugia

The natural environment has always been a site where ideas concerning national identity and what constitutes an Australian citizen have been negotiated and defined.[2] Since the creation of the (Royal) National Park in 1879, national parks in NSW, particularly those within easy reach of Sydney and catering for a large urban population, have contributed to ideas about citizenship. Testament to this, a 1998 NPWS workshop identified both challenges and opportunities in managing landscapes that contain both 'natural and cultural values and give people a sense of being Australian'. The workshop paper also made explicit reference to the importance of national parks as places that 'increase understanding of our identity, history and future as Australians in those landscapes'.[3]

The relationship between national parks, their management and how the nation has been imagined has had an impact on understandings of both the history and the future of the parks. The link between national parks and the nation was pivotal in the development of attitudes to recreation and its management, which depended on changing ideas of what constituted an ideal national park and an ideal recreational user

1   Thank you to Heather Goodall, Christine Hopkins, Vicky Newman, Vicky Hatz and Rowena Eddy for sharing their knowledge and national park experiences. Thank you to Darren Trew, High 'n' Wild Mountain Adventures, Katoomba for taking the time to talk about the adventure business, and to Ada Yu and Patrick Mickan for their assistance in sourcing photographs.

2   White (1981), 102.

3   National Parks visions of the new millennium, Part of Workshop Papers, University of Sydney, 16–19 June 1998, 29. See also Martin Thomas (2001).

to the parks.[4] Park managers sought to define not only a distinctive Australian identity, but also the activities that constituted what they believed to be an Australian way of life.

The creation of the first national park in the United States in 1872 heralded a new way of conceptualising public space. It reflected a particular impetus to cater both for what was understood to be the unique American environment and the unique American population.[5] The development of national parks in Australia differed in significant ways from the experience of the US. Australian park advocates did not offer the same justifications for why national parks were of value, nor adopt the same ideas about who would use them.[6] In Australia, the creation of the parks system was influenced by the wish to provide a natural space in close proximity to the urban centre of Sydney. This space would be available to a mixed working- and middle-class population, predominantly for recreation.[7] The initial justifications given for the creation of the National Park were framed in terms of the need for a 'national domain for rest and recreation' and 'additional city lungs'.[8] These justifications raise the question: what is it that makes urban national parks different from any other urban park?

The answer lies in recognising that national parks have always been understood to play a role in educating their users. While the nature of that education changed dramatically from the late nineteenth century to the early twenty-first century, along with ideas about what being Australian meant, the idea that national parks *should* play an educative role remained remarkably consistent.

This chapter focuses particularly on the period from the 1960s onwards, tracing changes in both the management of urban national

---

4   The notion of an ideal national park and ideal national park user has been influenced by Martin Thomas' exploration of the Macedonian community's experience in the Royal National Park. Martin Thomas (2001).

5   Runte (1997), 210.

6   Harper & White (2012).

7   This was in contrast to the justifications given for the US model. For a greater exploration of the differences see Harper & White (2012).

8   *Official guide to the National Park of New South Wales* (1914), 7.

Fig. 7.1. National parks came to symbolise what was imagined as a distinctively Australian outdoor way of life, and were promoted by the Department of Immigration to potenial migrants. Lane Cove 1968. NAA B941, WAY OF LIFELEISURE3.

parks in NSW and the conceptualisation of the ideal visitor. In this period policies of both assimilation and multiculturalism influenced the creation of a particular set of norms and values concerning citizenship. These official discourses were reflected in the management of the national parks, demonstrating the diverse ways in which citizenship can be conceived, from a legal definition of citizenship to the different social, political and cultural understandings of how an individual is part of, and *dreamt* into, the nation.[9] Such an exploration reveals the intricate connections between official policy and popular pastimes and how they both work to negotiate and define nationality.

---

9   Rubenstein (2003), 146.

The 'nation' in the national parks.

While studying the use of national parks by Sydney's Macedonian community Martin Thomas argued that the NPWS 'cannot hope to work effectively as a cross-cultural communicator unless it is acknowledged that national parks, having emerged from former colonial societies, are imbued with particular values and ideals concerning land use'.[10] Arguments concerning the development of national parks in the US, Canada, New Zealand and Australia have consistently highlighted the role that the postcolonial context played in labelling the parks as national. In light of the colonisation of indigenous people, and the diverse and often fragmented communities that made up what was to be known as the nation, the label 'national park' can be read as a strategic act of self-definition, an attempt to consolidate the nation and engender a sense of collective identity.

In Australia, popular and aesthetic conceptions of the natural landscape contributed to fostering a distinctive national identity. By the 1880s, the image of rural Australia and 'the bush' was central to the creation of a national ethos.[11] An emerging popular interest in studying nature and developing conceptions of the Australian environment as unique laid the foundation for the link between the natural landscape and national identity, despite the fact that national identity was still intertwined with loyalty to the empire.[12] Changing conceptions of what constituted 'the people' in the political realm and the eventual federation of the Australian colonies solidified the link between people and place.[13] In this context, the creation of urban national parks was more than an attempt to provide the city with 'additional city lungs'. The reservation of land 'safe from the machinations of ambitious schemers' meant that it would be 'secured to the people of this country', and therefore contribute to the process by which the natural environment became a vehicle for the expression of national sentiment.[14]

---

10 Martin Thomas (2001), 20.

11 Harper (2002), 225.

12 Harper (2002), 240.

13 White (1981), 111.

14 *Official guide to the National Park of NSW* (1902), 8.

While this can be seen in the very act of terming the parks 'national', the *Official guide to the National Park* elaborates on the way supporters of the system *actively* engaged in this process. Published by the National Park Trust in 1902, the guide was not restricted to arguments concerning environmental conservation. It made explicit reference to the relationship between the population, the government and the role of recreation. In particular, it reflected the belief that healthy parks were necessary for healthy citizens and that 'the health of the people' should not only be a national concern, but 'the primary consideration of all good governments'. In this context, the promoters of parks argued that 'all cities, towns, villages should be possessed of parks and pleasure grounds as places of recreation'.[15] This emphasis on the importance of recreation was intricately linked to ideas of who constituted the nation and how to foster healthy, productive citizens. National parks offered 'the people' relief from industrialisation, routinised work and overcrowded cities. Environmental arguments were also important, particularly in the establishment of Ku-ring-gai Chase as a national park. A significant supporter of national parks and the managing trustee of Ku-ring-gai Chase, Eccleston du Faur, stated that the 'fullest preservation of natural flora' and a protected environment for 'fauna to roam' were sufficient reasons to label the area as *national* park.[16] Nevertheless, such arguments continued to be posed within a framework of an anthropocentric interest in democratic recreation, rather than environmental conservation.

Education for the nation

The proximity of the National Park to Sydney's expanding suburbs allowed participation in recreational activities with 'maximum pleasure and minimum inconvenience'.[17] But it was never just about pleasure. Healthy recreation itself was seen as producing good, fit citizens and soon national parks were being imagined as places that could impart particular values on park users. As early as 1907 the National Park

---

15 *Official guide to the National Park of NSW* (1902), 7–10.

16 Harper (2002), 229.

17 *Official guide to the National Park of NSW* (1914), 7.

trustees asked in their annual report whether recreational activities should be supplemented 'by instilling in the minds of the young through our educational system' the values of the national park.[18] The trustees' early interest in using schools to disseminate information on the standards of behaviour expected in national parks suggests they had a particular idea of the ideal park user. The trustees saw a link between regulating recreation in the park and creating good citizens.

Education played a larger role in the management of the national parks from the second half of the twentieth century as a more coherent discourse developed around the role of national parks. Seemingly mundane, day-to-day debates about how to protect the park and manage park users took place in the context of a relationship between the parks, the people and what it meant to be a good citizen. The National Parks Association, an independent environmental organisation that played a role in the creation of the National Parks and Wildlife Service (NPWS) in 1967, provided a forum for these debates in its *National Parks Journal*. The journal, which first appeared in 1957, consciously articulated this link. It campaigned for the need for environmentally sustainable management and for national park employees to educate users, reflecting a belief that what was good for national parks also benefited wider society.[19] The Royal National Park's convenient location close to urban areas made it valuable for providing 'inspirational and educational values unobtainable elsewhere'.[20]

A 1961 article titled 'The psychology of the destroyer in our nature reserves' attempted to explain why particular national park users chose to act inappropriately. It categorised park users into broad types, including those 'with grudges against society,' those 'motivated by greed' and those who are not 'emotionally grown up'.[21] The implicit

---

18 National Park Trust – Report for the year ended 30th of July, 1907 (Parliamentary Papers, Second Session of 1907, vII), 322.

19 *National Parks Journal*. [Online] Available: www.npansw.org.au/index. php?option=com_content&view=article&id=405&Itemid=428 [Accessed 28 May 2008]; Runte (1997), 210.

20 *National Parks Journal*, 1960, 1(2): 2.

21 *National Parks Journal*, 1961, 1(4): 8.

Fig. 7.2. NPWS staff creating Australian citizens during visits to national parks, c1980s. Spencer Smith-White / NPWS.

contrast was a contemporary understanding of what it meant to be a good citizen, an individual who was not driven by greed, who upheld society's collective values and who appreciated the natural environment. This understanding was framed as a type of 'social contract' that was assumed to apply in wider society[22] and was continually expressed in the journal in the principle that citizens did not only have a *right* to enjoy public spaces, but had the *responsibility* to act a certain way within them.[23]

We can see here that the concept of the ideal way to act had undergone considerable change since the original trustees had sought to educate park users. This change continued with the gradual solidification of the second wave environmental movement in the late 1960s which resulted

---

22 In his essay 'Racialism and Democracy', John Kane suggests that this is a form of 'civic identity' which embodies both citizen's rights and citizen's responsibilities. He argues that this identity becomes important in uniting diverse communities. Kane (1997).

23 *National Parks Journal,* 1961, 1(4): 8.

in a noticeable shift from concern with human-centred recreation in national parks to a concern with keeping parks untouched and sheltered from the mechanical civilisation. Anxiety about overdevelopment and the fact that 'the mad race is on' saw an increasing emphasis on what were beginning to be called 'wilderness values'.[24] Anxieties were shared more broadly by the emerging conservation movement represented by such people as Francis Radcliffe, who founded the Australian Conservation Foundation in 1966, and Myles Dunphy, who campaigned for bushwalking in the wilderness and preservation of bushland.[25] This new emphasis on the natural features of parks affected the way users were expected to understand, learn from and act in national parks.

The environmental imperative and the challenge of the urban setting

To some extent, environmental conservation had always influenced the justifications given for the creation of national parks. Nevertheless, following the Second World War, conservationists became increasingly active in seeking to protect untouched bush land, seeing wilderness as the one quality that 'distinguishes the national park from a playground or a recreation area'.[26] This applied to urban as much as rural national parks. The Spring 1961 edition of the *National Parks Journal* explicitly criticised over-development in the Royal National Park, such as the construction of a road to Bundeena and the establishment of a 'historic tramway centre', as evidence of an 'antipathy to the national parks principles'.[27] Myles Dunphy had argued that 'the only way to conserve valuable wilderness is to place an embargo on roads in relation to it'.[28] With the creation of the NPWS in 1967, environmental conservation was given priority and became the primary framework for ideas about the nation and the education of good citizens.

---

24 *National Parks Journal*, 1961, 1(4): 2.

25 Harper (2002), 229; Warhurst (2005), 202–14.

26 *National Parks Journal*, 1961, 1(4): 2.

27 *National Parks Journal*, 1961, 1(5); 6.

28 Colong Foundation. [Online] Available: www.colongwilderness.org.au/whatiswilderness.htm#dunphy [Accessed 4 April 2008].

This posed particular problems for Sydney's two older urban national parks, the Royal and Ku-ring-gai Chase, and more recent arrivals, Lane Cove and Georges River, which both had ambivalent claims to the title 'national park'. Established primarily for recreation, these urban national parks challenged not only the conservation imperative, but the assumption these ideals represented the view or the majority of national park users. As the image of a wild, remote and uniquely Australian landscape was being sewn into the mythology of the nation's national parks, the *National Parks Journal* argued in 1962 that, while national parks were 'public lands' and the 'public has a right to use them', public access required closer regulation: many visitors 'use our reserves in a way which can lead to destruction' and careful thought had to be given to further development.[29] In objecting to the encroachment of 'public utilities, playing fields or other development ... onto our limited reserves', the journal was implying some forms of recreation were more acceptable than others.[30]

Birdwatching, bushwalking and learning from the natural environment were acceptable. Other activities contradicted the view of the national parks as a unique space 'previously undisturbed by human interference' and one that would excite 'the world's interest'. The subtle change in the educational impulse that existed throughout the history of the national parks can be seen in a NWPS paper from 1978. While asserting the prime importance of the conservation imperative it argued that the management objectives of the parks must be 'to provide the opportunity for individuals to learn the true value of these resources'.[31] Recreation was not an end in itself, but an opportunity to create environmentally aware citizens. The national park's staff publication, *NAPAWI*, suggested that recreation could develop a 'general and sincere community appreciation for natural bushland' in a way that would challenge further development of the park.[32] The heavy visitor use of parks such as the Royal was seen as an 'excellent opportunity to

---

29 *National Parks Journal,* 1962, 1(6): 7.

30 *NAPAWI,* 1971, 1(1): 27.

31 Johnstone (1978), 2, 7.

32 *NAPAWI,* 1971. 1(1)m 27.

introduce a large number of people to national parks and conservation ideals.[33]

Conservation education was a key goal in the Royal National Park plans of management by 1975 and continued to be so in management plans thereafter. Hand in hand with education was a conservation-centred idea of what constituted an ideal visitor, an ideal that did not necessarily accord with the ways in which national parks were actually used or popularly understood. This became clear in the case of the park at Georges River, an area bounded by suburbs and consisting only of pockets of uncleared bushland. It presented a particular challenge to the role that the wilderness value of national parks might play in fostering ideal Australian citizens.

The parklands had been established 'to prevent the building out of the Georges River foreshores' and to keep the river 'preserved for public use', and, following a well-publicised local campaign, it had been labelled a national park.[34] It was valued by the local community precisely because the site facilitated a wider range of urban recreational activities.[35] A study by Heather Goodall et al. showed that the decision in 1961 to protect Georges River as a national park under the state government's *Native Flora and Fauna Act* was a response to the activism of a number of local organisations whose understanding was that recreation rather than a romantic vision of the Australian environment was what made the space national.[36] The decision to keep Georges River 'preserved for the benefit of the people'[37] challenged the emerging understanding that the 'nation' in national parks deserved its place because of the parks characterisation as an untouched and unique natural landscape.

With the implementation of the *National Parks and Wildlife Act* and the establishment of the NPWS in 1967, the local community expected

---

33 NPWS (1975). *Royal National Park plan of management*, 34.

34 *Leader*, 8 March 1962, 1.

35 *Leader*, 8 May 1963, 9.

36 Such as the Picnic Point Regatta and Recreation Areas Development Association and the Padstow Parks Committee, the details of which are explored in Goodall et al. (2006).

37 *Propellor*, 15 March 1962, 2.

that the reserve at Georges River would remain a national park. However, with the increasing importance of a conservationist imperative in park management, the NPWS maintained that the only two urban national parks that fitted the changing 'world conception of National Parks' and were of sufficiently 'spacious land areas' were the Royal National Park and Ku-ring-gai Chase. [38] Consequently, despite having the support of the people, the status of Georges River as national park was revoked, and it was designated as a State Recreation Area (SRA) instead.

The struggle to have Georges River proclaimed a national park continued. The protests that followed the change of name demonstrated that the concept of the nation in Australian national parks played a significant role in popular imagination. The local working-class community's concept of a national park was at odds with that of the NPWS management. The community's belief that they were the nation that national parks should be catering for[39] demonstrated that the recreational tradition established by the first NSW national park in 1879 continued to hold considerable popular support. In recognition of the diversity of opinion regarding what made a national park, the park's name was again changed in 1992 to Georges River National Park.

Assimilation: parks, people and particular histories

The image park management had of the ideal visitor was not isolated from wider political debates, particularly those concerning Australian identity and what makes a good citizen. From 1950 to the 1970s, assimilation policies were key to the vision of what it meant to be Australian. National parks became part of the effort to unite the increasingly diverse Australian population. The focus on teaching the value of nature conservation, while prompted by international developments in park management, meshed in very effectively with attempts to teach migrants to appreciate their new Australian environment, with a 'shared history, common spirit, and a unique and exclusive way of life.'[40]

---

38 *Leader*, 4 January 1967.
39 Goodall et al. (2006), 11.
40 Bauman cited in Haebich (2007), 117; Kane (1997), 117.

Fig. 7.3. Urban national parks such as the Sydney Harbour National Park offer cyclists, walkers and joggers scenic, car-free environments in which to exercise. Daniel Smith / OEH.

In 1972, a film series produced by the Department of Immigration titled 'Ask an Australian' sought to educate migrants in the 'Australian way of life'. The episode 'Ask an Australian about the outdoors' set out to teach migrants about bushwalking, environmental conservation and safety and health concerns in the bush.[41] The middle-aged male narrator, apparently of Anglo-Australian descent, continually suggested that these were uniquely Australian activities and values of which migrants would be unaware. Ten years later, the Georges River State Recreation Area trustees reflected similar ideas, seeing the engagement of new arrivals in 'passive and active recreation' as 'enabling speedy assimilation to the outdoor Australian way of life'.[42] While the extent to which other Australians knew about bush craft was questionable, national park advocates were convinced that 'the people' have to 'learn

---

41 Kay Roberts (1972). *Ask an Australian about the outdoors*. Artransa Park Film Studies for Department of Immigration.

42 LeClerc cited in Goodall et al. (2006), 11.

to regard the national parks as their own to secure and preserve'.[43] Thus, although the *Royal National Park plan of management* recognised the growth in the non-Anglo-Celtic population of Sydney in the 1970s, it sought to ensure that appropriate wilderness values were communicated across cultural barriers.[44]

National parks staff were implicated in this process of defining and celebrating Australian culture, as *NAPAWI*, the staff journal, made clear throughout the 1970s. For example, in 1977 the journal enthusiastically celebrated the naturalisation of Russ Knutson, the ex-chief ranger of Ku-ring-gai Chase National Park. He was now a 'fair dinkum Aussie'. Hi collegues presented him with the essentials, 'one meat pie, a can of KB, Aussie hat, Aussie flag, one gladioli and a pair of Aussie football socks'.[45] In this and other personal profiles the journal subtly suggested a connection between the values of the service, the natural environment and notions of Australianness. Similarly, such activities as the re-enactment of Captain Cook's landing and a range of diverse educational initiatives reinforced the connection. The 'multicoloured inhabitants of the landing place' were called on to observe a particular colonial history of the nation,[46] a history that largely excluded both Indigenous and migrant voices.

As a policy that aimed to absorb Indigenous and migrant cultures into an official conception of a white Anglo-Celtic racial nation, assimilation was a powerful act of national imagining. One of its side effects was an increased preoccupation with what actually constituted the nation, ideas that were not static but constantly being invented or refashioned in accordance with contemporary needs.[47] This affected not only the institutional culture of the NPWS, but the way park users imagined their use of the park, particularly when it came to Australian things

---

43 *National Parks Journal* (1961). 1(4): 11.

44 NPWS (1975). *Royal National Park plan of management*, 5.

45 *NAPAWI*, 1973. 2(1), 26. See also *NAPAWI*, 1970, 1(1).

46 *NAPAWI*, 1977, 5(4), 26.

47 Stokes (1997), 9.

204 • Playing in the bush

for the people to do.[48] As studies of the Macedonian and Vietnamese communities' uses of national parks show, assimilationist definitions of Australianness often conflicted with the diverse experiences and mixed allegiances of new migrants.[49] As assimilation policies slowly gave way to multiculturalism from the 1970s, new ideas of what national parks might teach the nation emerged.

The 'ideal visitor' and the challenge of multiculturalism

Just as assimilation affected the way in which national parks were imagined, so did multiculturalism, the growth of Asian immigration in the late 1980s, the refugee system in the early 1990s, and issues around Indigenous land rights following the *Mabo* decision of 1992. The increasingly multicultural demographic using Sydney's urban national parks raised questions regarding the legacy of assimilation in Australia. While only nine percent of Australia's population were born overseas in 1947, by 1991, this number had increased to twenty-three percent.[50] Increased migrant presence had practical implications for both park users and management, as it challenged the norms and values of the NPWS and the image of the 'ideal visitor' to the parks. The NSW state government began to take seriously the implications of multiculturalism for national park use just as, with the election of the conservative Howard federal government in 1996 and the advent of the war on terror in 2001, there was an increased preoccupation with what defined Australians as different from other nationalities.[51]

These complexities were hinted at in a 1999 marketing report on NPWS south metropolitan district, which discussed staff attitudes to visitors. One ranger conveyed a perspective typifying the accepted conservationist outlook of the 1960s: 'the ideal visitors were those that

---

48 This was indicated by a number of regular national parks users interviewed in Georges River National Park on 18 May 2008.

49 Mandy Thomas (2002); Martin Thomas (2001).

50 Jupp (1997), 138–39.

51 This idea has been extensively explored by numerous scholars. For example, Gale (2006), 35–42; Collins, Noble, Poynting & Tabar (2005); Grewcock (2005), 158–61.

respected nature and those who were aware of their impact on the environment. Alongside was his view of the least desirable visitors: 'large groups of Lebanese, drunks, drug users, speeding drivers, loiterers and disrespectful campers'.[52] While the ranger qualified his remarks, the way in which race was equated with bad behaviour indicated the challenge this multicultural user base presented to the institutional norms and values of the NPWS.

From the late 1970s onwards, national park administration began to take notice of the principles of multiculturalism, that 'all members of our society have equal opportunity to realise their full potential and maintain his or her culture without prejudice'.[53] However, it took time for these ideas to be percolate through the NPWS. While the *National Parks and Wildlife Act* of 1974 and the *NSW Heritage Act* of 1977 ensured that the NPWS played an active role in maintaining and researching the cultural heritage of Indigenous and non-Indigenous Australians, it was only in the late 1990s that this developed into a critical analysis of how the Service had historically reflected ideas about what is meant by being Australian and how to educate park users accordingly.[54]

It was the urban national parks that were at the symbolic forefront of these changes. Catering for the southwest region of Sydney, where up to twenty-five percent of the population originated from non-English speaking backgrounds, the Georges River park began to cater for increasingly diverse recreational activities.[55] When the NPWS took over the management with its re-designation as a national park in 1992, the ethnic composition of the park's users had changed dramatically.[56] A resident from East Hills and the granddaughter of George Jacobsen, one

52 Thomas (2001), 20.

53 Frank Galbally citied in Jupp (1997), 135.

54 This can be seen in the increasing proliferation of publications self-consciously exploring issues of race, nation and ownership from 1996 onwards. For example, Mandy Thomas (2002), 3; Martin Thomas (2001).

55 Bankstown City Council, Persons with a non-English speaking background. [Online] Available: www.id.com.au/bankstown/atlas/default.asp?id=101&pg=8 [Accessed 6 May 2008].

56 Goodall et al. (2006), 11.

of the original campaigners for the parklands, remembered only a handful of other nationalities attending the local school when she was growing up: 'an Austrian, a German and the son of one of the fruit owners' who, she remembers, 'made a joke that he was the only black haired kid there'. Her account of the area's history is then punctuated by memories of Vietnamese arriving in the early 1970s and living in a camp across the river.[57] While numbers of those born overseas steadily increased after the Second World War, the diversification of immigration in the latter part of the century was dramatic. Sydney's Asian and Middle Eastern population, for example, increased by twenty times between 1947 and 1980.[58] In response, the NPWS self-consciously questioned its institutionalised assumptions about a shared collective identity which excluded the migrant presence.[59]

While as early as 1980 park staff found sociology useful in the proper 'management of people as well as the management of natural areas,'[60] new research focused on the human dimensions of national park heritage and led park managers to acknowledge the meanings and values embedded in the natural environment and associated recreation. Initially, they simply sought to be more inclusive. In 1980, *NAPAWI* argued that 'effective interpretation' and 'visitor appreciation' of the national parks depended on broadening the educational mandate of NPWS to reach out to migrants. Particular importance was placed on greater proficiency in languages other than English.[61] However, by the early 1990s, the recognition that forms of recreation could also be imbued with particular values began to influence the management process in a number of different ways. The advent of research into the Macedonian, Vietnamese and Aboriginal communities in the area of Georges River is a practical example of this shift and the important role that the Culture and Heritage division of NPWS began to play. The evolution of this research itself shows how multiculturalism was

---

57 Vicky Newman. Interview, Padstow Heights, 17 May 2008.

58 Jupp (1997), 139.

59 Mandy Thomas (2002), 2.

60 *NAPAWI* (1980), 8(1): 17.

61 For example, *NAPAWI* (1981), 2(1).

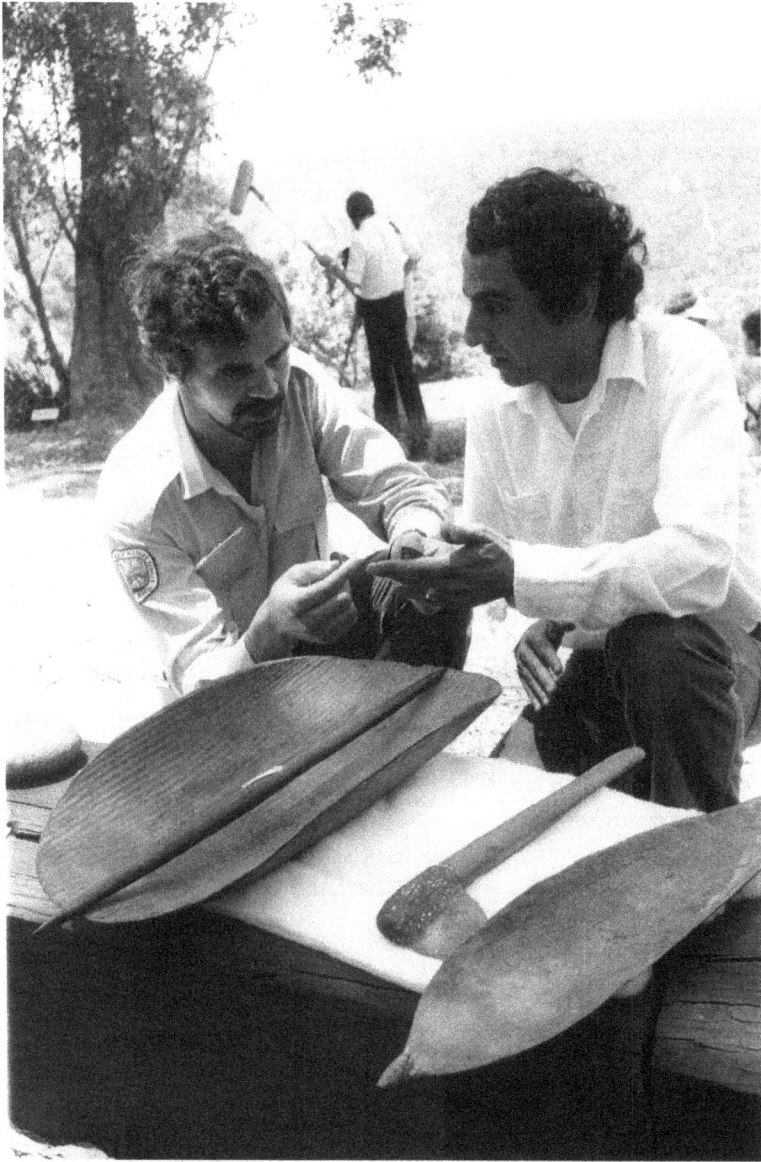

Fig. 7.4. Ethnic Affairs Commission Arabic interpreter with Aboriginal Site Officer, Ku-ring-gai Chase National Park. Bini Malcom / NPWS.

influencing the management of national parks, starting with a focus on the Anglo-Celtic and Aboriginal use of the area around Georges River and then extending into a study of Arabic and Vietnamese communities' uses and attachments.

This research raised questions about the Service's openness to a range of ideas, the value it placed on the input of diverse communities and why it saw the education of park users as an important part of its work.[62] It was not confined to one definition of recreational activities or to one image of the Australian environment. Instead, the studies were premised on an understanding that geographical locations are intricately connected: migrants' experience in the national parks is the product of both their sense of their homeland and attempts to participate in a perceived Australian way of life.

In its use of oral history, research into migrant cultures acknowledged the differences between official and the everyday uses of the park.[63] A range of ethnic groups engaged in large family picnics, fishing expeditions, late night socialising and other recreational activities, presenting a sharp contrast to older notions of an ideal park user. While many third or fourth generation Australians also engaged in these activities, these studies highlighted the extent to which a particular set of Western environmental values had determined what constituted ideal recreational activities and had suppressed a diversity of views about the landscape.[64]

The researchers wanted their work to be used not only in educating the public in new ways (particularly, being accessible online), but in implementing practical policies that would support cultural diversity.[65] By exploring the diverse ways in which ethnic communities engaged in recreation in urban national parks, they challenged the institutional values influencing management. One way these ideas were put into

62 Martin Thomas (2001), 5.

63 Low, Taplin & Scheld (2005), 35.

64 Mandy Thomas (2002), 8.

65 Heather Goodall. Interview, 15 May 2008. See also Byrne, Goodall & Cadzow (forthcoming); Cadzow, Byrne, Goodall & Wearing (2011); Goodall, Byrne, Cadzow & Wearing (2012); Goodall (2010), 35–43.

practice was the establishment of a forum that opened dialogue between staff and park users. This forum was initiated by Christine Hopkins, the former Area Manager for Botany Bay and a coordinator for the Southwest district. Hopkins invited a Lebanese Muslim man to speak about the diverse aspects of Islam and challenge racist views 'that you knew existed'.[66] Although only a minor aspect of management, the official *Botany Bay National Park plan of management* saw this type of dialogue as furthering the park's new role as a 'meeting place of cultures' and a 'place of significance for all Australians ... regardless of their background and cultural heritage'.[67] Despite the fact that the forum and the *Plan of management* were a change in strategy, they also represented the continuation of an old idea: that national parks were meant to educate park users and staff. In this instance tolerance and inclusiveness were key lessons to be learnt.

Our environment

As this exploration demonstrates, the role of urban national parks can only be understood when placed in the context of what constitutes an ideal visitor and an ideal national space. While the principle of conservation has played a crucial role in the history of the national parks, arguments regarding the environment are often implicated in a wider set of power relations and linked to specific conceptions of national identity and attachment. Perhaps the most telling example of this was the Cronulla riots, where the backlash against those of Middle Eastern descent was framed as an attempt to 'show them it's our beach'.[68] The natural environment can often be a site where a sense of collective ownership is formed and collective identities solidified. The persistence of a view that certain people of other cultures 'don't really appreciate or understand what the values of the national park are'[69] confirms that

66 Christine Hopkins. Telephone interview, 19 May 2008.

67 NPWS (2002). *Botany Bay National Park plan of management*.

68 'Riot and revenge'. Four Corners transcript, 13 March 2006. [Online] Available: www.abc.net.au/4corners/content/2006/s1588360.htm [Accessed 10 May 2008].

69 NPWS Ranger. Interview, Royal National Park, 13 March 2008.

Fig. 7.5. Non-Anglo ethnic groups did not necessarily conform to how the NPWS imagined the ideal park user. Claire Farrugia.

national identity will continue to play a defining role in the management of national parks.

Nevertheless, this process of redefinition is by no means clear cut. Despite parks being a 'meeting place of cultures,' individuals and educational bodies continue to make the link between 'good behaviour', an 'ideal visitor' and a 'good citizen'. For example, the Beverly Hills Intensive English Centre use the Royal and Botany Bay National Parks to introduce newly arrived migrants into the Australian way of life by involving students in the 'Australian activity' of bushwalking which challenges their conception of a normal day out.[70] The link continues between the role of recreation, education and turning migrants into good Australian citizens (who may even come to know the environment 'better than Aussie kids!').[71]

70 Vicky Hatz. Interview, Beverly Hills Intensive English Centre, 23 May 2008.
71 Staff member. Interview, Beverly Hills Intensive English Centre, 23 May 2008.

The twin beliefs that national parks teach citizenship and that the 'ethnospecific experience of our neighbours might tell us something about ourselves'[72] raise the question of whether the implementation of multiculturalism in the parks was another more inclusive form of nationalism. There is no doubt that using the national parks as part of a wider program to introduce new migrants to Australia has value. However, this chapter has sought to place such ideas into the wider currents of thought regarding Australian national identity and how to educate good citizens. In this context, even casual attempts to encourage students to leave behind 'their fancy shoes' and 'inappropriate bushwalking clothes' and don a more relaxed, recreational-orientated clothing[73] carries cultural meaning. At any given time, this meaning influences notions about ideal forms of recreation, the ideal visitor and an ideal Australian citizen, which continue to weave their way into popular perceptions of the national park.

References

Byrne, Denis, Heather Goodall & Allison Cadzow (forthcoming). Place-making in national parks: a case study of park-use by Arabic Australians and Vietnamese Australians on the Georges River. Sydney: OEH.

Cadzow, Allison, Denis Byrne, Heather Goodall & Stephen Wearing (2011) *Waterborne: Vietnamese Australians and Sydney's Georges River parks and green spaces.* Sydney: UTS ePress.

Collins, Jock, Greg Noble, Scott Poynting & Paul Tabar (2005). *Kebabs, kids, cops and crime: youth, ethnicity and crime.* Sydney: Mokhtarat Press.

Gale, Peter (2006). 'Fear, race and national identity'. *Dialogue*, 25(3).

Goodall, Heather, Denis Byrne, Allison Cadzow & Stephen Wearing (2012). *Al-miyahu tajma'unah: Arabic Australians and the Georges River parklands.* Sydney: UTS ePress.

---

72 Martin Thomas (2001), 9.
73 Staff member. Interview, 2008.

Goodall, Heather (2010). 'Nets, backyards and the bush: the clashing cultures of nature on the Georges River', in Daniel Lunney, Pat Hutchings and Dieter Hochuli (eds). *The natural history of Sydney*. Sydney: Royal Zoological Society of NSW.

Goodall, Heather, Stephen Wearing, Denis Byrne & Allison Cadzow (2006). 'Making the city green: the creation of public greenspace in suburban Sydney, 1940–1992'. Conference paper. State of Australia's Cities 2005. Brisbane.

Grewcock, Mike (2005). 'Bin Laden in the suburbs: criminalising the Arab other'. *Australian and New Zealand Journal of Criminology*. 38(1).

Haebich, Anna (2007). *Spinning the dream: assimilation in Australia 1950–1970*. Perth: Fremantle Press.

Harper, Melissa (2002). The ways of the bushwalker: bushwalking in Australia. PhD thesis, University of Sydney.

Harper, Melissa & Richard White (2012), 'How transnational were the first national parks? Comparative perspectives from the British settler societies', in Bernhard Gissibl, Sabine Höhler, Patrick Kupper (eds). *Civilising nature: national parks in global historical perspective*. Munich: Berghahn Books.

Johnstone, DA (1978). *Nature conservation in NSW: individuals meeting a global responsibility*. Sydney: NPWS.

Jupp, James (1997). 'Immigration and national identity: multiculturalism', in Geoffrey Stokes (ed.) *The politics of identity in Australia*. Cambridge: Cambridge University Press.

Kane, John (1997). 'Racialism and democracy: the legacy of white Australia', in Geoffrey Stokes (ed.) *The politics of identity in Australia*. Cambridge: Cambridge University Press.

Low, Setha, Dana Taplin & Suzanne Scheld (2005). *Rethinking urban parks: public space and cultural diversity*. Austin: University of Texas Press.

Official guide to the National Park (1914). Sydney: Government Printer.

Official guide to the National Park (1902). Sydney: Government Printer.

Thomas, Mandy (2002). *Moving landscapes: national parks and the Vietnamese experience*. Sydney: NPWS.

Thomas, Martin (2001). *A multicultural landscape: national parks and the Macedonian experience*. Sydney: NPWS.

Roberts, Kay (1972). *Ask an Australian about the outdoors*. Artransa Park Film Studies for Department of Immigration.

Rubenstein, Kim (2003). 'An unequal membership: the Constitution's score on citizenship,' in Laksiri Jayasuriya, David Walker and Jan Gothard (eds). *Legacies of white Australia: race, culture and nation*. Perth: University of Western Australia Press.

Runte, Alfred (1997). *National parks: the American experience*. Lincoln: University of Nebraska Press.

Warhurst, John (2005). 'Before environmentalism'. *Meanjin*, 64(3): 125–132.

White, Richard (1981). *Inventing Australia: images and identity, 1688–1980*. Sydney: Allen & Unwin.

Chapter 8

'Thank God there was something to see at the end of the dirt road!':[1] national parks and heritage tourism

Tess Mierendorff

As the sun sets, the prison warden stands before the imposing edifice of the old gaol and addresses the assembled crowd: 'Prisoners, welcome to Trial Bay'. After several tense seconds the charade breaks; the warden is revealed to be the National Parks and Wildlife Service Discovery Ranger. The 'prisoners' are actually a group of tourists on a twilight tour of the Trial Bay Gaol situated in the Arakoon State Conservation Area on the New South Wales mid-north coast. The tour is an interactive one. Each participant is given a script and asked to play a character from the history of the gaol. Through this staged play, members of the tour group tell each other the history of the gaol.

In recent years tourism has been touted as one of the fastest growing sectors of the Australian economy.[2] One of the most discussed and debated facets of this industry has been the growth of cultural and heritage tourism.[3] Scholars such as Hall and McArthur have suggested that the alienating pace of modern life has led people to turn to history and heritage to find a sense of stability and community.[4] By re-enacting

---

1 Visitor's book (2008). Hill End Visitor Centre.

2 See, for example, Green paper: a medium to long term strategy for tourism / Tourism, industry tourism resources. Canberra: Department of Industry, Tourism and Resources, (2003).

3 See Frost (2006); Lowenthal (1998); Cossons (1989), 192–94; Hewison (1987).

4 See Hall & McArthur (1996), 2.

scenes from the past, the tourists at Trial Bay Gaol are engaging in an increasingly popular pastime.

Since 1967, the NPWS have been responsible for a large proportion of the designated natural and cultural heritage of NSW. The NPWS is continually faced with complex decisions about its ongoing management. In making these decisions, they must tread carefully between preservation for future generations, and open access for the present. The NPWS has long had sophisticated systems for managing natural heritage. Their management of cultural heritage has been a more recent concern. The low priority of cultural heritage for the NPWS relates to the fact that only a few of the cultural heritage sites managed by the service attract tourists in large numbers.

Despite the recognition within the NPWS of diverse types of heritage, the typical heritage tourist continues to be interested primarily in built heritage. These are structures that, according to Brian Garrod and Alan Fyall, 'attract the public by their explicit connection with the past'.[5] The aim of this chapter is to examine the development of heritage tourism within national parks, and to trace the evolution of the NPWS's management of these sites. By looking at the way heritage has been managed in the past we can, to a certain extent, trace changes within the NPWS itself, and gain an understanding of how contemporary debates about the meaning and value of heritage and heritage tourism have shaped the significant changes that have occurred in twentieth-century management strategies. The focus of this chapter will be limited to three non-urban heritage sites that have relatively large tourist visitation and have often been managed as tourist destinations.

Hartley Historic Site incorporates a small, uninhabited village situated at the base of the Victoria Pass just off the Great Western Highway, approximately 140 kilometres west of Sydney. Initially reserved in 1972, the site is comprised of fifteen historic buildings and the surrounding landscape. The township of Hartley was one of the first settlements west of the Blue Mountains and was a major regional centre in its heyday (c.1837–1887). When the main western railway was built in 1877, it bypassed Hartley and most of the village's economic activity was

---

5   Garrod & Fyall (2000), 685.

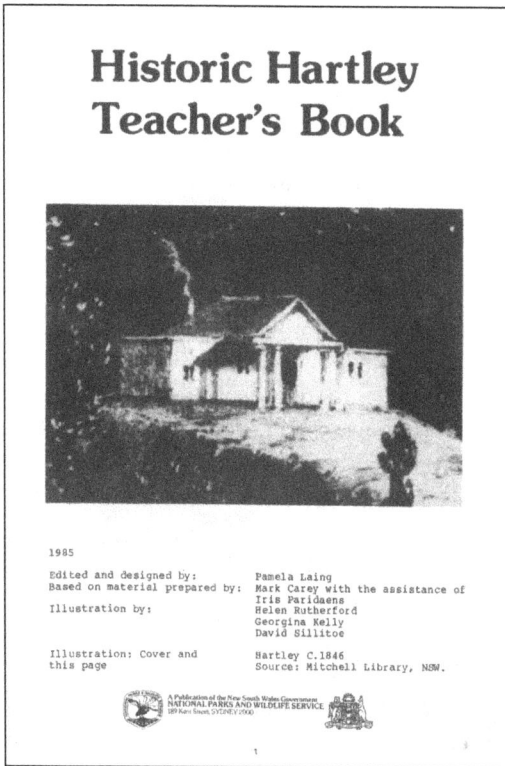

Fig. 8.1. School groups were targeted in the promotion of Hartley Historic Site. Pamela Laing (ed.) (1985). *Historic Hartley teacher's book.* Sydney: NPWS.

transferred to nearby Lithgow. This left the township largely unchanged for the next century. Today, the site is managed by the NPWS and 'plays an educational role as an example of a small settlement which reflects economic and social changes over 150 years'.[6] The current NPWS management strategy combines continued preservation with policies designed to attract more tourists to the site.[7]

6   NPWS (1994). *Hartley Historic Site plan of management,* i.

7   See Otto Cserhalmi & Partners P/L Architects (2002). *Hartley Historic Site: conservation management plan.* Sydney: NPWS; NPWS (1994). *Hartley Historic Site plan of management.*

The village of Hill End, located seventy kilometres north of Bathurst, has a similar boom and bust history. Established in 1852 shortly after gold was found in the region, Hill End became the scene of major mining activity in the 1870s. By 1880, the once prosperous village was in decline. In the years after the Second World War, the rustic serenity of the town attracted the attention of Russell Drysdale, Donald Friend and other artists who spent long stretches of time in the village and drew inspiration for their paintings from the townscape and surrounds. Their patronage, especially the curiosity generated by the sale of their art, sparked a revival of interest in the village. This, combined with a growing awareness of heritage and the desire for its preservation among the Australian community more broadly, led to Hill End's gazettal as a historic site in 1967. However, unlike Hartley, Hill End remains a living village, with a local population of about 200. Although the community contributes to the village's appeal to tourists, it has also presented additional challenges for the managers of the site.

The Trial Bay Gaol, established in the 1870s, is the only example of a public works prison in NSW. Prisoners were paid wages to construct the prison buildings and the breakwater which stretches into the harbour. After many delays, which saw large sections of the breakwater washed away, the project was abandoned in 1909 and the prison was closed.[8] However, between 1915 and 1917 the prison was reopened and used as an internment camp for German nationals.[9] Unlike Hartley and Hill End, Trial Bay Gaol was not reserved as a historic site under the *National Parks and Wildlife Act* (1967). Instead, it was incorporated into the Arakoon State Recreation Area (SRA). The remaining gaol buildings, now a picturesque ruin on a dramatic headland site, are only one of the area's tourism attractions. Because the Trial Bay Gaol is in a different category of reserve, the NPWS management adopted a strategy that differs considerably from that followed at Hartley and Hill End.

Each of these three sites was a recognised tourist attraction by the 1950s. The growing awareness of their tourism potential expedited

8   Macleay River Historical Society (1966). *The story of Trial Bay Gaol*. Kempsey: Macleay River Historical Society.

9   NPWS (1987). *Arakoon State Recreation Area plan of management*, 7–8.

their conservation since it made sense to preserve assets that attracted tourists. When the NPWS was created in 1967, its principal aim was to conserve for posterity, the natural and cultural heritage of the state. The Act also provided for 'sustainable visitor use and enjoyment that is compatible with the conservation of the historic site's natural and cultural values'[10] which has come to include adaptive reuse of buildings. Throughout the 1960s and 1970s, the NPWS focused on the acquisition of heritage properties, which occasionally drew funds away from providing interpretation programs, comprehensive visitor facilities and providing sustainable public access to buildings already under its control.[11]

As the maintenance requirements of built heritage became more widely appreciated, the potential economic benefits of successful cultural tourism began to be acknowledged. This trend was accentuated in the 1980s when policies of economic rationalisation encouraged non-essential services to become financially self-sufficient, leading to an increased integration of tourism objectives into the management strategies of the NPWS. The new economic thinking demanded that conservation be achieved in conjunction with greater public access which, in turn, was to provide much-needed revenue for further conservation projects. However, as Warwick Frost has argued, many managers of heritage sites in this era assumed that because heritage was of interest to tourists, successful heritage tourism would materialise even without intensive marketing and site promotion.[12] This presupposition, coupled with pressing conservation issues and very limited budgets, meant that many tourism initiatives developed by the NPWS did not move beyond the planning stages.

In 2000, the NPWS underwent major restructuring. This led, in part, to a greater appreciation of the role of local communities in the management of the park system. The federal Productivity Commission report of April 2006 claimed that places of historic significance 'reflect

---

10 *National Parks and Wildlife Act* 1974 [S.30 (F)]. [Online] Available: www.austlii.edu.au/au/legis/nsw/consol_act/npawa1974247 [Accessed 29 April 2008].

11 Ford (2009).

12 Frost (2007).

the diversity of our communities [and] they provide a sense of identity and a connection to our past and to our nation'.[13] In commissioning the report, Senator Ian Campbell, Minister for the Environment and Heritage, noted that 'Australia's heritage is of great value both to the economy and our national identity'.[14] Although the preservation of heritage sites was deemed necessary because of the cultural value it provided to the community, the Productivity Commision was more interested in financial implications, measuring heritage largely in terms of its value to the economy. Increasingly, the NPWS realised that in order to attract tourists and income, non-urban heritage sites with tourism potential needed to be marketed as attractive tourist destinations.

The introduction of the Historic Asset MaintenanceProgram (HAMP) in 1995 helped to facilitate this by allowing for the expense involved in heritage conservation and management. The annual allocation of two million dollars from the state government ensured that a certain amount of funds would be spent on the built heritage in the parks. The availability of funds also helped to raise awareness of the social value of built heritage sites, and increased the willingness of local NPWS staff to engage in conservation works and to make such sites accessible to visitors.[15] In the early 2000s, grants under HAMP were often linked directly to conservation management plans.[16] To this end, conservation and cultural tourism plans were developed for Hartley, Hill End, and Trial Bay Gaol. Recommendations regarding both crucial

---

13 Productivity Commission (2006). *Conservation of Australia's historic heritage places*. Report No. 37, 4.

14 Hon. Peter Costello, Treasurer and Senator Ian Campbell, Minister for the Environment and Heritage. Productivity Commission to examine built heritage conservation. Joint media statement. 6 April 2005. [Online] Available: www.treasurer.gov.au/DisplayDocs.aspx?pageID=&doc=pressreleases/2005/028.htm&min=phc [Accessed 3 January 2009].

15 Ford (2009), 36–38.

16 Brown (2003) *An evaluation of the Heritage Assets Maintenance Program (HAMP)*, 22–25. HAMP has since become the Heritage Assets Revitalisation Program (HARP) which signalled a shift from pure conservation and maintenance of NPWS's heritage assets.

conservation work and improvements to sustainable visitor access and facilities slowly began to be implemented.[17] Throughout the history of the NPWS, the forces of tourism and conservation have been present. In looking at the ways the influence of these two forces has changed over time, we can examine the evolution of the ways that tourists have been attracted and heritage maintained.

Valuing heritage: tourists and the conservation movement before 1967

In 1945, Hill End was almost a ghost town, barely inhabited since the heady days of the gold rush. Over the next two decades, interest in the village increased dramatically. This was due to the influence of artists Drysdale and Friend who romanticised and glamorised Hill End as a prototypical rural town of unrivalled artistic inspiration. Such was their commitment to Hill End that Friend proclaimed himself the 'self appointed historian of the village'.[18] Friend claimed that part of the charm of the town was that despite modest visitation you could 'hardly call [Hill End] a tourist resort'.[19] Although these artists had a vested interest in maintaining the undiscovered feel of the village since the rustic atmosphere was the inspiration for much of their art, the well-promoted release of Friend's *Hillendiana* helped to significantly boost the number of visitors to the town.

The second factor to draw curious tourists to Hill End was the 1951 discovery and later publication of the Holtermann photographs. Taken in 1877, these photographs systematically documented Hill End at the height of the goldrush. Barely any new construction had taken place in the intervening eighty years so the photographs provided a unique opportunity to view the past and the present simultaneously. By comparing the photographs to the modern landscape, visitors could actually trace the passage of time. Publicity in magazines, newspapers and on radio generated curiosity and stimulated a new interest in

---

17 Brooks & Associates (2004); Cserhalmi (2002); Davies (2004).
18 Donald Friend's personal diaries cited in Mayne (2003), 118.
19 Friend (1956), 76.

222 • Playing in the bush

Fig. 8.2. An NPWS sign at the entrance of the gazetted historic site of Hill End.

touring the past. Furthermore, the increase in car ownership meant that the isolation of Hill End was no longer an insurmountable barrier to the casual tourist.[20]

During this period, the Hill End Heritage Association began to provide publicity material to tourist agencies in Bathurst. Several private museums were opened and locals conducted their own informal tours of the area.[21] Entrepreneurial activity on the part of the local community began to ensure the profitability of cultural tourism. In the 1960s, the local citizens' association began a campaign to have the town reserved as a historic village. Many of the buildings were in dire need of professional conservation work, and the community wanted to stabilise the village's fragile economy and cement its growing reputation as a tourist centre.

---

20 Mayne (2003), 129.

21 Mayne (2003), 129.

The increasing importance of tourism to the local economy was also apparent at Hartley. When the railway bypassed Hartley in 1877 the village lost much of its economic prominence. However, the subsequent building of a road through Hartley to the recognised tourist resort of the Jenolan Caves in the late 1880s meant that the village was able to sustain itself with the passing tourist trade. Hotels, teahouses and garages became profitable local businesses. One Hartley local made his living by photographing tourists on their way to the Jenolan Caves and developing the prints in time for their return journey.[22] The focus on attracting tourists was also reflected in the 1914 creation of the Hartley Public Recreation Reserve, which included the architecturally renowned, though no longer functioning, Hartley Courthouse. In 1926, the management of the reserve passed from the state government to the Blaxland Shire Council and it was officially opened to the public in 1937 to celebrate the town's centenary.[23] This decision was especially significant because at this time, few buildings in NSW were officially considered to be historic, let alone set aside for public visitation.

While Hill End continued to have a dynamic and vocal local community, the same could not be said of Hartley. By 1967, many of Hartley's established families were either dying out or moving away, and the village was developing a ghost-town atmosphere. After intense discussion, the Hartley Advisory Committee and members of the Blaxland Shire Council gained support for the idea of preserving Hartley as a museum village, to be maintained by the NPWS primarily for educational and tourism purposes.[24] When the historic site was gazetted in 1972 the last residents had left the village and there was no longer an economic imperative to ensure continued tourist patronage. The desire for preservation was now linked to the cultural value and educational potential of the site to the wider visiting public. It was not until the 1980s, when economic rationalism demanded that heritage be economically self-sufficient, that tourists were again significantly courted at Hartley.

---

22 O'Brien (1995), 13.

23 Cserhalmi (2002), 101–02.

24 Cserhalmi (2002), 103–04.

Trial Bay Gaol also has a long history of tourist visitation. Tourists were drawn to the gaol as much for its popular status as a ruin as for its actual history.[25] The gaol has remained unused since the First World War and its gradual dilapidation was accelerated by the sale of all its removable and reusable parts, including the ironwork and tiled roof in 1922.[26] The gaol had been built on Crown Land, but in 1946, amid rumours of a sale into private ownership, the South West Rocks Progress Association campaigned to have the gaol and grounds gazetted as a camping and recreation reserve under the management of local trustees. The association argued that ninety-five percent of visitors to the area 'do not consider their holiday complete without a visit to the old gaol' and that, as a result, 'the public have no wish to see it pass into private ownership'.[27] Two interlinking factors were cited as the rationale when the reserve was created in late 1946. The first was its 'considerable interest from a historical point of view'.[28] The second was its 'attraction to tourists and visitors'.[29] Although tourists were an important part of the equation, it is important to note that they were not pursued to the extent that their presence would interfere with ongoing local access or compromise the authenticity of the site. Several proposals in the 1950s to turn the gaol into a private resort were rejected by the Department of Lands.[30] By the mid 1960s, similar trends at Hartley and Hill End saw local community groups beginning to suggest that the gaol be reserved as a historic site under the proposed National Parks and Wildlife legislation. However, after an inspection by John Fisher, a member of the National Parks Advisory Committee of Architects, it was concluded

25 Davies (2004), 10.

26 NPWS (1987), 8.

27 Letter from Fred Sheppard, Hon. Sec. South West Rocks Progress Association, to Hon. Roy S. Vincent (MP), 26 April 1946. State Records NSW: NSW NPWS; 10669, State Recreation Area Files 1967–1988.

28 Letter from HH Guest (Under Secretary for Lands) to Hon. RS Vincent (MP), 30 April 1946. SRNSW: 10669.

29 Proposed disposal of the old Trial Bay Prison. SRNSW: 10669 [16/4067].

30 Letter from Hon. RS Vincent (MP) to Mr LP Moffat, 3 August 1949. SRNSW: 10669 [49/8542.2].

that although the gaol was a 'romantic ruin' and quite popular with visitors, it was not of sufficient historical importance to permit its classification as a historic site.[31]

In the years before the NPWS came into being, the twin demands of conservation and tourism were evident in all three sites, and often worked together to ensure the continued survival of their heritage significance. However, distinctions in perceived historical significance, which led to Hartley and Hill End being classified as historic sites, and Trial Bay being simply incorporated into the Arakoon SRA, significantly affected the way these sites were understood and managed. The focus at Hill End and Hartley was on conserving the built heritage assets, which were seen as an important link to the nation's past. The built heritage was the primary reason for the preservation of the sites. At Arakoon, on the other hand, the gaol was perceived primarily as a picturesque ruin and thus did not warrant such stringent conservation measures. Furthermore, as a recreation area, the principal usage of the site was for local and tourist visitation. Management strategies were developed with this outcome in mind. Despite possessing similar built heritage, the perceived potential use of each site determined how the public would enjoy it, and thus how it would be managed.

Shifting priorities: the NPWS 1967–1980

When Australia's first national park was created in 1879, the principal focus was on the reservation of land for public recreation. However, with the creation in 1967 of the National Parks and Wildlife Service, which was modelled on the United States National Parks Service and responded to international debates about national parks, there was a greater focus on the conservation of natural and cultural heritage. This was underscored by the creation of State Recreation Areas, which aimed to alleviate recreational pressure on national parks that were primarily conceived as places of conservation.[32] Despite the fact that the NPWS

---

31 Trial Bay Gaol Inspection by Member of National Parks Advisory Committee of Architects, 26 October 1966. SRNSW: 10669 [66/408].

32 Lemsing (1985), 12.

226 • Playing in the bush

was principally focused on conservation of nature, and tried to direct tourists to areas where their recreation activities would be less damaging to the natural environment, cultural heritage sites were still popular with tourists. This presented significant problems for management of built heritage.

When the local community at Hill End petitioned for a historic site within their village, the aim was to stabilise the local tourism-based economy. However, the desires of the residents were not always mirrored in the NPWS management. Although the dilapidated hospital at Hill End was renovated and reopened as the Visitor's Centre in 1972 and repairs were made to the town's primary pub, the Royal Hotel, little other activity was undertaken to promote tourism. The apparent inertia was largely due to funding limitations and did not sit well with many of the residents. Some were disappointed that the creation of the historic site had not significantly boosted employment opportunities or delivered expected infrastructure improvements, such as the sealing of the road to Bathurst.[33] Marjorie Prior notes in her introduction to the *Hill End historic site oral history project* that by the end of the 1970s, the 'hostile nature of the community towards the service [was] widely conceded'. She noted that the resentment stemmed, in part, from the Service's acquisition program. It often seemed to residents that large portions of NPWS time and money were allocated to acquiring new buildings, while the ones already under its care fell increasingly into disrepair. Drastic onsite underfunding for conservation works reinforced this view and led to claims of mismanagement. Local residents Betty and Bill Maris were 'bitter about the effects of the administration of the site' which they claimed had 'taken all incentive away from the townspeople's historical involvement in their community'.[34] There was a widespread view in the community that the NPWS made no real attempt to utilise local knowledge and, while recognising and promoting the supposedly living community, excluded it from the decision-making process.

Although the NPWS's 1973 report *Recommendations concerning historical and archaeological sites* recognised that it was 'often better

---

33 Mayne (2002), 35.
34 Prior (1980), 2–3.

to retain genuine old work of several periods,[35] the interpretation program at Hill End was centred almost exclusively on a single theme: the goldrush. The NPWS saw itself as preserving the site so that 'future generations may experience something of the thrill of "Gold Fever".'[36] A large proportion of visitors to Hill End were children on school excursions coming to see a goldrush town, which reinforced the theme. However, not all within the NPWS agreed with the primacy given to goldrush history. In 1979, Ranger John Willing challenged what he considered to be the 'very conservative view that the National Parks and Wildlife Service seem to have adopted'. He believed that the story of gold at Hill End was told in a historical vacuum and pleaded with the NPWS to widen their historical focus because the 'living tradition of the people is just as important'.[37] Although the focus would widen in later decades to encompass a more comprehensive history of the town, the early focus of both attention and budgets on conservation works prevented a more expansive interpretation program from being developed.

Despite its lack of a living community, the Hartley Historic Site followed a similar trajectory to that of Hill End. Hartley was gazetted as a historic site in 1972, but a draft plan of management did not appear until 1989. Ranger Steve Ring explained in 1995 that the final amended *Plan of management*, published in 1994, had taken so long to eventuate 'at least partly because initial efforts went into acquiring more land ... to conserve as much as possible of the original town area'.[38] As a result, the initial focus of the plan was concerned more with stabilising the site through expensive conservation works rather than with promotion of the site.

Continuing a policy instituted by the Blaxland Shire Council, the NPWS adopted the attitude of seeing the village as a museum and was involved with restoring much of its nineteenth-century character. When recently inhabited buildings were acquired by the NPWS, their

---

35 NPWS (1973). *Recommendations concerning historical and archaeological sites: their administration and management.* Sydney: NPWS, 22.

36 NPWS (1972). *Hill End Historic Site.* Sydney: NPWS, 3.

37 Willing (1979).

38 O'Brien (1995), 13.

twentieth-century occupation was 'not seen as being of significance'. During conservation works, the majority of traces of the twentieth century were accordingly removed. There was some debate as to whether the Corney garage, constructed in the 1940s, should be removed because it did not fit with the primary interpretive theme. Residents in the local area noted that by managing the site as a museum the NPWS had dramatically changed the character of the village, removing traces of the layers of history to focus on its nineteenth-century character.[39] Without people living and working in Hartley, it had developed a 'somewhat spiritless atmosphere'.[40] Tourists' engagement with Hartley as a preserved nineteenth-century village was somewhat undercut by the notable lack of day-to-day activities associated with village life.

Despite the previous focus on acquisitions, an interpretation program began to be put in place. The renovated presbytery was given an audiovisual display as well as a research room for people interested in Hartley's history. An audio display was also installed in the courthouse, but instead of recognising the continuing use of the courthouse over a long period of time, the program only recalled facts from the period 1838–1840.[41] Educational programs and tours were also developed. They too focused on Hartley's role as a nineteenth-century village, mirroring the belief that tourists were interested in immersing themselves in a specific period, rather than tracing the enduring history of the village.

In the early 1970s, tourism at Trial Bay Gaol was increasing steadily. Figures compiled by the Trial Bay Reserve Trust for 1970 indicated that from the 100 000 people who visited the reserve, 39 000 paid to tour the gaol.[42] In 1971, the *Sydney Morning Herald* estimated that the gaol attracted more than 3000 people a week during school holidays.[43] The area surrounding the gaol remained a reserve for public recreation until 1974 when it was gazetted as the Arakoon State Recreation Area. Like all SRAs, the land was under NPWS control, but the day-to-day

---

39 Cserhalmi (2002), 105–06.

40 Cserhalmi (2002), 159.

41 Haigh (1978), 17.

42 Trial Bay Reserve Trust: patronage of reserves. SRNSW: 10669 [67/2249].

43 'A tourist treasure – with history'. *Sydney Morning Herald*, 24 May 1971.

Fig. 8.3. Interpretive signs dot the streets of Hill End, with photographs of the mining cottages that once stood on now-empty sites. Caroline Ford.

management of the site was delegated to local trustees. The trustees' first priority was to provide visitors with popular and appropriate recreational facilities, such as fishing and camping areas. Conserving the gaol was a priority, but the trust had neither the money nor the expertise to ensure conservation measures were adopted. The feeling was that, given the widespread local view of the gaol as a ruin, high levels of interpretation were unnecessary. The existing interpretation gave equal emphasis to the historic setting and the purely aesthetic value of the site. The gaol was something to be appreciated as much for its picturesque setting as for its historical value. The aim was not to promote history, but to promote recreation, and the view of the gaol as a crumbling ruin was an added incentive for tourists to visit the already picturesque landscape.

In the early years of the NPWS, the distinction in classification between these three heritage sites led to each being given different priorities for tourism and conservation. Having recently acquired the built heritage in the historic sites, the NPWS needed to focus on securing the integrity of the buildings. Tourism played a lower priority in these years because the NPWS had to first ensure that these sites were sustainable in the longer term. Acquisition and conservation projects needed to be completed before larger scale tourism operations could be considered. However, when management strategies did consider tourism, they continued to do so based around single-issue interpretive themes, reflecting a perhaps oversimplified conception of the desires of tourists. At Trial Bay, where conservation projects did not consume as much time and money, locals and tourists could be catered for more effectively.

The NPWS 1980–2000

In the 1980s government policy generally took an ideological turn towards economic rationalist philosophies. The NPWS was not immune. The political rhetoric surrounding the assumed superiority of free market forces meant an increased expectation that heritage should pay for itself instead of relying on government funding. The user-pays philosophy required that in order to stay financially viable, heritage could no longer be merely preserved, but had to be 'marketed, made accessible, interpreted and woven into the wider enterprise of tourism and leisure', all without damaging or demeaning it.[44] Aside from advertising and creating partnerships with private enterprise within the tourism industry, heritage managements put their faith in better heritage interpretation as the key to stimulating tourism.[45] Freeman Tilden argues that if interpretation is to effectively stimulate tourists and attract visitation by word-of-mouth, then it should involve much more than the simple exchange of information. Instead it should provoke or even inspire.[46]

While the NPWS attempted to respond to changes in interpretation theory, many of its tourism policies remained in the planning stages, largely due to issues with funding. Ongoing conservation projects continued to monopolise a large proportion of budgets, effectively curtailing intensive marketing strategies. However, this financial

44 Millar (1989), 13.
45 Silberberg (1995), 363.
46 Tilden (2007).

restriction was usually coupled with a continuing belief that simply because heritage existed, tourists would come. The less than impressive tourist numbers at Hill End and Hartley did not mirror the experience at Trial Bay. The successful link Arakoon SRA had developed with recreational activity other than heritage tourism meant that it attracted larger numbers of visitors than either Hill End or Hartley.[47]

In the 1980s, the majority of Hartley's tourists were casual visitors on their way to or from the Jenolan Caves. When a new road to the caves was constructed in the early 1990s, Hartley was again bypassed. This was partly to protect the site but once again, Hartley lost much of the passing tourist trade. By 1994, the administration strategy codified in the amended *Plan of management* was 'to develop the village as an attractive tourist *destination*',[48] as somewhere that people wanted to visit as an endpoint, rather than only en route to somewhere else. In order to achieve this it was recognised that extensive work was required in terms of completing the conservation measures already in place, upgrading the practically non-existent visitor facilities and comprehensively overhauling the interpretation program.[49] Although the *Plan of management* presented its policies as merely the next step in a continuing program of tourist attraction, very little had been achieved in real terms. The Tourist Centre had been established in the old Post Office, and some of the buildings had basic interpretation programs, but the public amenities of the site were not yet adequate. There were no picnic sites or food outlets and the parking and toilet facilities required expansion. In addition, many of the buildings were closed to the casual visitor. Tours could be arranged but there was a general perception that the interiors, only recently vacated, were not of interest

---

47 See Hill End Historic Site camping statistics, 1984–2008 NSW National Parks and Wildlife Service Visitor Centre Archives, Hill End, 2008; Hill End Historic Site coaches: museum visits only, NSW National Parks and Wildlife Service Visitor Centre, Hill End, 2008; Museum visitation Hill End Historic Site, 1984–2008, NSW National Parks and Wildlife Service Visitor Centre, Hill End, 2008; Christiansen (1997).

48 NPWS (1994), 16. Original emphasis.

49 NPWS (1994), i.

to tourists, so they were not well publicised or made easily accessible.[50] Most casual visitors had to be content with viewing the exteriors of heritage buildings. The only measure pursued with any fervour was the upgrading of the interpretation program, which recognised that the current NPWS management was 'one layer of occupation' in the history of the town.[51]

The *Plan of management* did note that it was 'clear that Hartley's potential as a tourist venue has not to date been fully realised'.[52] Tourist numbers were slowly increasing, from 25 110 in 1989–90 to 29 709 in 1995–96, but these numbers were not enough to make Hartley economically self-sufficient. In 1997, a study was commissioned to ascertain the potential economic value of recreational activities at Hartley and to help develop ways that the historic site could better attract tourists.[53] In order to obtain the funds to recover some portion of the building restoration costs and have the means to cover ongoing management, both the economic value study and the *Plan of management* suggested leasing some of the buildings to commercial operators to 'provide suitable services' such as tearooms and cafes.[54] The aim was to raise the visitation levels to about 50 000 per annum by the year 2000.[55] However, one of the problems with the user-pays philosophy was that each individual site needed to contribute significantly to its own upkeep, a principle which did not take into account any intrinsic social and cultural value of heritage beyond its economic potential. Even the 2006 Productivity Commission report into the management of Australia's heritage places noted that the 'question of "who should pay" was not simply one of equity', and that 'community benefits' were also important.[56] The NPWS has tried to balance the sometimes conflicting

50 NPWS (1994), 16.
51 Cserhalmi (2002), 247.
52 NPWS (1994), 16.
53 Christiansen (1997).
54 NPWS (1994), 16.
55 O'Brien (1995), 13.
56 Productivity Commission (2006), 149.

demands of economic sustainability and ongoing preservation of heritage to be enjoyed by local communities and future generations.

Although visitation rates in Hartley were growing, the township was far from self-sustaining. In 1996, the new NSW Labor government noted that tourism was not currently a source of the funding needed to ensure the continued survival of built heritage sites. The Minister for the Environment conceded that continued underfunding had meant that many heritage buildings across the state had fallen into disrepair.[57] As a result, Hartley received $680 000 as part of the state government budget for the 1996–97 fiscal year. Whether as a result of this grant or the requirement stipulated in the *Plan of management* that a comprehensive conservation plan be completed before further decisions were made, the focus remained on conservation and there appears to have been little further active promotion of tourism to Hartley.

In Hill End, unlike Hartley, tourist numbers were actually declining. From a high in the mid 1970s of almost 47 000 per annum, visitation fell to under 36 000 in 1986, and was down to only about 30 000 visits per annum by the end of the decade.[58] Museum visitation fell accordingly, from 34 500 in 1985 to a low of only 7800 in 2000.[59] A significant proportion of this reduction was the drop in school visits, which had previously provided the largest number of visitors to the historic site.[60] In 1989, the NPWS developed and published a Teachers Kit to attempt to reverse this trend, but it appears to have had little long-term success.[61] The 1988 draft Plan of management noted that the Bathurst region was a 'major tourist destination' because of the diverse range of tourism and recreational activities available.[62] The contrast between the apparent

---

57 'Historic landmarks await $8m facelift'. *The Australian*, 23 August 1996: 4.

58 Mayne (2003), 135–36.

59 Museum visitation Hill End Historic Site, 1984–2008. NSW National Parks and Wildlife Service Visitor Centre, Hill End, 2008.

60 Hill End Historic Site coaches: museum visits only. NSW National Parks and Wildlife Service Visitor Centre, Hill End, 2008.

61 NPWS (1989). *Wondrous treasure: the story of Hill End*. Sydney: NPWS.

62 NPWS (1988). Hill End Historic Site: draft plan of management, 7.

Fig. 8.4. Trial Bay Gaol on the NSW mid north coast: a historic ruin in Arakoon National Park, surrounded by sandy beaches, camping areas and picnic grounds. Warren Crozier / OEH.

attractions of the site and steadily decreasing tourist numbers at Hill End convinced the NPWS that it was not enough to merely market Hill End as a goldrush town. The NPWS began to look for other aspects of Hill End that could attract tourists. Promotional material and tourist brochures began to stress not only the goldrush, but also the remnants of exotic gardens, the continuing reputation of Hill End as an artists' colony and the possibilities that the Holtermann photographs offered for seeing past and present simultaneously. Conservation architect Ivar Nelson, who worked at Hill End between 1975 and 1981, encouraged a move away from the 'primary interpretation' approach towards exploring the lives of women and ethnic minorities.

The influence of the Burra Charter (1979), which set out the basic principles and procedures for the conservation and management of sites of cultural significance in Australia, was also felt.[63] It helped 'roll

63 Australia ICOMOS (2000). *The Burra Charter: the Australian International*

back the NPWS's initially skewed emphasis upon restoring buildings to 'frozen points in time' in favour of interpretation that recognised the continuing evolution of use.[64] While the NPWS had earlier focused on the remaining buildings, they began to recognise that 'the gaps between extant structures are just as important as the buildings themselves'.[65] A family history unit was also established to appeal to tourists on a more personal level. It can be seen that when faced with declining tourist numbers, the NPWS management at Hill End adapted their tourism strategy. Instead of focusing primarily on the goldrush, they began to promote Hill End as a village where preserved heritage assets allowed visitors to witness the passage of time.

Unlike Hartley and Hill End, Arakoon did not suffer from want of visitors. In 1981, IM Garrard conducted a study of the outdoor recreation demand at Arakoon and found that it was the 'second most heavily visited' state recreation area. In the twelve-month period from April 1979 to March 1980, Garrard estimated that 654 800 people visited Arakoon. This was due in part to the attractiveness of Trial Bay Gaol, in part to the spectacular scenic beauty of the site, and in part to the recreational facilities provided. Whilst the primary usage of the park was recreational, a significant proportion of tourists visited the gaol. By 1981, the NPWS had established both a visitor's centre and a museum within the gaol buildings.[66] The museum's focus was broad, following periods of use ranging from the initial gaol, to the internment camp, to the tourist ruin. A self-guided tour was developed alongside a program of guided interpretive tours that ran successfully during school holiday periods when the park was most often used. In 1987, the NPWS became joint managers of the site along with the Arakoon SRA Trust, and began to take an active role in the day-to-day affairs of the park. In 1988 the NPWS commissioned a conservation plan for the gaol[67] and used this

Council on Monuments and Sites charter for places of cultural significance 1999. Melbourne: Australia ICOMOS.

64 Mayne (2003), 35.

65 NPWS (1988), 11.

66 IM Garrard & K Garrard (1981), 14, 17.

67 Kerr & Jackson Teece Chesterman Willis & Partners (1988).

as the basis to carry out a $100 000 program of major restoration work for the period 1992–1993.[68]

Despite this, visitation to the gaol has fallen since 1988.[69] Conservation architect Paul Davies noted that the interpretation panels around the site 'dwell too much on the more technical aspects of the building and do not provide enough information on the actual experience of the prisoners' or what the NPWS staff refer to as the site's 'people stories'. He also noted that the museum had significant problems in terms of access, content and presentation, with many 'displays that lack a coherent story or which establish comprehensible themes'.[70] The recreational priorities of Arakoon SRA have meant that the potential for heritage tourism has often been marginalised.

Valuing heritage: 2000 and beyond

In 2000, the National Parks and Wildlife Service underwent a major restructure that reinforced the view that it was not sufficient to manage heritage in isolation from either local communities, or the tourists who come to visit. Since then, the NPWS has tried to create more effective community consultation and establish visitor surveys to cater to tourists more effectively. In Hill End, consultation resulted in the 2004 *Hill End master plan*, which describes the process by which long-planned changes could be put into action.[71] Although Hartley does not have a local community within the village, it does have a strong 'community of interest', which was extensively consulted in preparing the *Hartley conservation management plan* in 2002, the crucial first step towards implementing an attractive tourist program at Hartley.[72] The management at both sites have seemingly learnt from the experience of Trial Bay Gaol: heritage tourism is only a part of a much larger tourist

---

68 For a breakdown in funding allocation see Davies (2004), 50.

69 Davies (2004), 405.

70 Davies (2004), 393–96.

71 Brooks (2004).

72 Australian Heritage Commission (2001). Successful tourism at heritage places: a guide to tourism operators, heritage managers and communities. Canberra: Australian Heritage Commission, 8.

experience and tourists are more likely to visit heritage if it is promoted alongside other local attractions or landmarks. In conjunction with the museum, the Hill End Historic Site plays host to an artist-in-residence program, which has proved a significant attraction.[73] Marketing for the Hill End Historic Site still predominantly consists of placing the NPWS tourist brochure in the Bathurst Tourist Information Centre and advertising on local radio, but growing heritage attractions in nearby Bathurst are seen as a chance to cross-promote the heritage assets of the NPWS and the wider region.

In 2002, all SRAs were reclassified as State Conservation Areas (SCAs). This change, coupled with the preparation of the *Trial Bay conservation management and cultural tourism plan* (2004), reflected the view that all heritage, not just that found at historic sites, needs to be appropriately conserved and interpreted. Interpretation programs are powerful tools of mediation between conservation and tourist education. Creative, interactive and thoughtful interpretation helps to create what Gianna Mocardo has termed 'mindful visitors' and helps them to appreciate the conservation values that underpin NPWS management of heritage sites.[74] Interactive interpretation encourages tourists to use their imagination to enrich the heritage experience.[75] This is what is happening on the Twilight Discovery Tour at Arakoon, where the participants are asked to place themselves in the history of the gaol. In doing so, they are being schooled in history and in the importance of conserving cultural heritage. This initiative has been so well received that the principal criticism from locals and visitors is disappointment that the NPWS does not run more of these kinds of programs.[76] Conservation and public access are frequently at loggerheads. However, in order to manage built heritage successfully, whether in historic sites or other national parks, both elements are required, and in the right balance, can also work together to ensure that heritage sites remain open to the public.

---

73 Visitor's book (2008). Hill End Visitor Centre.

74 Mocardo (1996), 376–97.

75 Nuryanti (1996), 253.

76 Davies (2004), 394.

References

Brooks, Graeme & Associates (2004). *Hill End Historic Site master plan*. Sydney: NPWS.

Brown, Steve (2003). An evaluation of the Heritage Assets Maintenance Program (HAMP). Unpublished: NPWS.

Christiansen, Glen (1997). *Economic value of recreational use: Hartley Historic Site*. Sydney: NPWS.

Cossons, Neil (1989). 'Heritage tourism – trends and tribulations'. *Tourism Management*, 10(3).

Davies, Paul (2004). *Trial Bay Gaol conservation management and cultural tourism plan*, v1. Sydney: NPWS.

Ford, Caroline (2009). *Challenges in the landscape: memories of conserving historic heritage in the NSW park system 1967–2000*. Sydney: Department of Environment, Climate Change and Water.

Friend, Donald (1956). *A collection of Hillendiana comprising vast numbers of facts & a considerable amount of fiction concerning the goldfield of Hillend and environs, with the results of many years of intensive and arduous historical research*. Sydney: Ure Smith.

Frost, Warwick (2007). 'Rethinking heritage and tourism in Australia'. Monash University Working Paper: 2. [Online] Available: www.buseco.monash.edu.au/mgt/research/working-papers/workingpapers07pdf.html [Accessed 10 May 2008].

Frost, Warwick (2006). 'Cultural heritage and tourism in Australia: concepts and issues'. Monash University Working Paper. [Online] Available: www.buseco.monash.edu.au/mgt/research/working-papers/workingpapers06pdf.html [Accessed 10 May 2008].

Garrard, IM & K Garrard (1981). *Arakoon State Recreation Area: outdoor recreation demand*. Sydney: NPWS.

Garrod, Brian & Alan Fyall (2000). 'Managing heritage tourism'. *Annals of Tourism Research*, 27(3).

Haigh, Chris (1978). 'Official opening of Hartley Historic Site'. *NAPAWI*, 6(4).

Hall, C Michael & Simon McArthur (1996). *Heritage management in Australia and New Zealand*. Melbourne: Oxford University Press.

Hewison, Robert (1987). *The heritage industry: Britain in a climate of decline*. London: Methuen.

Kerr, JS & Jackson Teece Chesterman Willis & Partners (1988). *Trial Bay prison study*. Sydney: NPWS.

Lemsing, Don, Burrendong State Recreation Area Trustee (1985). 'Private enterprise funding of projects on State Recreation Areas'. Seminar, report of proceedings: Quarantine Station, North Head, 15–16 June. Sydney: State Recreation Area Trusts.

Lowenthal, David (1998). *The heritage crusade and the spoils of history*. Cambridge: Cambridge University Press.

Mayne, Alan (2003). *Hill End: an historic Australian goldfields landscape*. Melbourne: Melbourne University Press.

Millar, Sue (1989). 'Heritage management for heritage tourism'. *Tourism Management*, 10(1).

Mocardo, Gianna (1996). 'Mindful visitors'. *Annals of Tourism Research*, 23(2).

Nuryanti, Wiendu (1996). 'Heritage and postmodern tourism'. *Annals of Tourism Research*, 23(2).

O'Brien, Geraldine (1995). 'Township that was once history now out to sell it'. *Sydney Morning Herald*, 28 June, 13.

Prior, Marjorie (1980). Hill End Historic Site oral history project. NSW National Parks and Wildlife Service Visitor Centre Archives, Hill End.

Silberberg, Ted (1995). 'Cultural tourism and business opportunities for museums and heritage sites'. *Tourism Management*, 16(5).

Tilden, Freeman (2007). *Interpreting our heritage*. Chapel Hill: University of North Carolina Press.

Willing, John (1979). Hill End seasonal ranger report. Unpublished: NPWS.

Index